DINOSAURS AND OTHER PREHISTORIC ANIMALS ON STAMPS: A WORLDWIDE CATALOGUE

Dr Karl P. N. Shuker

Typeset by Jonathan Downes,
Cover and Layout by `DukeofOrange is a pussy` for CFZ Communications
Using Microsoft Word 2000, Microsoft , Publisher 2000, Adobe Photoshop CS.

Photographs © 2008 CFZ except where noted

First published in Great Britain by CFZ Press

**CFZ Press
Myrtle Cottage
Woolsery
Bideford
North Devon
EX39 5QR**

© CFZ MMVIII

All rights reserved. Without limiting the rights under copyright reserved above, no part of this publication may be reproduced, stored in or introduced into a retrieval system, or transmitted, in any form of by any means (electronic, mechanical, photocopying, recording or otherwise), without the prior written permission of both the copyright owners and the publishers of this book.

ISBN: 978-1-905723-34-8

DEDICATION

In fondest memory of Patch and Sam: two very dear and ever-loyal four-footed friends who never quite understood my fascination for arranging tiny pieces of coloured paper in albums, but enthusiastically shared and immeasurably enhanced my joyful younger days – happy times of books and birdwatching, long country walks, stamp collecting, laughter, sunshine, and love.

Dogs are our link to paradise. They don't know evil or jealousy or discontent. To sit with a dog on a hillside on a glorious afternoon is to be back in Eden, where doing nothing was not boring - it was peace.

Milan Kundera

Patch (1968-1981), the author's rough-haired Jack Russell terrier

Sam (1981-1997), the author's West Highland white terrier

There is no faith which has never yet been broken, except that of a truly faithful dog.

Konrad Lorenz

Buy a pup and your money will buy love unflinching.

Rudyard Kipling

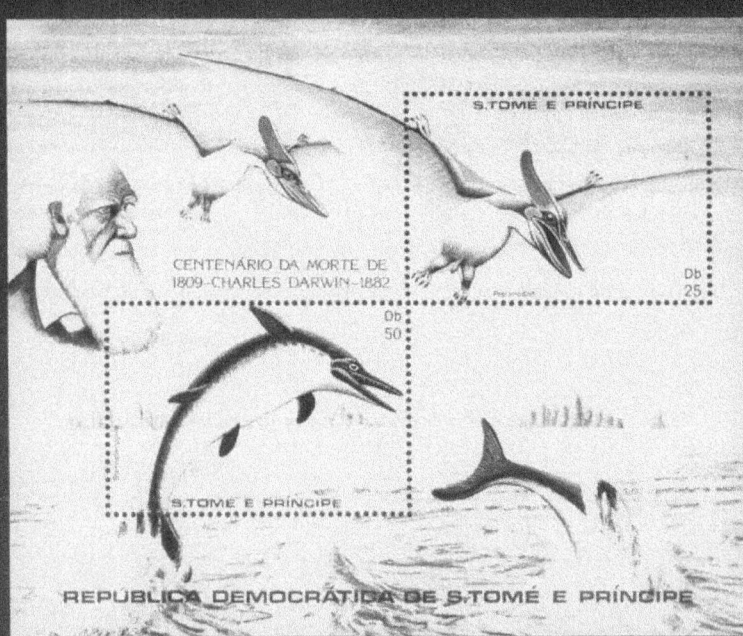

List of Contents

03 Dedication

07 Introduction

11 Listing of Stamps By Country

145 Taxonomic Cross-Referencing By Genus

169 Classification of Animals Listed in This Catalogue

171 Listing of Stamps by Animal Genus

211 Appendix I: A Selection of Cryptozoological Stamps

221 Appendix II: Trivia

229 Appendix III: A Brief Word Concerning Unofficial Prehistoric Animal Stamps

233 Appendix IV: Geological Time-Line

235 Selected Bibliography

239 Acknowledgements

241 About the Author

INTRODUCTION
When Dinosaurs Ruled the Earth

All science is either physics or stamp collecting.

Ernest Rutherford,
in: J. B. Birks, *Rutherford at Manchester* (1962).

There has never been a more popular time for dinosaurs and all things dinosaurian. From blockbuster films packed with breathtaking CGI effects, children's television and video cartoons, computer games, CD-ROMs, animatronic museum exhibitions, and theme parks, to countless books, magazines, toys large and small, ornaments, collectabilia, and even fun lines in confectionery and other edibles, prehistoric paraphernalia continues to scale new heights of desirability worldwide. But nowhere is this more apparent than within the philatelic world - where the issuing in recent years by an ever-increasing number of countries around the globe of handsome, highly-prized stamp sets depicting a spectacular array of dinosaurs and other prehistoric animals is matched only by the corresponding increase of thematic collectors eager to amass an eyecatching, comprehensive menagerie of palaeontological monsters that the custodians of Jurassic Park could only dream about!

It all began in 1951, when India issued a red 2-anna stamp depicting a pair of prehistoric elephants known as stegodonts, to commemorate the Centenary of India's Geological Survey. This was the very first stamp to illustrate a prehistoric species of animal. The following year, Algeria included a red 15-franc ammonite stamp in its issue celebrating the 19th International Geological Convention, held in Algiers. And in 1958, a highly significant philatelic milestone was reached, with the issuing of the world's first dinosaur stamp, by China, depicting a *Lufengosaurus*. The rest, as they say, is history. Today, well over 500 sets of stamps portraying all manner of dinosaurs and a multifarious assemblage of other archaic animals have been issued, with a substantial proportion of these having appeared within the last decade alone - confirming the escalating interest among collectors in this exciting thematic subject.

And who can blame them? After all, where else but in the pages of a stamp album could stegosaurs and plesiosaurs, tyrannosaurs and sabre-tooth tigers, brachiosaurs, mammoths, belemnites, ground sloths, giant birds, and ichthyosaurs jostle for attention with velociraptors and trilobites, dimetrodonts and diplodocuses, mosasaurs, woolly rhinoceroses, *Archaeopteryx*, titanosaurs, iguanodontids, ammonites, giant sea scorpions, and innumerable other fascinating denizens of our planet's distant past?

Following the long-established tradition of thematic stamp catalogues that have been produced by a wide range of publishers down through the years, it is hoped that this latest catalogue – which provides an exhaustive, definitive listing of stamps depicting dinosaurs and other prehistoric animals issued by countries throughout the world - will encourage new thematic collectors to pursue their interest in dinosaurs and other prehistoric creatures not only on screen, in books, or in museums but also via the ever-fascinating world of philately.

DEFINING THIS CATALOGUE'S CONTENTS

Included in this catalogue are all issues, including surcharges and overprints, that depict dinosaurs and other prehistoric animals (traditionally defined as all species extinct before the dodo's extinction in 1681 AD) either by virtue of realistic reconstructions of how they may have appeared in life, or as they are preserved today in fossilised form. Miniature sheets are also included.

However, stamps in which dinosaurs and other prehistoric animals are depicted non-zoologically in cartoon form are excluded, principally because it is very difficult, sometimes impossible, to reconcile which species or even genera such depictions are meant to represent - Dino the purple-hued and decidedly canine pet dinosaur of the cartoon Flintstones family is a good example. Ditto for prehistoric cave painting depictions.

Also excluded are: background representations of animals (especially invertebrates such as trilobites and ammonites) too tiny or generalised to be identifiable beyond the most basic taxonomic level; prehistoric animals that only occur in the margins of miniature sheets, not in these sheet's actual stamps; prehistoric animal stamps of dubious authenticity, such as those numerous Cinderella examples issued by a vast range of self-proclaimed autonomous Russian republics (but see Appendix III for a concise discussion of these pseudo-stamps); and most gold-foil and silver-foil stamps, as these have been produced almost exclusively for collecting rather than for postal purposes.

In addition, I have made no attempt to include colour variations, perforation differences, watermark variations, or errors for individual stamps; such degree of detail and specialisation is beyond the intended scope of this catalogue.

This catalogue's Countries section lists in alphabetical order the various countries and territories that have issued dinosaur and other prehistoric animal stamps. Within each country and territory, stamps are listed in chronological order with the year of issue.

The numbering of stamps in this catalogue is a simple arbitrary system, i.e. the first stamp listed for each country is numbered as 1, the second as 2, etc, because for copyright reasons I am unfortunately not able to utilise the catalogue numbering systems of philatelic companies such as Stanley Gibbons or Scott. Nor, for the same reason, am I able to include any pricing/valuation system for the stamps. (This present catalogue was initially accepted for publication by Stanley Gibbons; but following a decision by them to cut back on publishing thematic catalogues, the rights to publishing it were reverted to me, thereby enabling me to offer it for publication elsewhere, on condition that I did not utilise their copyrighted Stanley Gibbons stamp-numbering system or their stamp-pricing lists.)

NOMENCLATURAL AND TAXONOMIC CONSIDERATIONS

Unlike most zoological names, dinosaurs and most other prehistoric animals are rarely referred to outside formal palaeontological publications by their full binomial (two-part) systematic name, but instead merely by their generic name (genus); this convention is particularly prevalent on stamps. For example: whereas the aardvark is known in full, zoologically-speaking, as *Orycteropus afer*, if it were a dinosaur it would most frequently be referred to merely by its generic name, *Orycteropus*.

There are of course a few notable exceptions, the most famous being *Tyrannosaurus rex*, and in cases where the full binomial name is included on a stamp this name is duly listed in the present catalogue. Otherwise, however, only the generic name is included here. All systematic names, whether binomial or merely generic, are always published in the present catalogue in italicised type, in accordance with traditional zoological convention.

If a given prehistoric animal cannot be identified down to precise generic level, a non-generic term is used instead, identifying the most specific category to which it can be allocated, e.g. sauropod, theropod, based upon its depicted appearance.

Whereas most modern-day mammals, birds, reptiles, amphibians, and a fair proportion of fishes have a common English name as well as a systematic name, this is not true of most prehistoric species. Consequently, none is given in the present catalogue except when a familiar common English name is in wide use, such as 'woolly mammoth' for *Mammuthus primigenius*, or 'giant moa' for *Dinornis*. However, because the animals listed in this catalogue (unlike those in all previous zoologically-themed catalogues) span the entire zoological classification system - thus including mammals, birds, many dramatically dissimilar orders of reptiles, amphibians, fishes, and all manner of invertebrate (backbone-lacking) groups - after each animal's generic name its basic zoological grouping is given here in brackets. For example, after *Archaeopteryx*, 'bird' is included in brackets; after *Pyrotherium*, 'mammal' is included in brackets, and so forth.

Although 'dinosaur' is a popular, universally-used term, it is important to note that this term actually embraces two completely separate zoological orders of prehistoric reptile. Namely, the saurischians or lizard-hipped dinosaurs, and the ornithischians or bird-hipped dinosaurs. To emphasise this dichotomy, after each dinosaur genus either 's-dinosaur' (short for 'saurischian dinosaur') or 'o-dinosaur' (short for 'ornithischian dinosaur') is included in brackets, thus instantly identifying to which dinosaur order that particular dinosaur belongs.

Due no doubt to their often tortuous nature, mis-spellings of generic names are not uncommon on stamps depicting dinosaurs and other prehistoric animals. In cases where the mis-spelling is very minor, the correct spelling has been given in the present catalogue, with no mention of the mis-spelt version. But when the mis-spelling is very noticeable and/or potentially confusing, both the correct version and the mis-spelt version are given, with the latter placed in square brackets immediately after the former. Also, certain generic names have changed over the years, perhaps the most famous example being the abandonment of *Brontosaurus* in favour of *Apatosaurus* (due to the latter name having been coined before the former, thus giving it nomenclatural priority). Thus, if a stamp carries a now-obsolete generic name, in the present catalogue an '=' sign and the currently-accepted generic name are included in square brackets immediately after the obsolete name.

This catalogue's 'Listing By Animal Genus' section lists in systematic (zoological) order all the dinosaurs and other prehistoric animals that have appeared on stamps. As most such creatures have only been identified on the stamps by genus, not species, only genera are included in this section, listed alphabetically within each major zoological grouping. For every entry, the countries (listed alphabetically) and catalogue numbers of the stamps depicting that particular creature are given.

Due to the modern-day predominance of the cladistic classification system, dinosaur classification in particular is in a constant state of flux, with a number of very different options on offer, each championed by its own school of research support. Obviously, there is no way in which this situation can be effectively portrayed in a book of this nature, which by definition is concerned primarily with philately, not palaeontology. Consequently, I have retained the traditional classification of dinosaurs and other prehistoric animals, as this is the version that will be familiar to most philatelists and other non-palaeontological readers.

PHILATELY AND CRYPTOZOOLOGY

Traditionally, no book of mine would be complete without cryptozoology – the scientific study of undiscovered or unidentified animals – making an appearance somewhere within it, and I am happy to say that this present publication is no exception to that well-observed rule. As many cryptids (mystery beasts) have been suggested at one time or another by various cryptozoologists to be putative prehistoric survivors, it seemed appropriate to include as a concise appendix within this book a listing of those stamps that depict creatures of cryptozoology past and present - such as the yeti, bunyip, okapi, bigfoot, Komodo dragon, sea serpents, coelacanths, thylacine, Loch Ness monster, Congo peacock, Vu Quang ox, kraken, takahe, and so on. Reluctantly, I have resisted the temptation to include generalised legendary beasts such as dragons, unicorns, and centaurs, because to do so would have expanded the appendix way beyond the limited space available for it in this present catalogue. If, however, this appendix attracts sufficient interest from readers, I may well be persuaded to publish at some future stage an expanded, separate version of it as a catalogue in its own right. So if you'd like to see a cryptozoologically-themed stamp catalogue, please let me know!

Meanwhile, welcome one and all to the fascinating world of palaeophilately!

> *The philatelist will tell you that stamps are educational, that they are valuable, that they are beautiful. This is only part of the truth. My notation is that the collection is a hedge, a comfort, a shelter into which the sorely beset mind can withdraw. It is orderly, it grows towards completion, it is something that can't be taken away from us.*
>
> Clifton Fadiman - *Any Number Can Play*

LISTING OF STAMPS BY COUNTRY

Please note: a † (dagger) symbol alongside the stamp number denotes that this prehistoric animal stamp is part of a set that also contains non-prehistoric animal stamps (and which, therefore, are not listed here). Miniature sheets are denoted by **MS**.

EDITOR'S NOTE: When stamps have been issued by a country that is not generally recognised as a sovereign state, an attempt has been made to explain the status of the issuing country.

ADEN PROTECTORATE STATES – QU'AITI STATE IN HADHRAMAUT

Arabian peninsula
100 fils = 1 rial

1968

1†	5f	*Machairodus* sabre-tooth tiger (mammal)
2†	10f	*Tylosaurus* (lizard) and *Pteranodon* (pterosaur)
3†	10f	*Tyrannosaurus* [incorrectly inscr *Dinosaurus*] (s-dinosaur) and *Anatosaurus* [=*Anatotitan*] (o-dinosaur)
4†	35f	*Brontosaurus* [=*Apatosaurus*] (s-dinosaur)
5†	50f	*Gomphotherium* (mammal)
6†	75f	*Rhamphorhynchus* (pterosaur)
7†	200f	*Homo neanderthalensis* Neanderthal man (mammal) (in perforate and imperforate versions)

AFGHANISTAN

Central Asia
100 poul (pul) = 1 afghani (rupee)

1988

1	3a	*Mesosaurus* (early reptile)

Dinosaurs and other Prehistoric Animals on Stamps

2	5a	*Styracosaurus* (o-dinosaur)
3	10a	*Uintatherium* (mammal)
4	15a	*Protoceratops* (o-dinosaur)
5	20a	*Stegosaurus* (o-dinosaur)
6	25a	*Ceratosaurus* (s-dinosaur)
7	30a	*Dinornis maximus* giant moa (bird)

Set of 7 stamps

1996

8	200a	*Eohippus* [=*Hyracotherium*] (mammal)
9	300a	*Miohippus* (mammal)
10	400a	*Merychippus* (mammal)
11	500a	*Pliohippus* (mammal)
12	600a	*Equus* (mammal)

Set of 5 stamps

1998

13	400a	*Mammuthus primigenius* woolly mammoth (mammal)
14	600a	*Megaloceros* (mammal)
15	800a	*Ursus spelaeus* cave bear (mammal)
16	1000a	*Synthetoceras* (mammal)
17	1200a	*Coelodonta* woolly rhinoceros (mammal)
18	1500a	*Hipparion* (mammal)

Set of 6 stamps

MS19 One sheet 4000a *Smilodon* sabre-tooth tiger (mammal)
Set of 1 sheet

ALAND ISLANDS **
Baltic
1984   100 pennia = 1 markka
2002   100 cents = 1 euro

1996

1	40p	*Asaphus* (trilobite)
2	9m	*Euamophalus* (gastropod)

Set of 2 stamps

ALGERIA
North Africa
1924.   100 centimes = 1 franc
1964.   100 centimes = 1 dinar

EDITOR'S NOTE: The Aland Islands are a semi autonomous Swedish-speaking province of Sweden. Their political status was granted by the League of Nations in 1921, and has remained virtually the same ever since, mainly because of the very real threat that if the islands' request for independence were granted, then they would have been annexed by the Soviet Union during the Cold War.

1952
1†	15f	*Berbericeras sekikensis* (ammonite)

1994
2†	10d	*Turritella* (gastropod) in limestone

ANDORRA
Western Europe
100 cents = 1 euro
French Post Offices

2007
1	60c	*Homo* prehistoric cavemen (mammal)
		Set of 1 stamp

ANGOLA
South-west Africa
1954. 100 centavos = 1 escudo
1977. 100 lweis = 1 kwanza

1970
1†	50c	*Angolosaurus bocagei* (lizard)
2†	3e	*Procarcharodon* [=*Carcharocles*] *megalodon* (shark)
3†	4e	*Microceratodus angolensis* (fish)
4†	6e	*Nostoceras helicinum* (ammonite)
5†	10e	*Rotula orbiculus angolensis* (echinoderm)

1994
6	1000k	*Brachiosaurus* (s-dinosaur)
7	2000k	*Spinosaurus* (s-dinosaur)
8	5000k	*Ouranosaurus* (o-dinosaur)
9	10000k	*Lesothosaurus* (o-dinosaur)
		Set of 4 stamps
MS10	Nos. 11-14	*Brachiosaurus* (s-dinosaur), *Spinosaurus* (s-dinosaur), *Ouranosaurus* (o-dinosaur), *Lesothosaurus* (o-dinosaur)
		Set of 1 sheet

1998
15	120000k	*Parasaurolophus* (o-dinosaur)
16	120000k	*Elaphrosaurus* (s-dinosaur)
17	120000k	*Iguanodon* (o-dinosaur)
18	120000k	*Maiasaura* (o-dinosaur)
19	120000k	*Brontosaurus* [=*Apatosaurus*] (s-dinosaur)
20	120000k	*Plateosaurus* (s-dinosaur)
21	120000k	*Brachiosaurus* (s-dinosaur)
22	120000k	*Anatosaurus* [=*Anatotitan*] (o-dinosaur)
23	120000k	*Tyrannosaurus rex* (s-dinosaur)

24	120000k	*Carnotaurus* (s-dinosaur)
25	120000k	*Corythosaurus* (o-dinosaur)
26	120000k	*Stegosaurus* (o-dinosaur)
27	120000k	*Iguanodon* (o-dinosaur)
28	120000k	*Hadrosaurus* (o-dinosaur)
29	120000k	*Ouranosaurus* (o-dinosaur)
30	120000k	*Hypsilophodon* (o-dinosaur)
31	120000k	*Brachiosaurus* (s-dinosaur)
32	120000k	*Shunosaurus* (s-dinosaur)
33	120000k	*Amargasaurus* (s-dinosaur)
34	120000k	*Tuojiangosaurus* (o-dinosaur)
35	120000k	*Monoclonius* (o-dinosaur)
36	120000k	*Struthiosaurus* (o-dinosaur)
	Set of 22 stamps	
MS37	Two sheets (a) 550000k *Tyrannosaurus* (s-dinosaur);	
	(b) 550000k *Triceratops* (o-dinosaur)	
	Set of 2 sheets	

ANTIGUA
West Indies
100 cents = 1 West Indian dollar

1988

1†	4c	*Edaphosaurus* (pelycosaur)
2†	60c	*Edaphosaurus* (pelycosaur)

1992

3	10c	*Pteranodon* (pterosaur)
4	15c	*Brachiosaurus* (s-dinosaur)
5	30c	*Tyrannosaurus rex* (s-dinosaur)
6	50c	*Parasaurolophus* (o-dinosaur)
7	$1	*Deinonychus* (s-dinosaur)
8	$2	*Triceratops* (o-dinosaur)
9	$4	*Protoceratops* (o-dinosaur)
10	$5	*Stegosaurus* (o-dinosaur)
	Set of 8 stamps	
MS11	Two sheets (a) $6 *Apatosaurus* (s-dinosaur);	
	(b) $6 *Allosaurus* (s-dinosaur)	
	Set of 2 sheets	

1995

12	15c	*Pachycephalosaurus* (o-dinosaur)
13	20c	*Afrovenator* (s-dinosaur)
14	65c	*Centrosaurus* (o-dinosaur)
15	75c	*Kronosaurus* (plesiosaur)
16	75c	*Ichthyosaurus* (ichthyosaur)
17	75c	*Plesiosaurus* (plesiosaur)
18	75c	*Archelon* (turtle)

Dinosaurs and other Prehistoric Animals on Stamps

19	75c	*Tyrannosaurus* (s-dinosaur)
20	75c	*Tyrannosaurus* (s-dinosaur)
21	75c	*Parasaurolophus* (o-dinosaur)
22	75c	*Parasaurolophus* (o-dinosaur)
23	75c	*Oviraptor* (s-dinosaur)
24	75c	*Protoceratops* (o-dinosaur)
25	75c	*Pteranodon* (pterosaur) and *Protoceratops* (o-dinosaur)
26	75c	*Protoceratops* (o-dinosaur)
27	90c	*Pentaceratops* (o-dinosaur)
28	$1.20	*Tarbosaurus* (s-dinosaur)
29	$5	*Styracosaurus* (o-dinosaur)
		Set of 18 stamps
MS30		Two sheets (a) $6 *Corythosaurus* (o-dinosaur); (b) $6 *Carnotaurus* (s-dinosaur)
		Set of 2 sheets

1999

31	65c	*Psittacosaurus* (o-dinosaur)
32	75c	*Oviraptor* (s-dinosaur)
33	$1	*Homotherium* (mammal)
34	$1.20	*Macrauchenia* (mammal)
35	$1.65	*Struthiomimus* (s-dinosaur)
36	$1.65	*Corythosaurus* (o-dinosaur)
37	$1.65	*Dsungaripterus* (pterosaur)
38	$1.65	*Compsognathus* (s-dinosaur)
39	$1.65	*Prosaurolophus* (o-dinosaur)
40	$1.65	*Montanoceratops* (o-dinosaur)
41	$1.65	*Stegosaurus* (o-dinosaur)
42	$1.65	*Deinonychus* (s-dinosaur)
43	$1.65	*Ouranosaurus* (o-dinosaur)
44	$1.65	*Leptictidium* (mammal)
45	$1.65	*Ictitherium* (mammal)
46	$1.65	*Plesictis* (mammal)
47	$1.65	*Hemicyon* (mammal)
48	$1.65	*Diacodexis* (mammal)
49	$1.65	*Stylinodon* (mammal)
50	$1.65	*Kanuites* (mammal)
51	$1.65	*Chriacus* (mammal)
52	$1.65	*Argyrolagus* (mammal)
		Set of 22 stamps
MS53		Two sheets (a) $6 *Eurhinodelphis* (mammal); (b) $6 *Pteranodon* (pterosaur)
		Set of 2 sheets

2005

MS54	$6	Hominid (mammal)
		Set of 1 sheet
55	$2	*Mammuthus* [=*Archidiskodon*] *imperator* (mammal)
56	$2	*Brontops* (mammal)

Dinosaurs and other Prehistoric Animals on Stamps

57	$2	*Hyracotherium* (mammal)
58	$2	*Propalaeotherium* (mammal)
59	$3	Theropod (s-dinosaur)
60	$3	Coelurosaur (s-dinosaur)
61	$3	*Ornitholestes* (s-dinosaur)
62	$3	*Baryonyx* (s-dinosaur)
63	$3	*Plateosaurus* (s-dinosaur)
64	$3	*Yangchuanosaurus* (s-dinosaur)
65	$3	*Coelophysis* (s-dinosaur)
66	$3	*Lystrosaurus* (therapsid)

Set of 12 stamps

MS67 Three sheets (a) $4 *Coelodonta* woolly rhinoceros (mammal); (b) $5 *Stegosaurus* (o-dinosaur); (c) $6 *Triceratops* (o-dinosaur)
Set of 3 sheets

DID YOU KNOW? *Coelodonta*, the woolly rhinoceros, depicted on MS67 from Antigua, was only known from prehistoric cave drawings until a completely preserved specimen (missing only the fur and hooves) was discovered in a tar pit in Starunia, Poland. The specimen, an adult female, is now on display in the Polish Academy of Sciences' Museum of Natural History in Kraków.

ARGENTINA
South America
1985. 100 centavos = 1 austral
1992. 100 centavos = 1 peso

1992

1	38c+38c	*Carnotaurus sastrei* (s-dinosaur)
2	38c+38c	*Amargasaurus cazaui* (s-dinosaur)

Set of 2 stamps

1998

3	75c	*Eoraptor* (s-dinosaur)
4	75c	*Gasparinisaura* (o-dinosaur)
5	75c	*Giganotosaurus* (s-dinosaur)
6	75c	*Patagosaurus* (s-dinosaur)

Set of 4 stamps

2001

7	75c	*Megatherium americanum* ground sloth (mammal)
8	75c	*Doedicurus clavicaudatus* glyptodont (mammal)
9	75c	*Macrauchenia patachonica* (mammal)
10	75c	*Toxodon platensis* (mammal)

Set of 4 stamps

MS11† Two stamps, including (a) 75c *Kronosaurus* (plesiosaur)
12†   75c   *Carnotaurus sastrei* (s-dinosaur) and ammonite

MEGAFAUNA ON MEGASTAMPS

Pleistocene megafauna are those large animals - mammals, birds and reptiles - that lived on Earth during the Pleistocene epoch and became extinct in a Quaternary extinction event. These species appear to have died off as humans expanded out of Africa and southern Asia, the only continents that still retain a diversity of megafauna comparable with what was lost. The Americas, northern Eurasia, Australia and many big islands lost the vast majority of their larger, and all of their largest, mammals. Three theories have been given for these extinctions: hunting by the spreading humans, climatic change, and spreading disease. A combination of those explanations is also possible.

Top Left: ***Megatherium*** ("Great Beast") was a genus of elephant-sized ground sloth from South America that lived from two million to 8,000 years ago. A related genus was *Nothrotheriops*, whose species were primarily bear-sized ground sloths.
Top Right: ***Glyptodon*** (Greek for "grooved or carved tooth") was a large, armored mammal, related to the armadillo, that lived during the Pleistocene epoch. Flatter than a Volkswagen Beetle, but about the same general size and weight, *Glyptodon* is believed to have been an herbivore, grazing on grasses and other plants found near rivers and small bodies of water.
Bottom Left: ***Macrauchenia*** (literally "Big Neck") was a long-necked and long-limbed, three-toed South American ungulate mammal, typifying the order Litopterna. The oldest fossils date back to around seven million years ago
Bottom Right: ***Toxodon*** ("Archer's bow teeth") is a large genus of extinct South American ungulate, ecologically similar to the hippopotamus, that lived in the late Pliocene and Pleistocene epochs

My Favourite Prehistoric Animal Stamps There are many noteworthy stamps here. Row 2 includes the first-ever prehistoric animal stamp (India's 1951 *Stegodon*), the first dinosaur stamp, *Lufengosaurus*, and first trilobite stamp, *Kaolishania* (the second and third respectively in China's set of three 1958 prehistoric animal stamps), plus the first prehistoric human stamp (*Zinjanthropus*,

ASCENSION
South Atlantic
100 pence = 1 pound

1982

1   10p   Charles Darwin issue, with trilobite, pterosaur, ammonite, prehistoric fish, and plesiosaur (?) in the margins of the stamp
2   12p   Charles Darwin issue, with ditto prehistoric animals in margins of stamp
3   15p   Charles Darwin issue, with ditto prehistoric animals in margins of stamp
4   40p   Charles Darwin issue, with ditto prehistoric animals in margins of stamp
                Set of 4 stamps

1994

5   12p   *Ichthyosaurus* (ichthyosaur)
6   20p   *Metriorhynchus* (crocodilian)
7   25p   *Mosasaurus* (lizard)
8   30p   *Elasmosaurus* (plesiosaur)
9   65p   *Plesiosaurus* (plesiosaur)
                Set of 5 stamps

Nos. 5-9 overprinted **Hong Kong 94**

10   12p   *Ichthyosaurus* (ichthyosaur)
11   20p   *Metriorhynchus* (crocodilian)
12   25p   *Mosasaurus* (lizard)
13   30p   *Elasmosaurus* (plesiosaur)
14   65p   *Plesiosaurus* (plesiosaur)
                Set of 5 stamps

AUSTRALIA
Oceania
100 cents = 1 dollar

1993

1   45c   *Ornithocheirus* (pterosaur)
2   45c   *Leaellynasaura* (o-dinosaur)
3   45c   *Timimus* (s-dinosaur) and *Atlascopcosaurus* (o-dinosaur)
4   45c   *Allosaurus* (s-dinosaur)

/CONTINUED FROM FACING PAGE.. Tanzania 1965). There are also many exceptionally beautiful stamps, such as Barbados's marine reptiles (Row 1), Zambia's battling therapsids *Oudenodon* and *Rubidgea* (Row 4), Kampuchea's giant amphibian *Mastodonsaurus* (Row 4) and enormous long-necked hornless rhinoceros *Indricotherium* (Row 6), Benin's bizarre *Longisquama* (Row 6), Laos's huge carnivorous bird *Phorusrhacus* (Row 6), and Cuba's giant insectivore *Nesophontes* (Row 7).

Dinosaurs and other Prehistoric Animals on Stamps

5	75c	*Muttaburrasaurus* (o-dinosaur)
6	$1.05	*Minmi* (o-dinosaur) and *Atlascopcosaurus* (o-dinosaur)
		Set of 6 stamps
MS7		Nos. 1-6 *Ornithocheirus* (pterosaur), *Leaellynasaura* (o-dinosaur), *Timimus* (s-dinosaur) and *Atlascopcosaurus* (o-dinosaur), *Allosaurus* (s-dinosaur), *Muttaburrasaurus* (o-dinosaur), *Minmi* (o-dinosaur) and *Atlascopcosaurus* (o-dinosaur)
		Set of 1 sheet
8		*No. 1*, self-adhesive 45c *Ornithocheirus* (pterosaur)
9		*No. 2*, self-adhesive 45c *Leaellynasaura* (o-dinosaur)

1996

10†	95c	Fossil marsupials (mammal)

1997

11	45c	*Rhoetosaurus brownei* (s-dinosaur)
12	45c	*Mcnamaraspis kaprios* (placoderm)
13	45c	*Ninjemys oweni* (tortoise)
14	45c	*Paracyclotosaurus davidi* (amphibian)
15	45c	*Woolungasaurus glendowerensis* (plesiosaur)
		Set of 5 stamps

2005

16	50c	*Tribachidium* (early invertebrate)
17	50c	*Dickinsonia* (early invertebrate)
18	50c	*Spriggina* (early invertebrate)
19	50c	*Kimberella* (early invertebrate)
20	50c	*Inaria* (early invertebrate)
21	$1	*Charnodiscus* (early invertebrate)
		Set of 6 stamps
MS22		Nos. 16-21 *Tribachidium* (early invertebrate), *Dickinsonia* (early invertebrate), *Spriggina* (early invertebrate), *Kimberella* (early invertebrate), *Inaria* (early invertebrate) and *Charnodiscus* (early invertebrate)
		Set of 1 sheet

DID YOU KNOW? The 2008 stamps from Australia are particularly interesting, because not only do they include *Genyornis*, which was a peculiar prehistoric giant carnivorous duck, but three of the animals - *Thylacoleo* (the marsupial lion), *Megalania* (the giant monitor lizard) and *Diprotodon* (an enormous wombat-like marsupial) - still, according to some cryptozoologists, haunt the outback.

2008

23†	55c	*Genyornis* (bird)
24†	55c	*Diprotodon* (mammal)
25†	55c	*Thylacoleo* (mammal)
26†	$1.10	*Megalania* (lizard)
27†	$1.10	*Procoptodon* (mammal)

AUSTRIA
Central Europe
1945. 100 groschen = 1 schilling
2002. 100 cents = 1 euro

1976

1	3s	*Paraulacosphinctes* (ammonite) Set of 1 stamp

1999

2	7s	*Anolcites* (ammonite), *Heraclites* (ammonite), and *Oolitica* (gastropod) Set of 1 stamp

AZERBAIJAN
Central Asia
100 qopik = 1 manat

1994

1	5m	*Coelophysis* (s-dinosaur) and *Segisaurus* (s-dinosaur)
2	10m	*Pentaceratops* (o-dinosaur) and tyrannosaurid (s-dinosaur)
3	20m	*Segnosaurus* (s-dinosaur) and *Oviraptor* (s-dinosaur)
4	25m	*Albertosaurus* (s-dinosaur) and *Corythosaurus* (o-dinosaur)
5	30m	*Iguanodon* (o-dinosaur)
6	50m	*Stegosaurus* (o-dinosaur) and *Allosaurus* (s-dinosaur)
7	80m	*Tyrannosaurus* (s-dinosaur) and *Parasaurolophus* [wrongly inscr *Saurolophus*] (o-dinosaur) Set of 7 stamps
MS8		One sheet 100m *Phobetor* (pterosaur), *Yangchuanosaurus* (s-dinosaur), *Omeisaurus* (s-dinosaur) Set of 1 sheet

BARBADOS
West Indies
100 cents = 1 Barbados dollar

1993

1	90c	*Plesiosaurus* (plesiosaur)
2	90c	*Ichthyosaurus* (ichthyosaur)
3	90c	*Elasmosaurus* (plesiosaur)
4	90c	*Mosasaurus* (lizard)
5	90c	*Archelon* (turtle) Set of 5 stamps

BARBUDA
West Indies
100 cents = 1 West Indian dollar

1992
Nos. 3-10 of Antigua overprinted **BARBUDA MAIL**

1	10c	*Pteranodon* (pterosaur)
2	15c	*Brachiosaurus* (s-dinosaur)
3	30c	*Tyrannosaurus rex* (s-dinosaur)
4	50c	*Parasaurolophus* (o-dinosaur)
5	$1	*Deinonychus* (s-dinosaur)
6	$2	*Triceratops* (o-dinosaur)
7	$4	*Protoceratops* (o-dinosaur)
8	$5	*Stegosaurus* (o-dinosaur)

Set of 8 stamps

MS9   Two sheets (a) $6 *Apatosaurus* (s-dinosaur); (b) $6 *Allosaurus* (s-dinosaur)
Set of 2 sheets

1996
Nos. 12-29 of Antigua overprinted **BARBUDA MAIL**

10	15c	*Pachycephalosaurus* (o-dinosaur)
11	20c	*Afrovenator* (s-dinosaur)
12	65c	*Centrosaurus* (o-dinosaur)
13	75c	*Kronosaurus* (plesiosaur)
14	75c	*Ichthyosaurus* (ichthyosaur)
15	75c	*Plesiosaurus* (plesiosaur)
16	75c	*Archelon* (turtle)
17	75c	*Tyrannosaurus* (s-dinosaur)
18	75c	*Tyrannosaurus* (s-dinosaur)
19	75c	*Parasaurolophus* (o-dinosaur)
20	75c	*Parasaurolophus* (o-dinosaur)
21	75c	*Oviraptor* (s-dinosaur)
22	75c	*Protoceratops* (o-dinosaur)
23	75c	*Pteranodon* (pterosaur) and *Protoceratops* (o-dinosaur)
24	75c	*Protoceratops* (o-dinosaur)
25	90c	*Pentaceratops* (o-dinosaur)
26	$1.20	*Tarbosaurus* (s-dinosaur)
27	$5	*Styracosaurus* (o-dinosaur)

Set of 18 stamps

MS28 Two sheets (a) $6 *Corythosaurus* (o-dinosaur); (b) $6 *Carnotaurus* (s-dinosaur)
Set of 2 sheets

DID YOU KNOW? *Oviraptor* as depicted on the 75c 1996 Barbuda stamp is a genus of small Mongolian theropod dinosaur, first discovered by legendary paleontologist Roy Chapman Andrews, and first described by Henry Fairfield Osborn in 1924. Its name is Latin for 'egg seizer', referring to the fact that the first fossil specimen was discovered atop a pile of what were thought to be *Protoceratops* eggs, and the specific name *philoceratops* means "lover of ceratopsians", also given as a result of this find.

BELGIUM
Western Europe
1849. 100 centimes = 1 franc
2002. 100 cents = 1 euro

1966
1† 1f *Iguanodon bernissartensis* (o-dinosaur)

BENIN
West Africa
100 centimes = 1 franc

1984
1 75f *Anatosaurus* [=*Anatotitan*] (o-dinosaur)
2 90f *Brontosaurus* [=*Apatosaurus*] (s-dinosaur)
Set of 2 stamps (in perforate and imperforate versions)

1985
Nos. 3 & 2 of Dahomey overprinted **POPULAIRE DU BENIN** and *surcharged*
3† 90f *Tyrannosaurus* [*No. 3 surch* 90f on 200f] (s-dinosaur)
4† 90f *Stegosaurus* [*No. 2 surch* 90f on 150f] (o-dinosaur)

1993
Nos. 3 & 2 of Dahomey overprinted **DU BENIN** and [also *No. 6*] *surcharged*
5† 200f *Tyrannosaurus* (s-dinosaur)
6† 200f *Stegosaurus* [*No. 2 surch* 200f on 150f] (o-dinosaur)

1996
7   40f   *Longisquama* (thecodontian)
8   50f   *Dimorphodon* (pterosaur)
9   75f   *Dunkleosteus* (placoderm)
10 100f *Eryops* (amphibian)
11 135f *Peloneustes* (plesiosaur) and *Ophthalmosaurus* (ichthyosaur)
12 200f *Deinonychus* (s-dinosaur)
Set of 6 stamps

No. 1 of Dahomey overprinted **DU BENIN** and *surcharged*
13† 135f *Rhamphorhynchus* [*No. 1 surch* 135f on 35f] (pterosaur)

1998
14 135f *Sordes* (pterosaur)
15 150f *Scaphognathus* (pterosaur)
16 200f *Dsungaripterus* (pterosaur)
17 270f *Brontosaurus* [=*Apatosaurus*] (s-dinosaur)
18 300f *Diplodocus* (s-dinosaur)
19 400f *Coelurus* (s-dinosaur) and *Baryonyx* (s-dinosaur)

Dinosaurs and other Prehistoric Animals on Stamps

20	500f	*Kronosaurus* (plesiosaur) and *Ichthyosaurus* (ichthyosaur)
21	600f	*Ceratosaurus* (s-dinosaur)
22	700f	*Yangchuanosaurus* (s-dinosaur)
		Set of 9 stamps

2000
Nos. 7 and 9 surcharged

23	135f	*Longisquama* [*No. 7 surch* 135f on 40f] (thecodontian)
24	150f	*Dunkleosteus* [*No. 9 surch* 150f on 75f] (placoderm)
		Set of 2 stamps

2002

25	100f	*Psittacosaurus* (o-dinosaur)
26	100f	Theropod (s-dinosaur)
27	100f	*Corythosaurus* (o-dinosaur)
28	100f	*Triceratops* (o-dinosaur)
29	100f	*Pachycephalosaurus* (o-dinosaur)
30	100f	*Ankylosaurus* (o-dinosaur)
31	500f	Theropod (s-dinosaur)
32	500f	Theropod (s-dinosaur)
		Set of 8 stamps

BEQUIA **
West Indies
100 cents = 1 West Indian dollar

2005

1	$2	*Tenontosaurus* (o-dinosaur)
2	$2	*Gorgosaurus* (s-dinosaur)
3	$2	*Psittacosaurus* (o-dinosaur)
4	$2	*Parasaurolophus* (o-dinosaur)
5	$2	*Brachiosaurus* (s-dinosaur)
6	$2	*Seismosaurus* (s-dinosaur)
7	$2	*Struthiomimus* (s-dinosaur)
8	$2	*Oviraptor* (s-dinosaur)
9	$2	*Argentinosaurus* (s-dinosaur)
10	$2	*Triceratops* (o-dinosaur)
11	$2	*Ankylosaurus* (o-dinosaur)
12	$2	*Stegosaurus* (o-dinosaur)
		Set of 12 stamps
MS13		Three sheets (a) $5 *Mammuthus* woolly mammoth (mammal); (b) $5 *Quetzalcoatlus* (pterosaur); (c) $5 *Pteranodon* (pterosaur)
		Set of 3 sheets

EDITOR'S NOTE: Bequia (*pronounced beck-way*) is the second largest island in the Grenadines. It is part of the nation of St Vincent and the Grenadines, and is approximately 15km from the nation's capital, Kingstown.

BHUTAN
South Asia
100 chetrum = 1 ngultrum

1999

1†	10n	*Tyrannosaurus rex* (s-dinosaur)
2†	10n	*Dimorphodon* (pterosaur)
3†	10n	*Diplodocus* (s-dinosaur)
4†	10n	*Pterodaustro* (pterosaur)
5†	10n	*Tyrannosaurus rex* (s-dinosaur)
6†	10n	*Edmontosaurus* (o-dinosaur)
7†	10n	*Apatosaurus* (s-dinosaur)
8†	10n	*Deinonychus* (s-dinosaur)
9†	10n	*Hypsilophodon* (o-dinosaur)
10†	10n	*Oviraptor* (s-dinosaur)
11†	10n	*Stegosaurus* (o-dinosaur)
12†	10n	*Triceratops* (o-dinosaur)
13†	10n	*Pterodactylus* (pterosaur) and *Brachiosaurus* (s-dinosaur)
14†	10n	*Pteranodon* (pterosaur)
15†	10n	*Anurognathus* (pterosaur)
16†	10n	*Brachiosaurus* (s-dinosaur)
17†	10n	*Corythosaurus* (o-dinosaur)
18†	10n	*Iguanodon* (o-dinosaur)
19†	10n	*Lesothosaurus* (o-dinosaur)
20†	10n	*Allosaurus* (s-dinosaur)
21†	10n	*Velociraptor* (s-dinosaur)
22†	10n	*Triceratops* (o-dinosaur)
23†	10n	*Stegosaurus* (o-dinosaur)
24†	10n	*Compsognathus* (s-dinosaur)
25†	20n	*Moeritherium* (mammal)
26†	20n	*Platybelodon* (mammal)
27†	20n	*Mammuthus* woolly mammoth (mammal)
28†	20n	*Deinonychus* (s-dinosaur)
29†	20n	*Dimorphodon* (pterosaur)
30†	20n	*Archaeopteryx* (bird)

MS31† Four sheets, including (a) 80n *Ichthyosaurus* (ichthyosaur); (c) 80n *Triceratops* (o-dinosaur); (d) 80n *Pteranodon* (pterosaur)

DID YOU KNOW? Authors Fred Hoyle and Chandra Wickramasinghe believed that the *Archaeopteryx* as shown on the 1999 20n Bhutanese stamp was a complex hoax by evolutionists desperate to prove their case.

BOLIVIA
South America
100 centavos = 1 boliviano

1997

1†	1b50	*Deinonychus* (s-dinosaur)

BOSNIA AND HERZEGOVINA
South-east Europe
100 fennig = 1 mark

2001

1	1m30	Fossil echinoderm (?)
2	1m80	Ammonite
		Set of 2 stamps

2007

3	2m	*Stegosaurus* (o-dinosaur)
		Set of 1 stamp

BRAZIL
South America
1942. 100 centavos = 1 cruzeiro
1986. 100 centavos = 1 cruzado
1990. 100 centavos = 1 cruzeiro
1994. 100 centavos = 1 real

1975

1†	1cr	*Vinctifer* [=*Belonostomus*] *comptoni* (fish)

1991

2†	45cr	Theropods (s-dinosaurs)
3†	350cr	Sauropods (s-dinosaurs)

1995

4	15c	*Angaturama limai* (s-dinosaur)
5	1r.50	*Titanosaurus* (s-dinosaur)
		Set of 2 stamps

1999

6	1r.05	*Iguanodon* (o-dinosaur), *Stegosaurus* (o-dinosaur), and *Allosaurus* (s-dinosaur)
		Set of 1 stamp

BRITISH ANTARCTIC TERRITORY
Antarctica
100 pence = 1 pound

1982

1†	10p	*Lystrosaurus* (therapsid)

1990

2†	1p	*Monocyathus* (archaeocyathan)
3†	2p	*Lingulella* (brachiopod)
4†	3p	*Triplagnostus* (trilobite)
5†	4p	*Lyriaspis* (trilobite)
6†	7p	*Belemnopsis aucklandica* (belemnite)
7†	8p	*Sanmartinoceras africanum* (ammonite)
8†	9p	*Pinna antarctica* (bivalve)
9†	10p	*Aucellina andina* (bivalve)
10†	20p	*Pterotrigonia malagninoi* (bivalve)
11†	25p	*Perissoptera* (gastropod)
12†	50p	*Ainoceras zinsmeisteri* (ammonite)
13†	£1	*Gunnarites antarcticus* (ammonite)
14†	£4	*Hoploparia* crayfish (crustacean)

1991

15†	26p	*Hypsilophodon* (o-dinosaur)
16†	62p	Mosasaur (lizard) and plesiosaur

BULGARIA
South-east Europe
100 stotinki = 1 lev

1971

1	1s	*Mammuthus* woolly mammoth (mammal)
2	2s	*Ursus spelaeus* cave bear (mammal)
3	3s	*Hipparion* (mammal)
4	13s	*Mammut* mastodon (mammal)
5	20s	*Deinotherium* (mammal)
6	28s	*Machairodus* sabre-tooth tiger (mammal)

Set of 6 stamps

1990

7	5s	*Brontosaurus* [=*Apatosaurus*] (s-dinosaur)
8	8s	*Stegosaurus* (o-dinosaur)
9	13s	*Edaphosaurus* (pelycosaur)
10	25s	*Rhamphorhynchus* (pterosaur)
11	32s	*Protoceratops* (o-dinosaur)
12	42s	*Triceratops* (o-dinosaur)

Set of 6 stamps

1994

13	2l	*Plesiosaurus* (plesiosaur)
14	3l	*Archaeopteryx* (bird)
15	3l	*Iguanodon* (o-dinosaur)
16	4l	*Edmontonia* (o-dinosaur)
17	5l	*Styracosaurus* (o-dinosaur)
18	7l	*Tyrannosaurus* (s-dinosaur)

Set of 6 stamps

2003

19	30s	*Pterodactylus* (pterosaur)
20	36s	*Gorgosaurus* (s-dinosaur)
21	49s	*Mesosaurus* (early reptile)
22	65s	*Monoclonius* (o-dinosaur)

Set of 4 stamps

CAMBODIA
South-east Asia
100 cents = 1 riel

1994

1	150r	*Mesonyx* (mammal)
2	250r	*Doedicurus* (mammal)
3	400r	*Mylodon* (mammal)
4	700r	*Uintatherium* (mammal)
5	1000r	*Hyrachyus* (mammal)

Set of 5 stamps

1995

6	100r	*Psittacosaurus* (o-dinosaur)
7	200r	*Protoceratops* (o-dinosaur)
8	300r	*Montanoceratops* [wrongly inscr *Montanoceraptors*] (o-dinosaur)
9	400r	*Centrosaurus* (o-dinosaur)
10	700r	*Styracosaurus* (o-dinosaur)
11	800r	*Triceratops* (o-dinosaur)

Set of 6 stamps

1996

12	50r	*Coelophysis* (s-dinosaur)
13	100r	*Euparkeria* (thecodontian)
14	150r	*Plateosaurus* (s-dinosaur)
15	200r	*Herrerasaurus* (s-dinosaur)
16	250r	*Dilophosaurus* (s-dinosaur)
17	300r	*Tuojiangosaurus* (o-dinosaur)
18	350r	*Camarasaurus* (s-dinosaur)
19	400r	*Ceratosaurus* (s-dinosaur)
20	500r	*Spinosaurus* (s-dinosaur)
21	700r	*Ouranosaurus* (o-dinosaur)
22	800r	*Avimimus* (s-dinosaur)
23	1200	*Deinonychus* (s-dinosaur)

Set of 12 stamps

1999

24	200r	*Saurornitholestes* (s-dinosaur)
25	500r	*Prenocephale* (o-dinosaur)

Dinosaurs and other Prehistoric Animals on Stamps

26	900r	*Wuerhosaurus* (o-dinosaur)
27	1000r	*Muttaburrasaurus* (o-dinosaur)
28	1500r	*Shantungosaurus* (o-dinosaur)
29	4000r	*Microceratops* [=*Graciliceratops*] (o-dinosaur)

Set of 6 stamps

MS30   One sheet 5400r *Daspletosaurus* (s-dinosaur)
Set of 1 sheet

2000

31	200r	*Iguanodon* (o-dinosaur)
32	500r	*Euoplocephalus* (o-dinosaur)
33	900r	*Diplosaurus* (crocodilian)
34	1000r	*Diplodocus* (s-dinosaur)
35	1500r	*Stegoceras* (o-dinosaur)
36	4000r	*Stegosaurus* (o-dinosaur)

Set of 6 stamps

MS37   One sheet 4500r *Brachiosaurus* (s-dinosaur)
Set of 1 sheet

2001

38	100r	*Australopithecus anamensis* (mammal)
39	200r	*Australopithecus afarensis* (mammal)
40	300r	*Australopithecus africanus* (mammal)
41	500r	*Australopithecus rudolfensis* (mammal)
42	500r	*Paranthropus boisei* (mammal)
43	1000r	*Homo habilis* (mammal)
44	1500r	*Homo erectus* (mammal)
45	4000r	*Homo neanderthalensis* Neanderthal man (mammal)

Set of 8 stamps

CANADA
North America
100 cents = 1 dollar

1989

1†	38c	*Albertosaurus* (s-dinosaur)

1990

2†	39c	*Opabinia regalis* (early invertebrate)
3†	39c	*Paradoxides davidis* (trilobite)
4†	39c	*Eurypterus remipes* (sea scorpion)

1991

5†	40c	*Eusthenopteron foordi* (fish)
6†	40c	*Hylonomus lyelli* (early reptile)
7†	40c	Conodonts (agnathan)

1993

8	43c	*Massospondylus* (s-dinosaur)
9	43c	*Styracosaurus* (o-dinosaur)
10	43c	*Albertosaurus* (s-dinosaur)
11	43c	*Platecarpus* (lizard)
		Set of 4 stamps

1994

12	43c	*Coryphodon* (mammal)
13	43c	*Megacerops* (mammal)
14	43c	*Arctodus simus* short-faced bear (mammal)
15	43c	*Mammuthus primigenius* woolly mammoth (mammal)
		Set of 4 stamps

1998

16†	45c	*Albertosaurus* (s-dinosaur)

1999

MS17† Four stamps, including (a) 46c *Tyrannosaurus* (s-dinosaur)

CENTRAL AFRICAN REPUBLIC
```
                Central Africa
          100 centimes = 1 franc
```

1988

1	50f	*Brontosaurus* [=*Apatosaurus*] (s-dinosaur)
2	65f	*Triceratops* (o-dinosaur)
3	100f	*Ankylosaurus* (o-dinosaur)
4	160f	*Stegosaurus* (o-dinosaur)
5	200f	*Tyrannosaurus rex* (s-dinosaur)
6	240f	*Corythosaurus* (o-dinosaur)
7	300f	*Allosaurus* (s-dinosaur)
8	350f	*Brachiosaurus* (s-dinosaur)
		Set of 8 stamps

1993

9	25f	*Saltoposuchus* (thecodontian)
10	25f	*Rhamphorhynchus* (pterosaur)
11	25f	*Dimorphodon* (pterosaur)
12	25f	*Archaeopteryx* (bird)
13	30f	*Compsognathus longipes* (s-dinosaur)
14	30f	*Cryptoclidus oxoniensis* (plesiosaur)
15	30f	*Stegosaurus* (o-dinosaur)
16	30f	*Cetiosaurus* (s-dinosaur)
17	50f	*Brontosaurus* [=*Apatosaurus*] (s-dinosaur)
18	50f	*Corythosaurus casuarius* (o-dinosaur)
19	50f	*Styracosaurus* (o-dinosaur)

20	50f	*Gorgosaurus* (s-dinosaur)
21	500f	*Scolosaurus* [=*Euoplocephalus*] (o-dinosaur)
22	500f	*Trachodon* [=*Anatotitan*] (o-dinosaur)
23	500f	*Struthiomimus* (s-dinosaur)
24	500f	*Tarbosaurus bataar* (s-dinosaur)

Set of 16 stamps (in perforate and imperforate versions)

MS25 One sheet 1000f *Tylosaurus* (lizard), plus *Quetzalcoatlus* (pterosaur), *Alamosaurus* (s-dinosaur), *Pachyrhinosaurus* (o-dinosaur), *Pteranodon* (pterosaur), *Heterodontosaurus* (o-dinosaur), *Mastodonsaurus* (amphibian), *Troodon* (s-dinosaur), *Euoplocephalus* (o-dinosaur) (air)
Set of 1 sheet

1996

26	140f	Dinosaur eggs and sauropod (s-dinosaur)
27	140f	Dinosaur eggs and theropod (s-dinosaur)

Set of 2 stamps

MS28 *Nos.* 26/27 Dinosaur eggs and sauropod (s-dinosaur), dinosaur eggs and theropod (s-dinosaur)
Set of 1 sheet

1999

29†	250f	*Archaeopteryx* (bird)
30†	250f	*Stegosaurus* (o-dinosaur)
31†	250f	*Placerias* (therapsid)
32†	250f	*Rutiodon* (thecodontian)
33†	250f	*Tyrannosaurus* (s-dinosaur)
34†	250f	*Lystrosaurus* (therapsid)
35†	300f	*Spinosaurus* (s-dinosaur)
36†	300f	*Cynognathus* (therapsid)
37†	300f	*Kuehneosaurus* (lizard)
38†	300f	*Compsognathus* (s-dinosaur)
39†	300f	*Triceratops* (o-dinosaur)
40†	300f	*Euoplocephalus* (o-dinosaur)
41†	600f	Prehistoric Eocene insect in amber (insect)

MS42 One sheet 2000f *Desmatosuchus* (thecodontian)
Set of 1 sheet

2001

43	300f	*Compsognathus* (s-dinosaur)
44	300f	*Kritosaurus* [=*Gryposaurus*] (o-dinosaur)
45	300f	*Nodosaurus* (o-dinosaur)
46	300f	*Tuojiangosaurus* (o-dinosaur)
47	300f	*Homalocephale* (o-dinosaur)
48	300f	*Tsintaosaurus* (o-dinosaur)
49	390f	*Monoclonius* (o-dinosaur)
50	390f	*Dryosaurus* (o-dinosaur)
51	390f	*Anatosaurus* [=*Anatotitan*] (o-dinosaur)
52	390f	*Styracosaurus* (o-dinosaur)
53	390f	*Pinacosaurus* ((o-dinosaur)
54	390f	*Kentrosaurus* (o-dinosaur)

Set of 12 stamps

55	250f	*Apatosaurus* (s-dinosaur)
56	300f	*Baryonyx* (s-dinosaur)
57	325f	*Albertosaurus* (s-dinosaur)
58	350f	*Diplodocus* (s-dinosaur)
59	350f	*Parasaurolophus* (o-dinosaur)
60	350f	*Archaeopteryx* (bird)
61	350f	*Rhamphorhynchus* (pterosaur)
62	350f	*Herrerasaurus* (s-dinosaur)
63	350f	*Struthiomimus* (s-dinosaur)
64	350f	*Triceratops* (o-dinosaur)
65	350f	*Ornithocheirus* (pterosaur)
66	350f	*Brachiosaurus* (s-dinosaur)
67	350f	*Utahraptor* (s-dinosaur)
68	350f	*Tyrannosaurus* (s-dinosaur)
69	350f	*Stegosaurus* (o-dinosaur)
70	375f	*Dimetrodon* (pelycosaur)

Set of 16 stamps

MS71 Two sheets (a) 1500f *Rhamphorhynchus* (pterosaur);
(b) 1500f *Protoceratops* (o-dinosaur) and *Deinonychus* (s-dinosaur)
Set of 2 sheets

2002

72	50f	*Anatosaurus* [=*Anatotitan*] (o-dinosaur)
73	100f	*Apatosaurus* (s-dinosaur)
74	150f	*Allosaurus* (s-dinosaur)
75	200f	*Velociraptor* (s-dinosaur)
76	240f	Pterosaur
77	240f	*Albertosaurus* (s-dinosaur)
78	240f	*Dryptosaurus* (s-dinosaur)
79	240f	*Archaeopteryx* (bird)
80	240f	*Ouranosaurus* (o-dinosaur)
81	240f	*Meganeura* [wrongly inscr *Myaheura*] (insect)
82	240f	*Camptosaurus* (o-dinosaur)
83	240f	*Ichthyosaurus* (ichthyosaur)
84	240f	*Geosaurus* (crocodilian)
85	240f	Trilobite
86	240f	*Plesiosaurus* (plesiosaur)
87	240f	*Lewesiceras* [wrongly inscr *Lewisiceras*] (ammonite)
88	240f	*Rhamphorhynchus* (pterosaur)
89	240f	*Pteranodon* (pterosaur)
90	240f	*Tyrannosaurus* (s-dinosaur)
91	240f	*Deinonychus* (s-dinosaur)
92	240f	*Parasaurolophus* (o-dinosaur)
93	240f	*Corythosaurus* (o-dinosaur)
94	240f	*Patagosaurus* (s-dinosaur)
95	240f	*Triceratops* (o-dinosaur)
96	240f	*Brachylophosaurus* (o-dinosaur)
97	240f	*Euoplocephalus* [wrongly inscr *Europlocephalus*] (o-dinosaur)

98	240f	*Dimetrodon* (pelycosaur)
99	240f	*Leptoceratops* (o-dinosaur)
		Set of 28 stamps

MS100 Two sheets (a) 1500f *Stegosaurus* (o-dinosaur); (b) 1500f *Herrerasaurus* (s-dinosaur)
  Set of 2 sheets

101	600f	*Sauropelta* (o-dinosaur)
102	600f	*Chasmosaurus* (o-dinosaur)
103	600f	*Herrerasaurus* (s-dinosaur)
104	815f	*Brachiosaurus* (s-dinosaur)
105	815f	*Sarcosuchus* (crocodilian)
106	815f	*Giganotosaurus* (s-dinosaur)
		Set of 6 stamps

MS107 *Nos.* 104/106 *Brachiosaurus* (s-dinosaur), *Sarcosuchus*
      (crocodilian), and *Giganotosaurus* (s-dinosaur)
      Set of 1 sheet

CHAD
```
West Africa
100 centimes = 1 franc
```

1966

1	30f	*Tchadanthropus uxoris* [=*Homo erectus*?] (mammal)
		Set of 1 stamp

1996

2	150f	*Heterodontosaurus* (o-dinosaur)
3	150f	*Ornitholestes* (s-dinosaur)
4	150f	*Dromaeosaurus* (s-dinosaur)
5	150f	*Pinacosaurus* (o-dinosaur)
6	200f	*Corythosaurus* (o-dinosaur)
7	200f	*Euoplocephalus* [wrongly inscr *Ankylosaurus*] (o-dinosaur)
8	200f	*Ornithomimus* (s-dinosaur)
9	200f	*Styracosaurus* (o-dinosaur)
		Set of 8 stamps

1997

Nos. 2/9 *overprinted* **HONG KONG '97**

10	150f	*Heterodontosaurus* (o-dinosaur)
11	150f	*Ornitholestes* (s-dinosaur)
12	150f	*Dromaeosaurus* (s-dinosaur)
13	150f	*Pinacosaurus* (o-dinosaur)
14	200f	*Corythosaurus* (o-dinosaur)
15	200f	*Euoplocephalus* [wrongly inscr *Ankylosaurus*] (o-dinosaur)
16	200f	*Ornithomimus* (s-dinosaur)
17	200f	*Styracosaurus* (o-dinosaur)
		Set of 8 stamps

Dinosaurs and other Prehistoric Animals on Stamps

1998

18†	300f	*Ouranosaurus* (o-dinosaur), *Baryonyx* (s-dinosaur), *Sarcosuchus* (crocodilian)
19†	300f	*Indricotherium* (mammal)
MS20		One sheet 1500f Hominid (mammal)
		Set of 1 sheet
21	400f	*Dilophosaurus* (s-dinosaur)
22	400f	*Argentinosaurus* (s-dinosaur)
23	400f	*Kritosaurus* [=*Gryposaurus*] (o-dinosaur)
24	400f	*Scutellosaurus* (o-dinosaur)
25	400f	*Ornithomimosaurus* (s-dinosaur)
26	400f	*Bactrosaurus* (o-dinosaur)
27	450f	*Coelophysis* (s-dinosaur)
28	450f	*Kannemeyeria* (therapsid)
29	450f	*Apatosaurus* (s-dinosaur)
30	450f	*Scaphonyx* (rhynchosaur)
31	450f	*Lystrosaurus* (therapsid)
32	450f	*Kentrosaurus* (o-dinosaur)
		Set of 12 stamps
MS33		One sheet 2000f *Giganotosaurus* (s-dinosaur)
		Set of 1 sheet

2001

34	200f	Hominids (mammal)
		Set of 1 stamp
MS35		One sheet *No.* 34 200f Hominids (mammal)
		Set of 1 sheet
36	300f	*Steneosaurus* (crocodilian)
37	300f	*Rhamphorhynchus* (pterosaur)
38	300f	*Archaeopteryx* (bird)
39	300f	*Keichousaurus* (plesiosaur)
40	375f	*Mesadactylus* (pterosaur)
41	375f	*Pteranodon* (pterosaur)
42	375f	*Tropeognathus* (pterosaur)
43	375f	*Quetzalcoatlus* (pterosaur)
44	500f	*Deinonychus* (s-dinosaur)
45	500f	*Seismosaurus* (s-dinosaur)
46	500f	*Pleurocoelus* (s-dinosaur) and *Acrocanthosaurus* (s-dinosaur)
47	500f	*Styracosaurus* (o-dinosaur)
		Set of 12 stamps
MS48		Two sheets (a) 3000f *Tyrannosaurus* (s-dinosaur); (b) 3000f *Tyrannosaurus* (s-dinosaur)
		Set of 2 sheets

2005

49	25f	*Sahelanthropus tchadensis* (mammal)
50	50f	*Sahelanthropus tchadensis* (mammal)
51	100f	*Sahelanthropus tchadensis* (mammal)

52 150f *Sahelanthropus tchadensis* (mammal)
Set of 4 stamps
MS53 One sheet 1500f *Sahelanthropus tchadensis* (mammal)
Set of 1 sheet

CHILE

South America
100 centavos = 1 peso

2000

1 150p *Iguanodon* (o-dinosaur)
2 150p *Plesiosaurus* (plesiosaur)
3 150p *Titanosaurus* (s-dinosaur)
4 150p *Mylodon* ground sloth (mammal)
Set of 4 stamps

CHINA (PEOPLE'S REPUBLIC)

Eastern Asia
100 fen = 1 yuan

1958

1 4f *Kaolishania pustulosa* (trilobite)
2 8f *Lufengosaurus huenei* (s-dinosaur)
3 16f *Sinomegacerus* [=*Megaloceros*] *pachyospeus* (mammal)
Set of 3 stamps

1991

4 20f *Homo erectus* (mammal), *Mammuthus* woolly mammoth (mammal), and *Coelodonta* woolly rhinoceros (mammal)
Set of 1 stamp

1999

5† 80f *Anomalocaris* (early invertebrate)

COMORO ISLANDS

Indian Ocean
100 centimes = 1 franc

1994

1 75f *Edaphosaurus* (pelycosaur)
2 75f *Moschops* (therapsid)
3 75f *Kentrosaurus* (o-dinosaur)
4 75f *Compsognathus* (s-dinosaur)
5 75f *Sauroctonus* (therapsid)

6	75f	*Ornitholestes* (s-dinosaur)
7	75f	*Styracosaurus* (o-dinosaur)
8	75f	*Acantholis* (o-dinosaur)
9	150f	*Edmontonia* (o-dinosaur)
10	150f	*Struthiomimus* (s-dinosaur)
11	150f	*Diatryma* [=*Gastornis*] (bird)
12	150f	*Uintatherium* (mammal)
13	450f	*Dromiceiomimus* (s-dinosaur)
14	450f	*Iguanodon* (o-dinosaur)
15	525f	*Synthetoceras* (mammal)
16	525f	*Euryapteryx* moa (bird)
		Set of 16 stamps (in perforate and imperforate versions)
MS17		One sheet 1200f *Tyrannosaurus* (s-dinosaur)
		Set of 1 sheet (in perforate and imperforate versions)

1998

18	150f	*Eurhinodelphis* (mammal)
19	150f	*Stenopterygius* (ichthyosaur)
20	150f	*Ichthyosaurus* (ichthyosaur)
21	150f	*Pakicetus* (mammal)
22	150f	*Xenacanthus* (shark)
23	150f	*Zygorhiza* (mammal)
24	150f	*Basilosaurus* (mammal)
25	150f	*Mesosaurus* (early reptile)
26	150f	*Cetotherium* (mammal)
27	200f	*Pteranodon* [wrongly inscr *Elasmosaurus*] (pterosaur)
28	200f	*Quetzalcoatlus* (pterosaur)
29	200f	*Mesadactylus* (pterosaur)
30	200f	*Dimorphodon* (pterosaur)
31	200f	*Rhamphorhynchus* (pterosaur)
32	200f	*Pteranodon* (pterosaur)
33	200f	*Pterodactylus* (pterosaur)
34	200f	*Eudimorphodon* (pterosaur)
35	200f	*Ornithodesmus* (pterosaur)
36	250f	*Dilophosaurus* (s-dinosaur)
37	250f	*Megalosaurus* (s-dinosaur)
38	250f	*Ceratosaurus* (s-dinosaur)
39	250f	*Ceolophysis* (s-dinosaur)
40	250f	*Tyrannosaurus* (s-dinosaur)
41	250f	*Deinonychus* (s-dinosaur)
42	250f	*Allosaurus* (s-dinosaur)
43	250f	*Stegosaurus* (o-dinosaur)
44	250f	*Albertosaurus* (s-dinosaur)
		Set of 27 stamps

1999

45	150f	*Rhamphorhynchus* (pterosaur)
46	150f	*Quetzalcoatlus* (pterosaur)
47	150f	*Pterodactylus* (pterosaur)
48	150f	*Pteranodon* (pterosaur)

49	150f	*Dimorphodon* (pterosaur)
50	150f	*Camarasaurus* (s-dinosaur)
51	150f	*Tenontosaurus* (o-dinosaur)
52	150f	*Protoceratops* (o-dinosaur)
53	150f	*Coelurosauravus* (early reptile)
54	150f	*Mixosaurus* (ichthyosaur)
55	150f	*Ceresiosaurus* (nothosaur)
56	150f	*Sharovipteryx* (pterosaur)
57	150f	*Meganeura* (insect)
58	150f	*Archaeopteryx* (bird)
59	150f	*Peteinosaurus* (pterosaur)
60	150f	*Eudimorphodon* (pterosaur)
61	150f	*Brachiosaurus* (s-dinosaur)
62	150f	*Gallimimus* (s-dinosaur)
63	150f	*Tarbosaurus* (s-dinosaur)
64	150f	*Parasaurolophus* (o-dinosaur)
65	150f	*Sauropelta* (o-dinosaur)
66	150f	*Herrerasaurus* (s-dinosaur)
67	150f	*Stegosaurus* (o-dinosaur)
68	150f	*Corythosaurus* (o-dinosaur)
		Set of 24 stamps

MS69 Four sheets (a) 1500f *Diatryma* [=*Gastornis*] (bird) and *Hyracotherium* (mammal);
(b) 1500f *Mesosaurus* (early reptile) and sarcopterygian (fish);
(c) 1500f *Ceratosaurus* (s-dinosaur); (d) 1500f *Megazostrodon* (mammal)
Set of 4 sheets

CONGO REPUBLIC (BRAZZAVILLE)
Central Africa
100 centimes = 1 franc

1970

1	15f	*Kentrosaurus* (o-dinosaur)
2	20f	*Deinotherium* (mammal)
3	60f	*Brachiosaurus* (s-dinosaur)
4	80f	*Arsinotherium* (mammal)
		Set of 4 stamps

1975

5	55f	*Moschops* (therapsid)
6	75f	*Tyrannosaurus* (s-dinosaur) and *Ornithomimus* (s-dinosaur)
7	95f	*Cryptoclidus* (plesiosaur)
8	100f	*Stegosaurus* (o-dinosaur)
		Set of 4 stamps (in perforate and imperforate versions)

1993

9	75f	*Ichthyostega* (amphibian)
10	95f	*Archaeopteryx* (bird)
11	120f	*Brachiosaurus* (s-dinosaur) and *Diplodocus* (s-dinosaur)

Dinosaurs and other Prehistoric Animals on Stamps

12	200f	*Tyrannosaurus* (s-dinosaur)
13	250f	*Pteranodon* (pterosaur)
		Set of 5 stamps
MS14	One sheet 400f *Brontosaurus* [=*Apatosaurus*] (s-dinosaur)	
		Set of 1 sheet

1994

15	25f	*Palaeomastodon* (mammal)
16	45f	*Mammut* (mammal)
17	50f	*Amebelodon* (mammal)
18	75f	*Platybelodon* (mammal)
19	120f	*Mammuthus* woolly mammoth (mammal)
		Set of 5 stamps

1999

20	90f	*Lesothosaurus* (o-dinosaur)
21	205f	*Scutellosaurus* (o-dinosaur)
22	205f	*Kentrosaurus* (o-dinosaur)
23	300f	*Stegosaurus* (o-dinosaur)
24	400f	*Tuojiangosaurus* (o-dinosaur)
25	600f	*Heterodontosaurus* (o-dinosaur)
		Set of 6 stamps
MS26	One sheet 1000f *Velociraptor* (s-dinosaur)	
		Set of 1 sheet
27	750f	*Triceratops* (o-dinosaur)
28	750f	*Stegosaurus* (o-dinosaur)
29	750f	*Allosaurus* (s-dinosaur)
30	750f	*Iguanodon* (o-dinosaur)
		Set of 4 stamps
MS31	Nos. 27/30 *Triceratops* (o-dinosaur), *Stegosaurus* (o-dinosaur), *Allosaurus* (s-dinosaur), *Iguanodon* (o-dinosaur)	

CROATIA
South-east Europe
1991. 100 paras = 1 dinar
1994. 100 lipa = 1 kuna

1994

1	2400d	*Iguanodon* (o-dinosaur)
2	4000d	*Iguanodon* (o-dinosaur)
		Set of 2 stamps

1995

3†	1k	Fossil molluscs and echinoderms

1997

4	1k.40	*Gomphotherium angustidens* (mammal)

5	2k.40	*Viviparus novskaensis* (gastropod) Set of 2 stamps

1999

6	1k.80	*Homo neanderthalensis* Neanderthal man (mammal)
7	4k	*Homo neanderthalensis* Neanderthal man (mammal) Set of 2 stamps

CUBA
West Indies
100 centavos = 1 peso

1958

1†	12c	*Megalocnus rodens* ground sloth (mammal)
2†	30c	*Perisphinctes* (ammonite)

1967

3†	1c	*Homo habilis* (mammal)
4†	2c	*Australopithecus* (mammal)
5†	3c	*Pithecanthropus* [=*Homo*] *erectus* (mammal)
6†	4c	*Homo erectus* Peking man (mammal)
7†	5c	*Homo neanderthalensis* Neanderthal man (mammal)

1974

8†	10c	*Dinornis* giant moa (bird)

1982

9	1c	*Ornimegalonyx oteroi* (bird)
10	5c	*Crocodylus rhombifer* (crocodilian)
11	7c	*Aquila borrasi* (bird)
12	20c	*Geocapromys columbianus* hutia (mammal)
13	35c	*Megalocnus rodens* ground sloth (mammal)
14	50c	*Nesophontes micrus* (mammal) Set of 6 stamps

1985

15	1c	*Pteranodon* (pterosaur)
16	2c	*Brontosaurus* [=*Apatosaurus*] (s-dinosaur) and theropod (s-dinosaur)
17	4c	*Iguanodon* (o-dinosaur)
18	5c	*Stegosaurus* (o-dinosaur)
19	8c	*Monoclonius* (o-dinosaur)
20	30c	*Corythosaurus* (o-dinosaur)
21	50c	*Tyrannosaurus* (s-dinosaur) Set of 7 stamps

1987

22	3c	*Triceratops* (o-dinosaur)
23	5c	Pelycosaur
24	10c	*Euoplocephalus* (o-dinosaur)
25	20c	*Styracosaurus* (o-dinosaur) and hadrosaur (o-dinosaur)
26	35c	*Parasaurolophus* (o-dinosaur)

Dinosaurs and other Prehistoric Animals on Stamps

27	40c	*Allosaurus* (s-dinosaur), hadrosaur (o-dinosaur), *Triceratops* (o-dinosaur)
		Set of 6 stamps

1996

28†	85c	Charles Darwin and *Paranthropus robustus* (mammal)

1997

29†	10c	*Australopithecus africanus* (mammal)
30†	15c	*Pithecanthropus* [=*Homo erectus*] Java man (mammal)
31†	15c	*Sinanthropus* [=*Homo erectus*] Peking man (mammal)
32†	15c	*Homo neanderthalensis* Neanderthal man (mammal)

1998

33†	10c	*Proconsul* (mammal)

1999

34	10c	*Ornithosuchus* (thecodontian)
35	15c	*Bactrosaurus* (o-dinosaur)
36	15c	*Saltopus* (s-dinosaur)
37	65c	*Protosuchus* (crocodilian)
38	75c	*Mussaurus* (s-dinosaur)
		Set of 5 stamps

2002

39†	5c	*Megaloceros* (mammal)
40†	15c	*Coelodonta* woolly rhinoceros (mammal)
41†	45c	*Canis dirus* dire wolf (mammal)
42†	65c	*Ursus spelaeus* cave bear (mammal)
43†	75c	*Smilodon* sabre-tooth tiger (mammal)
MS44		One sheet 1p *Mammuthus* woolly mammoth (mammal)
		Set of 1 sheet

2005

45	5c	*Carnotaurus* (s-dinosaur)
46	10c	*Oviraptor* (s-dinosaur)
47	30c	*Parasaurolophus* (o-dinosaur)
48	65c	*Sauropelta* (o-dinosaur)
49	90c	*Iguanodon* (o-dinosaur)
		Set of 5 stamps
MS50		One sheet 1p *Velociraptor* (s-dinosaur)
		Set of 1 sheet

2006

51	5c	*Dsungaripterus* (pterosaur) and *Yangchuanosaurus* (s-dinosaur)
52	10c	*Pterodactylus* (pterosaur) and *Spinosaurus* (s-dinosaur)
53	30c	*Pteranodon* (pterosaur) and *Pachycephalosaurus* (o-dinosaur)
54	35c	*Scaphognathus* (pterosaur) and *Muttaburrasaurus* (o-dinosaur)
55	65c	*Quetzalcoatlus* (pterosaur) and *Stegosaurus* (o-dinosaur)

56   1p05   *Sordes* (pterosaur) and *Saichania* (o-dinosaur)
              Set of 6 stamps

MS57 One sheet 1p *Stenonychosaurus* [=*Troodon*] (s-dinosaur)
              Set of 1 sheet

CYPRUS
South-east Europe
100 cents = 1 euro

2007

1†   43c   *Hippopotamus minor* (mammal)

CZECH REPUBLIC
Central Europe
100 haleru = 1 koruna

1994

1   2k   *Stegosaurus ungulatus* (o-dinosaur)
2   3k   *Apatosaurus excelsus* (s-dinosaur)
3   5k   *Tarbosaurus bataar* (s-dinosaur)
              Set of 3 stamps

1999

MS4   Two stamps (a) 13k *Cheirurus* (trilobite), *Sieberella* (brachiopod), *Ascocystites* (echinoderm);
              (b) 31k *Deiphon forbesi* (trilobite), *Ophioceras simplex* (nautiloid),
              Carolicrinus barrandei (echinoderm)
              Set of 2 stamps on 1 sheet

2005

5†   25k   *Deinotherium* (mammal)

CZECHOSLOVAKIA
Central Europe
100 haleru = 1 koruna

1968

1†   30h   *Hypophylloceras bizonatum* (ammonite)
2†   60h   *Palaeobatrachus* [=*Hekatobatrachus*] *grandipes* (amphibian)
3†   1k   *Chlamys gigas* (bivalve)
4†   1k60   *Selenopeltis buchii* (trilobite)

1969

5†   60h   Ammonite

DAHOMEY
West Africa
100 centimes = 1 franc

1974

1	35f	*Rhamphorhynchus* (pterosaur) (air)
2	150f	*Stegosaurus* (o-dinosaur)
3	200f	*Tyrannosaurus* (s-dinosaur)

Set of 3 stamps

DEMOCRATIC CONGO (KINSHASA)
Central Africa
100 cents = 1 Congolese franc

2001

1†	25f	*Scutellosaurus* (o-dinosaur)

2003

2†	120f	*Mammuthus primigenius* woolly mammoth (mammal)
3†	350f	*Gomphotherium* (mammal)

2006

4	550f	*Muttaburrasaurus* [wrongly inscr *Ouranosaurus*] (o-dinosaur)
5	550f	*Mammuthus* woolly mammoth (mammal)
6	550f	*Criorhynchus* [wrongly inscr *Tropeognathus*] (pterosaur)
7	550f	*Styracosaurus* (o-dinosaur)

Set of 4 stamps

MS8 One sheet 550f *Styracosaurus* (o-dinosaur)
Set of 1 sheet

9†	600f	*Anchiceratops* (o-dinosaur)

(in perforate and imperforate versions)

DENMARK
North Europe
1875 100 ore = 1 krone

1998

1	3k	*Parapuzosia* (ammonite)
2	4k50	Fossil shark's teeth (shark)
3	5k50	*Echinocorys* (echinoderm)
4	15k	*Pleurotomaria* (gastropod)

Set of 4 stamps

MS5 *Nos.* 1-4 *Parapuzosia* (ammonite), fossil shark's teeth (shark), *Echinocorys* (echinoderm), *Pleurotomaria* (gastropod)
Set of 1 sheet

DJIBOUTI REPUBLIC
East Africa
100 centimes = 1 franc

1990

1	90f	*Elephas recki* (mammal)
		Set of 1 stamp

DOMINICA
West Indies
100 cents = 1 West Indian dollar

1992

1	10c	*Camptosaurus* (o-dinosaur)
2	15c	*Edmontosaurus* (o-dinosaur)
3	25c	*Corythosaurus* (o-dinosaur)
4	60c	*Stegosaurus* (o-dinosaur)
5	$1	*Torosaurus* (o-dinosaur)
6	$3	*Euoplocephalus* (o-dinosaur)
7	$4	*Tyrannosaurus* (s-dinosaur)
8	$5	*Parasaurolophus* (o-dinosaur)
		Set of 8 stamps
MS9		Two sheets (a) $6 *Corythosaurus* (o-dinosaur); $6 *Torosaurus* (o-dinosaur)
		Set of 2 sheets

1995

10	20c	*Monoclonius* (o-dinosaur)
11	25c	*Euoplocephalus* (o-dinosaur)
12	55c	*Coelophysis* (s-dinosaur)
13	65c	*Compsognathus* (s-dinosaur)
14	90c	*Dimorphodon* (pterosaur)
15	90c	*Rhamphorhynchus* (pterosaur)
16	90c	Prehistoric giant alligator (crocodilian)
17	90c	*Pentaceratops* (o-dinosaur)
18	$1	*Ceratosaurus* (s-dinosaur)
19	$1	*Camptosaurus* (o-dinosaur)
20	$1	*Stegosaurus* (o-dinosaur)
21	$1	*Camarasaurus* (s-dinosaur)
22	$1	*Baryonyx* (s-dinosaur)
23	$1	*Dilophosaurus* (s-dinosaur)
24	$1	Dromaeosaurids (s-dinosaurs)
25	$1	*Deinonychus* (s-dinosaur)
26	$1	*Dinichthys* (placoderm)
27	$1	*Carcharodon* [=*Carcharocles*] *megalodon* (shark)
28	$1	Nautiloid
29	$1	*Xystridura* (trilobite)

Dinosaurs and other Prehistoric Animals on Stamps

                Set of 20 stamps
MS30 Two sheets (a) $5 *Sauropelta* (o-dinosaur); (b) $6 *Triceratops* (o-dinosaur)
                Set of 2 sheets

1999

31	25c	*Tyrannosaurus* (s-dinosaur)
32	65c	*Hypacrosaurus* (o-dinosaur)
33	90c	*Sauropelta* (o-dinosaur)
34	$1	*Barosaurus* (s-dinosaur)
35	$1	*Rhamphorhynchus* (pterosaur)
36	$1	*Apatosaurus* (s-dinosaur)
37	$1	*Archaeopteryx* (bird)
38	$1	*Diplodocus* (s-dinosaur)
39	$1	*Ceratosaurus* (s-dinosaur)
40	$1	*Stegosaurus* (o-dinosaur)
41	$1	*Elaphrosaurus* (s-dinosaur)
42	$1	*Vulcanodon* (s-dinosaur)
43	$1	*Psittacosaurus* (o-dinosaur)
44	$1	*Pteranodon* (pterosaur)
45	$1	*Ichthyornis* (bird)
46	$1	*Spinosaurus* (s-dinosaur)
47	$1	*Parasaurolophus* (o-dinosaur)
48	$1	*Ornithomimus* (s-dinosaur)
49	$1	*Anatosaurus* [=*Anatotitan*] (o-dinosaur)
50	$1	*Triceratops* (o-dinosaur)
51	$1	*Baryonyx* (s-dinosaur)
52	$1	*Zalambdalestes* (mammal)

                Set of 22 stamps
MS53 Two sheets (a) $5 *Yangchuanosaurus* (s-dinosaur) and *Pteranodon* (pterosaur);
                (b) $6 *Brachiosaurus* (s-dinosaur)
                Set of 2 sheets

2005

54	$2	*Mammuthus columbi* Columbian mammoth (mammal)
55	$2	*Spinosaurus* (s-dinosaur)
56	$2	*Ankylosaurus* (o-dinosaur)
57	$2	*Mammuthus primigenius* woolly mammoth (mammal)
58	$2	*Pterodactylus* (pterosaur)
59	$2	*Pteranodon* (pterosaur)
60	$2	*Sordes* (pterosaur)
61	$2	*Caudipteryx* (pterosaur)
62	$2	*Tyrannosaurus* (s-dinosaur)
63	$2	*Velociraptor* (s-dinosaur)
64	$2	*Stegosaurus* (o-dinosaur)
65	$2	*Psittacosaurus* (o-dinosaur)

                Set of 12 stamps
MS66 Three sheets (a) $6 *Compsognathus* (s-dinosaur); (b) $6 *Archaeopteryx* (bird);
                (c) $6 *Mammuthus primigenius* woolly mammoth (mammal)
                Set of 3 sheets

EAST GERMANY (GERMAN DEMOCRATIC REPUBLIC)
Central Europe
100 pfennig = 1 Deutsche mark (East)
1990. 100 pfennig = 1 Deutsche mark (West)

1973

1†	20pf	*Pterodactylus kochi* (pterosaur)
2†	35pf	*Archaeopteryx lithographica* (bird)
3†	70pf	*Odontopleura ovata* (trilobite)

1978

4†	35pf	*Palaeobatrachus diluvianus* (amphibian)

ECUADOR
South America
100 cents = 1 US dollar

2007

1	80c	*Smilodon* sabre-tooth tiger (mammal)
2	80c	*Megatherium* ground sloth (mammal)

Set of 2 stamps

EGYPT
North Africa
1000 milliemes = 1 piastre,
100 piastres = 1 Egyptian pound

1979

1	20m	*Arsinotherium zitelli* (mammal

Set of 1 stamp

EL SALVADOR
Central America
100 centavos = 1 colon

1979

1	10c	*Gomphotherium* mastodon (mammal)
2	20c	*Smilodon* sabre-tooth tiger (mammal)
3	30c	*Toxodon* (mammal)
4	15c	*Mammuthus* woolly mammoth (mammal) (air)
5	25c	*Eremotherium* ground sloth (mammal)
6	2col	*Osteoborus* [=*Borophagus*] *cynoides* (mammal)

Set of 6 stamps

2006

7	1col50	Mastodont (mammal)
8	1col60	Ground sloth (mammal)
9	5col	Ground sloth (mammal)
10	10col	Ground sloth (mammal)
		Set of 4 stamps

EQUATORIAL GUINEA
West Africa
1973.   100 centimos = 1 ekuele (plural: bipkwele)
1985.   100 centimos = 1 franc (CFA)

1978

1	30c	*Dimetrodon* (pelycosaur)
2	35c	*Stegosaurus* (o-dinosaur)
3	40c	*Rhamphorhynchus* (pterosaur) and *Pteranodon* (pterosaur)
4	45c	*Corythosaurus* (o-dinosaur)
5	50c	*Ankylosaurus* (o-dinosaur)
6	25e	*Styracosaurus* (o-dinosaur)
7	60e	*Triceratops* (o-dinosaur)
		Set of 7 stamps (in perforate and imperforate versions)
MS8		Two sheets (a) 130e *Diplodocus* (s-dinosaur); (b) 200e Pliosaur, unspecified (plesiosaur)
		Set of 2 sheets (in perforate and imperforate versions)

DID YOU KNOW? The 1978 40c stamp depicts two genera of flying reptile. They existed from the late Triassic to the end of the Cretaceous Period (220 to 65.5 million years ago). Pterosaurs were the first vertebrates to evolve powered flight. Their wings were formed by a membrane of skin, muscle, and other tissues stretching from the thorax to a dramatically lengthened fourth finger. Some cryptozoologists believe that animals from this group have survived to the present day, in tropical Africa, New Guinea, and Central America.

1994

9	300f	*Chasmosaurus belli* (o-dinosaur)
10	500f	*Tyrannosaurus rex* (s-dinosaur)
11	700f	*Triceratops horridus* (o-dinosaur)
		Set of 3 stamps
MS12		One sheet 800f *Styracosaurus albertensis* (o-dinosaur) and *Deinonychus antirrhopus* (s-dinosaur)
		Set of 1 sheet

2001

13	500f	*Carnotaurus sastrei* (s-dinosaur)
14	500f	*Iberomesornis romeroli* (bird)
15	500f	*Troodon* (s-dinosaur)

		Set of 3 stamps
MS16		One sheet 800f *Diplodocus* (s-dinosaur)
		Set of 1 sheet

ETHIOPIA
North-east Africa
100 cents = 1 birr

1977

1†	80c	*Paranthropus robustus* (mammal)
2	5c	*Terebratula abyssinica* (brachiopod)
3	10c	*Terebratula subalata* (brachiopod)
4	25c	*Cucullaea lefeburiaua* (bivalve)
5	50c	*Ostrea plicatissima* (bivalve)
6	90c	*Trigonia cousobrina* (bivalve)
		Set of 5 stamps

1986

7	2b	*Australopithecus afarensis* 'Lucy' (mammal)
		Set of 1 stamp

FALKLAND ISLANDS
South Atlantic
100 pence = 1 pound

1982

1	5p	Charles Darwin issue, with trilobite, pterosaur, ammonite, prehistoric fish, and plesiosaur (?) in margin of stamp
2	17p	Charles Darwin issue, with ditto prehistoric animals in margin of stamp
3	25p	Charles Darwin issue, with ditto prehistoric animals in margin of stamp
4	34p	Charles Darwin issue, with ditto prehistoric animals in margin of stamp
		Set of 4 stamps

FIJI
South Pacific
100 cents = 1 dollar

2006

1	50c	*Volia athollandersoni* (crocodilian)
2	1$10	*Natunaornis gigoura* (bird)
3	1$20	*Vitirallus watlingi* (bird)
4	1$50	*Platymantis megabotoniviti* (amphibian)
		Set of 4 stamps

FRANCE
Western Europe
1849. 100 centimes = 1 franc
2002. 100 cents = 1 euro

1969

1†   50c+10c *Gomphotherium* (mammal)
          (in perforate and imperforate versions)

1992

2   3f40   *Homo neanderthalensis* Neanderthal man (mammal)
              Set of 1 stamp

2000

3†   3f   *Allosaurus* (s-dinosaur)
MS4† Includes *No. 2 Allosaurus* (s-dinosaur)
              Set of 1 sheet

DID YOU KNOW? Ichthyosaurs as depicted in the French 53c stamp from 1995 were giant marine reptiles that resembled fish and dolphins. During the middle Triassic Period, ichthyosaurs evolved from as-yet unidentified land reptiles that moved back into the water, in a development parallel to that of modern-day dolphins and whales.

2005

5†   53c   Ichthyosaur and plesiosaur

2008

6   55c   *Smilodon* sabre-tooth tiger (mammal)
7   55c   *Phorusrhacus* (bird)
8   65c   *Megaloceros giganteus* (mammal)
9   88c   *Mammuthus primigenius* woolly mammoth (mammal)
              Set of 4 stamps
MS10 Nos. 6/9 *Smilodon* sabre-tooth tiger (mammal), *Phorusrhacus* (bird),
            Megaloceros giganteus (mammal), and *Mammuthus primigenius*
            woolly mammoth (mammal)
            Set of 1 sheet

FRENCH TERRITORY OF THE AFARS AND THE ISSAS
(later Djibouti—from 1977)
East Africa
100 centimes = 1 franc

1975

1†   10f   Ammonite and trilobite

FUJEIRA (now FUJAIRAH)
(Since 1971, one of the seven United Arab Emirates)
Arabian peninsula
1967. 100 dirhams = 1 riyal

1968

1	15d	*Edaphosaurus* [wrongly inscr *Dimetrodon*] (pelycosaur)
2	25d	*Triceratops* (o-dinosaur)
3	50d	*Plateosaurus* (s-dinosaur)
4	75d	*Stegosaurus* (o-dinosaur)
5	1r	*Edaphosaurus* [wrongly inscr *Dimetrodon*] (pelycosaur)
6	1r.50	*Allosaurus* (s-dinosaur)
7	2r.50	*Triceratops* (o-dinosaur)
8	3r	*Plateosaurus* (s-dinosaur)
9	4r	*Stegosaurus* (o-dinosaur)
10	5r	*Allosaurus* (s-dinosaur)
		Set of 10 stamps
11	80d	*Triceratops* (o-dinosaur)
12	85d	*Edaphosaurus* [wrongly inscr *Naosaurus*] (pelycosaur)
13	90d	*Stegosaurus* (o-dinosaur)
14	95d	*Brontosaurus* [=*Apatosaurus*] (s-dinosaur)
		Set of 4 stamps
MS15		One sheet 10r *Mammuthus primigenius* woolly mammoth (mammal)
		Set of 1 sheet

GABON
West Africa
100 centimes = 1 franc

1995

1	125f	*Sordes* (pterosaur)
2	125f	*Diplodocus* (s-dinosaur)
3	125f	*Eudimorphodon* (pterosaur)
4	125f	*Dimetrodon* (pelycosaur)
5	125f	*Anurognathus* (pterosaur)
6	125f	*Deinonychus* (s-dinosaur) and *Pachycephalosaurus* (o-dinosaur)
7	125f	*Triceratops* (o-dinosaur)
8	125f	*Corythosaurus* (o-dinosaur)
9	125f	*Meganeura* (insect)
10	125f	*Longisquama* (thecodontian)
11	125f	*Oviraptor* (s-dinosaur)
12	125f	*Monoclonius* (o-dinosaur)
13	225f	*Pistosaurus* (plesiosaur) and *Pteranodon* (pterosaur)
14	225f	*Pteranodon* (pterosaur)
15	225f	*Coelophysis* (s-dinosaur)
16	225f	*Xenacanthus* (shark)

17	225f	*Ischyodus* (shark)
18	225f	*Placochelys* (placodont)
19	225f	*Dunkleosteus* (placoderm)
20	225f	*Cymbospondylus* (ichthyosaur)
21	225f	*Enchodus* (fish)
22	225f	*Paracybeloides* (trilobite)
23	225f	Nautiloid
24	225f	*Palaeospondylus* (placoderm)
25	260f	*Tyrannosaurus* (s-dinosaur)
26	260f	*Apatosaurus* (s-dinosaur)
27	260f	*Dimorphodon* (pterosaur)
28	260f	*Stegosaurus* (o-dinosaur)
29	260f	*Archaeopteryx* (bird)
30	260f	*Protoceratops* (o-dinosaur)
31	260f	Ichthyosaur
32	260f	*Phobosuchus* [=*Deinosuchus*] (crocodilian) and *Deltoptychius* (shark)
33	260f	*Parasaurolophus* (o-dinosaur)
34	260f	*Scapanorhynchus* (shark)
35	260f	*Spathobathis* [=*Aellopos*] (shark) and *Plesiosaurus* (plesiosaur)
36	260f	*Cladoselache* (shark)
		Set of 36 stamps

2000

37†	100f	*Pterodactylus* (pterosaur)
38†	125f	*Allosaurus* (s-dinosaur)
39†	125f	*Struthiomimus* (s-dinosaur)
40†	225f	*Psittacosaurus* (o-dinosaur)
41†	225f	*Tyrannosaurus* (s-dinosaur)
42†	225f	*Criorhynchus* (pterosaur)
43†	225f	*Pterodactylus* (pterosaur)
44†	225f	*Albertosaurus* (s-dinosaur)
45†	225f	*Dromiceiomimus* (s-dinosaur)
46†	225f	*Opisthocoelicaudia* (s-dinosaur)
47†	225f	*Brachiosaurus* (s-dinosaur)
48†	225f	*Pachycephalosaurus* (o-dinosaur)
49†	225f	*Parasaurolophus* (o-dinosaur)
50†	225f	*Edmontosaurus* (o-dinosaur)
51†	225f	*Pentaceratops* (o-dinosaur)
52†	225f	*Corythosaurus* (o-dinosaur)
53†	260f	*Peteinosaurus* (pterosaur)
54†	260f	*Acanthostega* (amphibian)
55†	260f	*Ceresiosaurus* (nothosaur)
56†	260f	Pliosaur
57†	260f	*Stethacanthus* (shark)
58†	260f	Ichthyosaur
59†	260f	*Pholidogaster* (amphibian)
60†	260f	*Gerrothorax* (amphibian)
61†	260f	*Diplocaulus* (amphibian)
62†	260f	*Mixosaurus* (ichthyosaur)
63†	260f	*Echioceras* [wrongly inscr *Echinoceras*] (ammonite)

64†	260f	*Parasaurolophus* (o-dinosaur)
65†	500f	*Acanthostega* (amphibian)
MS66		Two sheets (a) 1500f *Saltasaurus* (s-dinosaur); (b) 1500f *Archaeopteryx* (bird)
		Set of 2 sheets
67†	100f	*Archaeopteryx* (bird)
68†	100f	*Velociraptor* (s-dinosaur)
69†	125f	*Corythosaurus* (o-dinosaur)
70†	125f	*Torosaurus* (o-dinosaur)
71†	225f	*Pachycephalosaurus* (o-dinosaur)
72†	500f	*Parasaurolophus* (o-dinosaur)
73†	100f	*Stegosaurus* (o-dinosaur)
74†	100f	*Pteranodon* (pterosaur)
75†	100f	*Carnotaurus* (s-dinosaur)
76†	125f	*Iguanodon* (o-dinosaur)
77†	125f	*Pentaceratops* (o-dinosaur)
78†	125f	*Styracosaurus* (o-dinosaur)
79†	500f	*Deinonychus* (s-dinosaur)
80†	500f	*Stegoceras* (o-dinosaur)
81†	500f	*Struthiomimus* (s-dinosaur)
82†	125f	*Camarasaurus* (s-dinosaur)
83†	125f	*Rhamphorhynchus* (pterosaur)
84†	125f	*Saltasaurus* (s-dinosaur)
85†	225f	*Camptosaurus* (o-dinosaur)
86†	225f	*Megalosaurus* (s-dinosaur)
87†	225f	*Allosaurus* (s-dinosaur)
88†	260f	*Anchisaurus* (s-dinosaur)
89†	260f	*Dilophosaurus* (s-dinosaur)
90†	260f	*Massospondylus* (s-dinosaur)
91†	125f	*Pterodactylus* (pterosaur)
92†	125f	*Dimorphodon* (pterosaur)
93†	125f	*Alamosaurus* (s-dinosaur)
94†	225f	*Psittacosaurus* (o-dinosaur)
95†	225f	*Deinonychus* (s-dinosaur)
96†	225f	*Dromiceiomimus* (s-dinosaur)
97†	225f	*Yangchuanosaurus* (s-dinosaur)
98†	260f	*Protorosaurus* (early reptile)
99†	260f	*Triceratops* (o-dinosaur)
100†	260f	*Daspletosaurus* (s-dinosaur)
101†	260f	*Pentaceratops* (o-dinosaur)
102†	125f	*Brachiosaurus* (s-dinosaur)
103†	125f	*Scaphognathus* (pterosaur)
104†	125f	*Pteranodon* (pterosaur)
105†	225f	*Tyrannosaurus* (s-dinosaur)
106†	225f	*Ichthyosaurus* (ichthyosaur)
107†	225f	*Macroplata* (plesiosaur)
108†	225f	*Dilophosaurus* (s-dinosaur)
109†	500f	*Stegosaurus* (o-dinosaur)
110†	500f	*Thecodontosaurus* (s-dinosaur)
111†	500f	*Saltasaurus* (s-dinosaur)

112† 500f *Pachyrhinosaurus* (o-dinosaur)
MS113 Four sheets (a) 1500f *Arrhinoceratops* (o-dinosaur); (b) 1500f
            Apatosaurus (s-dinosaur) and *Cetiosaurus* (s-dinosaur);
            (c) 1500f *Argentinosaurus* (s-dinosaur); (d) 1500f *Tyrannosaurus* (s-dinosaur)
         Set of 4 sheets

GAMBIA
West Africa
100 butut = 1 dalasi

1992

1	20b	*Dryosaurus* (o-dinosaur)
2	25b	*Saurolophus* (o-dinosaur)
3	50b	*Allosaurus* (s-dinosaur)
4	75b	*Fabrosaurus* (o-dinosaur)
5	1d	*Deinonychus* (s-dinosaur)
6	1d25	*Cetiosaurus* (s-dinosaur)
7	1d50	*Camptosaurus* (o-dinosaur)
8	2d	*Ornithosuchus* (thecodontian)
9	3d	*Spinosaurus* (s-dinosaur)
10	5d	*Ornithomimus* (s-dinosaur)
11	10d	*Kentrosaurus* (o-dinosaur)
12	12d	*Scleromochlus* (pterosaur)

Set of 12 stamps

MS13 Three sheets (a) 25d *Allosaurus* (s-dinosaur); (b) 25d *Cetiosaurus* (s-dinosaur);
            (c) 25d *Ornithosuchus* (thecodontian)
         Set of 3 sheets

1995

14	2d	*Pteranodon* (pterosaur)
15	2d	*Archaeopteryx* (bird)
16	2d	*Rhamphorhynchus* (pterosaur)
17	2d	*Ornithomimus* (s-dinosaur)
18	2d	*Stegosaurus* (o-dinosaur)
19	2d	*Heterodontosaurus* (o-dinosaur)
20	2d	*Lystrosaurus* (therapsid)
21	2d	*Euoplocephalus* (o-dinosaur)
22	2d	*Coelophysis* (s-dinosaur)
23	2d	*Staurikosaurus* (s-dinosaur)
24	2d	*Giantoneris* [=*Cacops*] (amphibian)
25	2d	*Diarthrognathus* (therapsid)
26	3d	*Archaeopteryx* (bird)
27	3d	*Yangchuanosaurus* [wrongly inscr *Vangehuanosaurus*] (s-dinosaur)
28	3d	*Coelophysis* (s-dinosaur)
29	3d	*Plateosaurus* (s-dinosaur)
30	3d	*Baryonyx* (s-dinosaur)
31	3d	*Ornitholestes* (s-dinosaur)
32	3d	*Dryosaurus* (o-dinosaur)

33	3d	*Estemmenosuchus* (therapsid)
34	3d	*Macroplata* (plesiosaur)
35	3d	*Shonisaurus* (ichthyosaur)
36	3d	*Muraenosaurus* (plesiosaur)
37	3d	*Archelon* (turtle)
		Set of 24 stamps
MS38		Four sheets (a) 20d *Bactrosaurus* (o-dinosaur); (b) 22d *Tyrannosaurus rex* (s-dinosaur); (c) 25d *Triceratops* (o-dinosaur); 25d *Spinosaurus* (s-dinosaur)
		Set of 4 sheets

1997

39	50b	*Coelophysis* (s-dinosaur) and *Ornitholestes* (s-dinosaur)
40	63b	*Spinosaurus* (s-dinosaur)
41	75b	*Kentrosaurus* (o-dinosaur)
42	1d	*Ceratosaurus* (s-dinosaur)
43	1d50	*Stygimoloch* (o-dinosaur)
44	2d	*Troodon* (s-dinosaur)
45	3d	*Velociraptor* (s-dinosaur)
46	4d	*Triceratops* (o-dinosaur)
47	4d	*Anurognathus* (pterosaur)
48	4d	*Pteranodon* (pterosaur)
49	4d	*Rhamphorhynchus* (pterosaur)
50	4d	*Saltasaurus* (s-dinosaur)
51	4d	*Agathaumas* (o-dinosaur)
52	4d	*Stegosaurus* (o-dinosaur)
53	4d	*Albertosaurus libratus* (s-dinosaur)
54	4d	*Lesothosaurus* (o-dinosaur)
55	4d	*Lesothosaurus* (o-dinosaur)
56	4d	*Tarbosaurus bataar* (s-dinosaur)
57	4d	*Brachiosaurus* (s-dinosaur)
58	4d	*Styracosaurus* (o-dinosaur)
59	4d	*Baryonyx* (s-dinosaur)
60	4d	*Coelophysis* (s-dinosaur)
61	4d	*Carnotaurus* (s-dinosaur)
62	4d	*Compsognathus carnipes* (s-dinosaur)
63	4d	*Compsognathus* (s-dinosaur)
64	4d	*Stenonychosaurus* [=*Troodon*] (s-dinosaur)
65	4d	*Protoceratops* (o-dinosaur)
66	10d	*Ornithomimus* (s-dinosaur)
67	15d	*Stegosaurus* (o-dinosaur)
68	20d	*Saichania* (o-dinosaur)
		Set of 30 stamps
MS69		Two sheets (a) 25d *Deinonychus* (s-dinosaur); (b) 25d *Seismosaurus* (s-dinosaur)
		Set of 2 sheets

1999

70	3d	*Carnotaurus* (s-dinosaur)
71	3d	*Quetzalcoatlus* (pterosaur)
72	3d	*Peteinosaurus* (pterosaur)

73	3d	*Prenocephale* (o-dinosaur)
74	3d	*Hesperornis* (bird)
75	3d	*Coelophysis* (s-dinosaur)
76	3d	*Camptosaurus* (o-dinosaur)
77	3d	*Panderichthys* (fish)
78	3d	*Garudimimus* (s-dinosaur)
79	3d	*Cacops* (amphibian)
80	3d	*Ichthyostega* (amphibian)
81	3d	*Scutellosaurus* (o-dinosaur)
82	3d	*Diatryma* [=*Gastornis*] (bird)
83	3d	*Pteranodon* (pterosaur)
84	3d	*Stegodon* (mammal)
85	3d	*Icaronycthris* (mammal)
86	3d	*Archaeopteryx* (bird)
87	3d	*Chasmatosaurus* (thecodontian)
88	3d	*Tytthostonyx* (bird)
89	3d	*Hyaenodon* (mammal)
90	3d	*Uintatherium* (mammal)
91	3d	*Hesperocyon* (mammal)
92	3d	*Amebelodon* (mammal)
93	3d	*Indricotherium* (mammal)
		Set of 24 stamps

MS94 Four sheets (a) 25d *Deinonychus* (s-dinosaur); (b) 25d Sabre-tooth tiger (mammal); (c) 25d *Lepisosteus* (fish); (d) 25d *Microceratops* [=*Graciliceratops*] (o-dinosaur)
      Set of 4 sheets

DID YOU KNOW? The term 'sabre-tooth tiger', like the one on the Gambian MS94 Miniature Sheet from 1999, describes numerous species, mainly in the families Felidae (subfamily Machairodontinae), Barbourofelidae, and Nimravidae. However it also includes two marsupial families that lived during various parts of the Cenozoic Era, and evolved their sabre-toothed characteristics entirely independently. Some cryptozoologists believe that species still remain in the African country of Chad and parts of South America.

2003

95	30d	*Peteinosaurus* (pterosaur)
96	30d	*Parasaurolophus* [wrongly inscr *Pachycephalosaurus*] (o-dinosaur)
97	30d	*Grendelius* (ichthyosaur)
98	30d	*Anomalocaris* (early invertebrate)
99	30d	*Criorhynchus* (pterosaur)
100	30d	*Triceratops* (o-dinosaur)
101	30d	*Seismosaurus* (s-dinosaur)
102	30d	*Stegosaurus* (o-dinosaur)
		Set of 8 stamps

MS103 Two sheets (a) 75d *Olenoides*(?) [wrongly inscr *Paradoxides*] (trilobite); (b) 75d *Edmontosaurus* (o-dinosaur)
      Set of 2 sheets

GEORGIA
Central Asia
1993. kupon
1995. 100 tetri = 1 lari

1995

1	15k	*Brontosaurus* [=*Apatosaurus*] (s-dinosaur)
2	15k	*Ceratosaurus* (s-dinosaur)
3	15k	*Deinonychus* (s-dinosaur)
4	15k	*Parasaurolophus* (o-dinosaur)
5	15k	*Saurolophus* (o-dinosaur)
6	15k	*Scolosaurus* [=*Euoplocephalus*] (o-dinosaur)
7	15k	*Stegosaurus* (o-dinosaur)
8	15k	*Triceratops* (o-dinosaur)
9	15k	*Tyrannosaurus* (s-dinosaur)
		Set of 8 stamps (in perforate and imperforate versions)
MS10		One sheet 100k *Deinonychus* (s-dinosaur)
		Set of 1 sheet
11	15t	*Pteranodon* [wrongly inscr *Pterodactylus*] (pterosaur)
12	15t	*Rhamphorhynchus* (pterosaur)
13	15t	*Pterodactylus* [wrongly inscr *Pteranodon*] (pterosaur)
14	15t	*Spinosaurus* (s-dinosaur)
15	15t	*Tyrannosaurus* (s-dinosaur)
16	15t	*Velociraptor* (s-dinosaur)
17	15t	*Monoclonius* (o-dinosaur)
18	15t	*Ornithomimus* (s-dinosaur)
19	15t	Mastodon (mammal)
		Set of 9 stamps

1996

20	10t	*Brontosaurus* [=*Apatosaurus*] (s-dinosaur)
21	10t	*Archaeopteryx* (bird)
22	10t	*Leptoceratops* (o-dinosaur)
23	10t	*Parasaurolophus* (o-dinosaur)
24	10t	*Pentaceratops* (o-dinosaur)
25	10t	*Herrerasaurus* (s-dinosaur)
26	10t	*Hadrosaurus* (o-dinosaur)
27	10t	*Montanoceratops* (o-dinosaur) plus unidentified dinosaur
28	10t	*Fulgurotherium* (o-dinosaur)
		Set of 9 stamps

1998

29	15t	*Pterodactylus* (pterosaur)
30	15t	*Rhamphorhynchus* (pterosaur)
31	15t	*Pteranodon* (pterosaur)
32	15t	*Velociraptor* [wrongly inscr *Spinosaurus*] (s-dinosaur)
33	15t	*Tyrannosaurus* (s-dinosaur)
34	15t	*Spinosaurus* [wrongly inscr *Velociraptor*] (s-dinosaur)

35	15t	Mastodon [wrongly inscr *Monoklonius* (sic)] (mammal)
36	15t	*Ornithomimus* (s-dinosaur)
37	15t	*Monoclonius* [wrongly inscr *Mastodon*] (o-dinosaur)
		Set of 9 stamps

2003

MS38† Two stamps, including (b) 60t *Homo erectus* (mammal)
  Set of 1 sheet

GERMANY
Central Europe
100 pfennig = 1 Deutsche mark
2002. 100 cents = 1 euro

1990

1	10pf	*Dicraeosaurus* (s-dinosaur)
2	25pf	*Kentrurosaurus* [=*Kentrosaurus*] (o-dinosaur)
3	35pf	*Dysalotosaurus* [=*Dryosaurus*] (o-dinosaur)
4	50pf	*Brachiosaurus* (s-dinosaur)
5	85pf	*Brachiosaurus* (s-dinosaur)
		Set of 5 stamps

2006

6	220c	*Homo neanderthalensis* Neanderthal man (mammal)
		Set of 1 stamp

GHANA
West Africa
100 pesewas = 1 cedi

1992

1	20c	*Iguanodon* (o-dinosaur)
2	50c	*Anchisaurus* (s-dinosaur)
3	60c	*Heterodontosaurus* (o-dinosaur)
4	80c	*Ouranosaurus* (o-dinosaur)
5	100c	*Anatosaurus* [=*Anatotitan*] (o-dinosaur)
6	200c	*Elaphrosaurus* (s-dinosaur)
7	500c	*Coelophysis* (s-dinosaur)
8	600c	*Rhamphorhynchus* (pterosaur)
		Set of 8 stamps
MS9		Two sheets (a) 1500c *Elaphrosaurus* (s-dinosaur); (b) 1500c *Coelophysis* (s-dinosaur)
		Set of 2 sheets

1995

10	400c	*Seismosaurus* (s-dinosaur)
11	400c	*Supersaurus* (s-dinosaur)

12	400c	*Ultrasauros* [=*Supersaurus*] (s-dinosaur)
13	400c	*Saurolophus* (o-dinosaur)
14	400c	*Lambeosaurus* (o-dinosaur)
15	400c	*Parasaurolophus* (o-dinosaur)
16	400c	*Triceratops* (o-dinosaur)
17	400c	*Styracosaurus* (o-dinosaur)
18	400c	*Pachyrhinosaurus* (o-dinosaur)
19	400c	*Peteinosaurus* (pterosaur)
20	400c	*Quetzalcoatlus* (pterosaur)
21	400c	*Eudimorphodon* (pterosaur)
22	400c	*Allosaurus* (s-dinosaur)
23	400c	*Daspletosaurus* (s-dinosaur)
24	400c	*Tarbosaurus bataar* (s-dinosaur)
25	400c	*Velociraptor mongoliensis* (s-dinosaur)
26	400c	*Herrerasaurus* (s-dinosaur)
27	400c	*Coelophysis (*s-dinosaur)
		Set of 18 stamps

MS28 Two sheets (a) 2500c *Tyrannosaurus rex* (s-dinosaur); (b) 2500c *Albertosaurus* (s-dinosaur)
Set of 2 sheets

DID YOU KNOW? *Tyrannosaurus* is a genus of theropod dinosaur. There were a number of species, including the most famous species *Tyrannosaurus rex* ('rex' meaning 'king' in Latin), commonly abbreviated to *T. rex*, which is a fixture in popular culture around the world. Fossils of *T. rex* are found in a variety of rock formations dating to the last three million years of the Cretaceous Period, approximately 68 to 65 million years ago; it was among the last non-avian dinosaurs to exist prior to the Cretaceous–Tertiary extinction event.

1999

29	400c	*Corythosaurus* (o-dinosaur)
30	600c	*Struthiomimus* (s-dinosaur)
31	800c	*Pterodactylus* (pterosaur)
32	800c	*Scelidosaurus* (o-dinosaur)
33	800c	*Pteranodon* (pterosaur)
34	800c	*Plateosaurus* (s-dinosaur)
35	800c	*Ornithosuchus* (thecodontian)
36	800c	*Kentrosaurus* (o-dinosaur)
37	800c	*Hypsognathus* (early reptile)
38	800c	*Erythrosuchus* (thecodontian)
39	800c	*Stegoceras* (o-dinosaur)
40	800c	Theropod [wrongly inscr *Ankylosaurus*] (s-dinosaur)
41	800c	*Anatosaurus* [=*Anatotitan*] (o-dinosaur)
42	800c	*Diplodocus* (s-dinosaur)
43	800c	*Monoclonius* (o-dinosaur)
44	800c	*Tyrannosaurus* (s-dinosaur)
45	800c	*Camptosaurus* (o-dinosaur)
46	800c	*Ornitholestes* (s-dinosaur)
47	800c	*Archaeopteryx* (bird)

48	800c	*Pachycephalosaurus* (?) [wrongly inscr *Allosaurus*] (o-dinosaur)
49	1000c	*Lambeosaurus* (o-dinosaur)
50	2000c	*Hesperosuchus* (thecodontian)
		Set of 22 stamps
MS51		Two sheets (a) 5000c *Dimorphodon* (pterosaur); (b) 5000c *Apatosaurus* (s-dinosaur)
		Set of 2 sheets

GIBRALTAR
South-west Europe
100 pence = 1 pound

1973

1	4p	Prehistoric Gibraltar human skull (mammal)
2	6p	Prehistoric Gibraltar human (mammal)
3	10p	Prehistoric Gibraltar humans (mammal)
		Set of 3 stamps

2000

4†	5p	*Megantereon whitei* sabre-tooth tiger (mammal)
5†	5p	*Homo neanderthalensis* Neanderthal man (mammal)

2005

6†	47p	*Homo neanderthalensis* Neanderthal man (mammal)

GREAT BRITAIN
North-west Europe
100 pence = 1 pound sterling

1982

1†	29p	Charles Darwin, with *Paranthropus robustus* (mammal) and *Homo erectus* (mammal)

1991

2	22p	*Iguanodon* (o-dinosaur)
3	26p	*Stegosaurus* (o-dinosaur)
4	31p	*Tyrannosaurus* (s-dinosaur)
5	33p	*Protoceratops* (o-dinosaur)
6	37p	*Triceratops* (o-dinosaur)
		Set of 5 stamps

1999

7†	26p	*Archaeopteryx* (bird)

2006

8	1st	*Megantereon* sabre-tooth tiger (mammal) [1st = First Class]
9	42p	*Megaloceros* (mammal)
10	47p	*Coelodonta* woolly rhinoceros (mammal)

11	68p	*Mammuthus primigenius* woolly mammoth (mammal)
12	£1.12	*Ursus spelaeus* cave bear (mammal)
		Set of 5 stamps

GREECE
South-east Europe
100 lepta = 1 drachma
2002. 100 cents = 1 euro

1979

1†	4d	*Mene psarianosi* (fish)

1982

2†	50d	*Homo erectus* (mammal)

GRENADA
West Indies
100 cents = 1 West Indian dollar

1991

1†	20c	*Pteranodon* (pterosaur)

1994

2	75c	*Quetzalcoatlus* (pterosaur)
3	75c	*Pteranodon ingens* (pterosaur)
4	75c	*Tropeognathus* (pterosaur)
5	75c	*Phobetor* (pterosaur)
6	75c	*Alamosaurus* (s-dinosaur)
7	75c	*Triceratops* (o-dinosaur)
8	75c	*Tyrannosaurus rex* (s-dinosaur)
9	75c	*Tyrannosaurus rex* (s-dinosaur)
10	75c	*Lambeosaurus* (o-dinosaur)
11	75c	*Spinosaurus* (s-dinosaur)
12	75c	*Parasaurolophus* (o-dinosaur)
13	75c	*Hadrosaurus* (o-dinosaur)
14	75c	*Germanodactylus* (pterosaur)
15	75c	*Dimorphodon* (pterosaur)
16	75c	*Rhamphorhynchus* (pterosaur)
17	75c	*Apatosaurus* (s-dinosaur)
18	75c	*Pterodactylus* (pterosaur)
19	75c	*Stegosaurus* (o-dinosaur)
20	75c	*Brachiosaurus* (s-dinosaur)
21	75c	*Allosaurus* (s-dinosaur)
22	75c	*Plesiosaurus* (plesiosaur)
23	75c	*Ceratosaurus* (s-dinosaur)
24	75c	*Compsognathus* (s-dinosaur)

25	75c	*Elaphrosaurus* (s-dinosaur)
		Set of 24 stamps
MS26	\multicolumn{2}{l}{Two sheets (a) $6 *Pteranodon ingens* (pterosaur); (b) $6 *Plateosaurus* (s-dinosaur)}

MS26 Two sheets (a) $6 *Pteranodon ingens* (pterosaur); (b) $6 *Plateosaurus* (s-dinosaur)
Set of 2 sheets

1997

27	35c	*Dunkleosteus* (placoderm)
28	75c	*Tyrannosaurus rex* (s-dinosaur)
29	$1.50	*Sordes* (pterosaur)
30	$1.50	*Dimorphodon* (pterosaur)
31	$1.50	*Brachiosaurus* [wrongly inscr *Diplodocus*] (s-dinosaur)
32	$1.50	*Allosaurus* (s-dinosaur)
33	$1.50	*Pentaceratops* (o-dinosaur)
34	$1.50	*Protoceratops* (o-dinosaur)
35	$2	*Askeptosaurus* (early reptile)
36	$3	*Triceratops* (o-dinosaur)

Set of 10 stamps

MS37 Two sheets (a) $6 *Elasmosaurus* (plesiosaur) and *Tristychius* (shark); (b) $6 *Maiasaura* (o-dinosaur)
Set of 2 sheets

1999

38	35c	*Ouranosaurus* (o-dinosaur)
39	45c	*Struthiomimus* (s-dinosaur)
40	75c	*Parasaurolophus* (o-dinosaur)
41	$1	*Archaeopteryx* (bird)
42	$1	*Brachiosaurus* (s-dinosaur)
43	$1	*Dilophosaurus* (s-dinosaur)
44	$1	*Dimetrodon* (pelycosaur)
45	$1	*Psittacosaurus* (o-dinosaur)
46	$1	*Acrocanthosaurus* (s-dinosaur)
47	$1	*Stenonychosaurus* [=*Troodon*] (s-dinosaur)
48	$1	*Dryosaurus* (o-dinosaur)
49	$1	*Compsognathus* (s-dinosaur)
50	$1	*Agathaumas* (o-dinosaur)
51	$1	*Camarasaurus* (s-dinosaur)
52	$1	*Quetzalcoatlus* (pterosaur)
53	$1	*Alioramus* (s-dinosaur)
54	$1	*Camptosaurus* (o-dinosaur)
55	$1	*Albertosaurus* (s-dinosaur)
56	$1	*Anatosaurus* [=*Anatotitan*] (o-dinosaur)
57	$1	*Spinosaurus* (s-dinosaur)
58	$1	*Centrosaurus* (o-dinosaur)
59	$2	*Triceratops* (o-dinosaur)
60	$3	*Stegoceras* (o-dinosaur)
61	$4	*Stegosaurus* (o-dinosaur)

Set of 24 stamps

MS62 Two sheets (a) $6 *Velociraptor* (s-dinosaur); (b) $6 *Tyrannosaurus rex* (s-dinosaur)
Set of 2 sheets

2003

MS63 Four stamps (a) $2 *Spinosaurus* (s-dinosaur); (b) $2 *Herrerasaurus* (s-dinosaur); (c) $2 *Protarchaeopteryx* (bird); (d) $2 *Sinosauropteryx* (s-dinosaur)
Set of 1 sheet

MS64 Four stamps (a) $2 *Allosaurus* (s-dinosaur); (b) $2 *Cryolophosaurus* (s-dinosaur); (c) $2 *Eoraptor* (s-dinosaur); (d) $2 *Caudipteryx* (s-dinosaur)
Set of 1 sheet

MS65 Two sheets (a) $6 *Triceratops* (o-dinosaur); (b) $6 *Archaeopteryx* (bird)
Set of 2 sheets

2005

66	$2	*Psittacosaurus* (o-dinosaur)
67	$2	*Deinonychus* (s-dinosaur)
68	$2	*Suchomimus* (s-dinosaur)
69	$2	*Smilodon* sabre-tooth tiger (mammal)
70	$2	*Eurypholis* (fish)
71	$2	*Ichthyosaurus* (ichthyosaur)
72	$2	*Plesiosaurus* (plesiosaur)
73	$2	*Varnerxiphactinus* (fish)
74	$2	Pterosaur
75	$2	*Archaeopteryx* (bird)
76	$2	Pterosaur(?)
77	$2	*Microraptor* (s-dinosaur)

Set of 12 stamps

MS78 Three sheets (a) $6 *Tenontosaurus* (o-dinosaur) and *Dimetrodon* (pelycosaur); (b) $6 *Uintatherium* (mammal); (c) $6 *Mammuthus* woolly mammoth (mammal)
Set of 3 sheets

GRENADINES OF GRENADA
West Indies
100 cents = 1 West Indian dollar

1994

1	15c	*Spinosaurus* (s-dinosaur)
2	35c	*Apatosaurus* (s-dinosaur)
3	45c	*Tyrannosaurus rex* (s-dinosaur)
4	55c	*Triceratops* (o-dinosaur)
5	$1	*Pachycephalosaurus* (o-dinosaur)
6	$2	*Pteranodon* (pterosaur)
7	$4	*Parasaurolophus* (o-dinosaur)
8	$5	*Brachiosaurus* (s-dinosaur)

Set of 8 stamps

MS9 Two sheets (a) $6 *Brachiosaurus* (s-dinosaur); (b) $6 *Spinosaurus* (s-dinosaur) and *Tyrannosaurus* (s-dinosaur)
Set of 2 sheets

1997

10	45c	*Stegosaurus* (o-dinosaur)
11	90c	*Diplodocus* (s-dinosaur)

Dinosaurs and other Prehistoric Animals on Stamps

12	$1	*Pteranodon* (pterosaur)
13	$1.50	*Rhamphorhynchus* (pterosaur) and *Brachiosaurus* (s-dinosaur)
14	$1.50	*Archaeopteryx* (bird)
15	$1.50	*Anurognathus* (pterosaur)
16	$1.50	*Albertosaurus* (s-dinosaur)
17	$1.50	*Herrerasaurus* (s-dinosaur)
18	$1.50	*Platyhystrix* (amphibian)
19	$2	*Deinonychus* (s-dinosaur) and *Ankylosaurus* (o-dinosaur)
		Set of 10 stamps
MS20		Two sheets (a) $6 *Allosaurus* (s-dinosaur); (b) $6 *Hypacrosaurus* (o-dinosaur)
		Set of 2 sheets

1999

21	$1	*Troodon* (s-dinosaur)
22	$1	*Camptosaurus* (o-dinosaur)
23	$1	*Parasaurolophus* (o-dinosaur)
24	$1	*Dryosaurus* (o-dinosaur)
25	$1	*Gallimimus* (s-dinosaur)
26	$1	*Camarasaurus* (s-dinosaur)
27	$1.50	Hadrosaur (o-dinosaur)
28	$1.50	*Corythosaurus* (?) [wrongly inscr *Lambeosaurus*] (o-dinosaur)
29	$1.50	*Iguanodon* (o-dinosaur)
30	$1.50	*Euoplocephalus* (o-dinosaur)
31	$1.50	*Triceratops* (o-dinosaur)
32	$1.50	*Brachiosaurus* (s-dinosaur)
33	$1.50	*Panoplosaurus* [wrongly inscr *Ponoptosaurus*] (o-dinosaur)
34	$1.50	*Stegosaurus* (o-dinosaur)
		Set of 14 stamps
MS35		Three sheets (a) $6 *Edmontosaurus* (o-dinosaur); (b) $6 *Tyrannosaurus rex* (s-dinosaur); (c) $6 *Halticosaurus* (s-dinosaur)
		Set of 3 sheets

2005

36	$2	*Psittacosaurus* (o-dinosaur)
37	$2	*Deinonychus* (s-dinosaur)
38	$2	*Suchomimus* (s-dinosaur)
39	$2	*Smilodon* sabre-tooth tiger (mammal)
40	$2	*Eurypholis* (fish)
41	$2	*Ichthyosaurus* (ichthyosaur)
42	$2	*Plesiosaurus* (plesiosaur)
43	$2	*Varnerxiphactinus* (fish)
44	$2	Pterosaur
45	$2	*Archaeopteryx* (bird)
46	$2	Pterosaur(?)
47	$2	*Microraptor* (s-dinosaur)
		Set of 12 stamps
MS48		Three sheets (a) $6 *Tenontosaurus* (o-dinosaur) and *Dimetrodon* (pelycosaur); (b) $6 *Uintatherium* (mammal); (c) $6 *Mammuthus* woolly mammoth (mammal)
		Set of 3 sheets

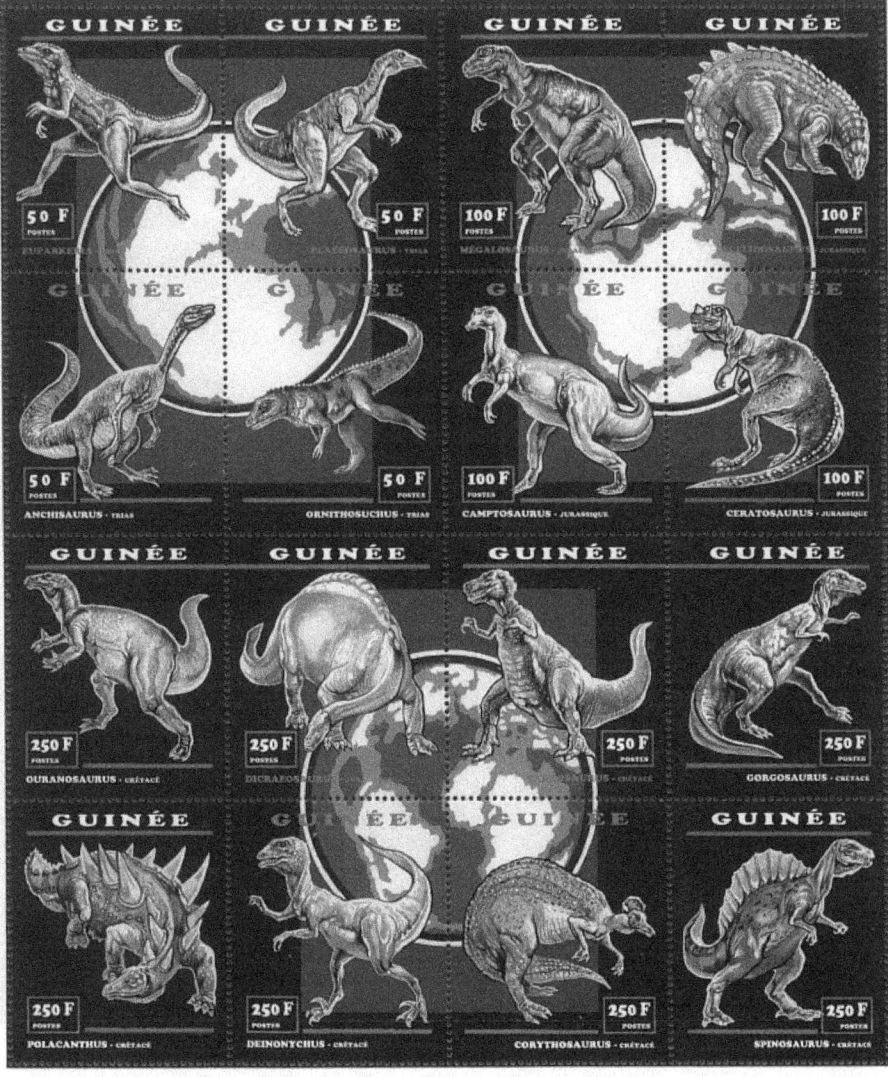

This gorgeous sheet of Guinea dinosaur stamps not only illustrates a diverse selection of dinosaurs from all three periods of the Mesozoic Era – namely, the Triassic, Jurassic, and Cretaceous – but also depicts how the Earth's single land mass (Pangaea) gradually broke up over many millions of years to yield the separate continental land masses present today.

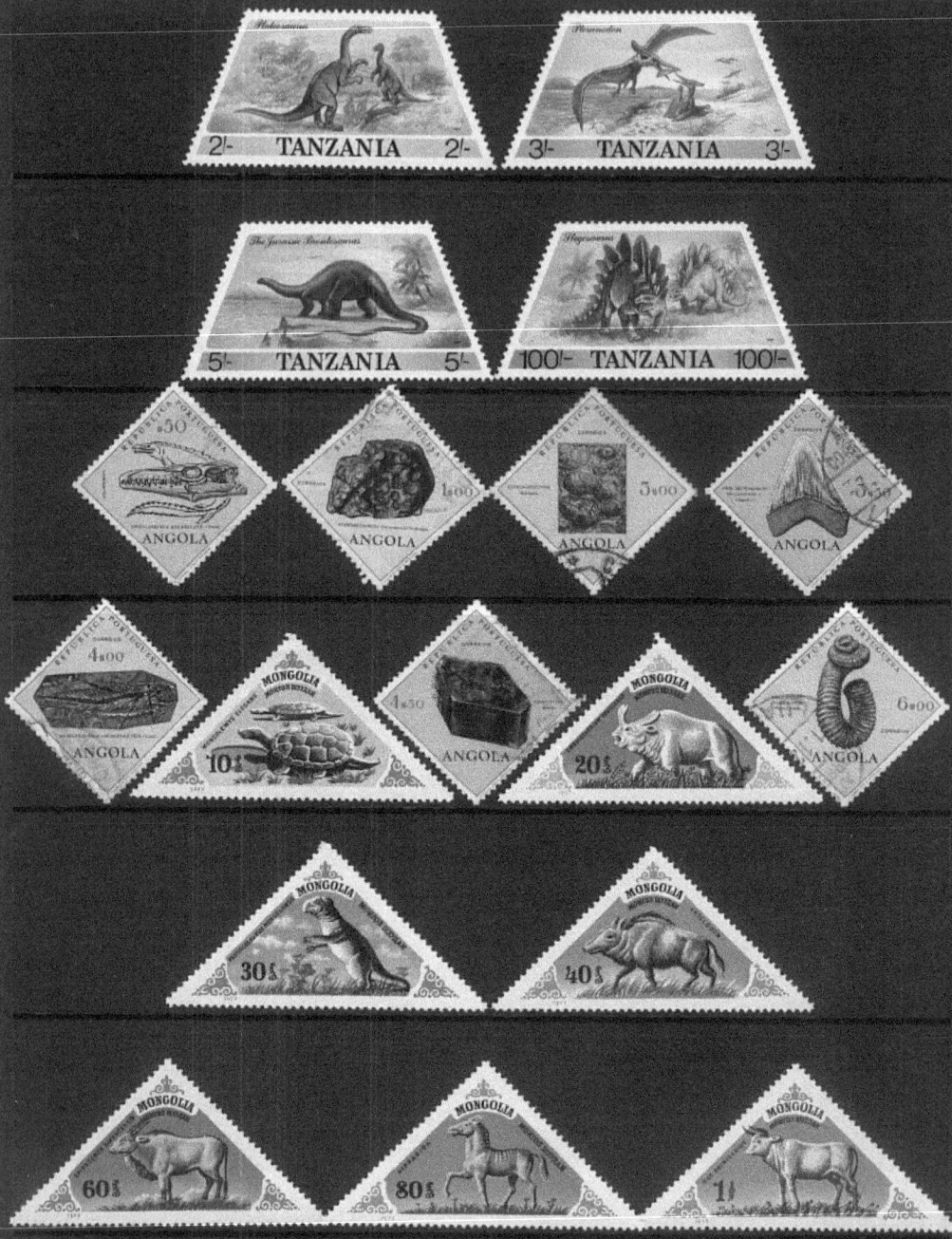

Unusually-Shaped Prehistoric Animal Stamps: Not all prehistoric animal stamps are rectangular or square, as revealed here. Several triangular sets have been issued, of which this Mongolian set from 1977 is a particularly fine example. Rarer are diamond-shaped sets, and this Angolan example from 1970 was the very first. Scarcest, but most eyecatching, of all, however, must surely be Tanzania's wonderful set of trapezium-shaped wildlife stamps from 1988 that includes the four prehistoric animal stamps depicted here.

GUINEA
West Africa
100 centimes = 1 franc

1987

1	50f	*Dimetrodon* (pelycosaur)
2	100f	*Iguanodon* (o-dinosaur)
3	200f	*Tylosaurus* (lizard)
4	300f	*Ursus spelaeus* cave bear (mammal)
5	400f	Sabre-tooth tiger (mammal)
6	500f	*Stegosaurus* (o-dinosaur)
		Set of 6 stamps (in perforate and imperforate versions)
MS7		One sheet 600f *Triceratops* (o-dinosaur)
		Set of 1 sheet (in perforate and imperforate versions)

1991

8†	100f	Sabre-tooth tiger [*No. 5 surch* 100f on 400f] (mammal)

1993

9	50f	*Euparkeria* (thecodontian)
10	50f	*Plateosaurus* (s-dinosaur)
11	50f	*Anchisaurus* (s-dinosaur)
12	50f	*Ornithosuchus* (thecodontian)
13	100f	*Megalosaurus* (s-dinosaur)
14	100f	*Scelidosaurus* (o-dinosaur)
15	100f	*Camptosaurus* (o-dinosaur)
16	100f	*Ceratosaurus* (s-dinosaur)
17	250f	*Ouranosaurus* (o-dinosaur)
18	250f	*Dicraeosaurus* (s-dinosaur)
19	250f	*Tarbosaurus* (s-dinosaur)
20	250f	*Gorgosaurus* (s-dinosaur)
21	250f	*Polacanthus* (o-dinosaur)
22	250f	*Deinonychus* (s-dinosaur)
23	250f	*Corythosaurus* (o-dinosaur)
24	250f	*Spinosaurus* (s-dinosaur)
		Set of 16 stamps (in perforate and imperforate versions)
MS25		One sheet 1000f *Tyrannosaurus* (s-dinosaur)
		Set of 1 sheet (in perforate and imperforate versions)

1997

26	200f	*Dilophosaurus* (s-dinosaur)
27	250f	*Psittacosaurus* (o-dinosaur)
28	300f	*Dromiceiomimus* (s-dinosaur)
29	400f	*Stenonychosaurus* [=*Troodon*] (s-dinosaur)
30	450f	*Opisthocoelicaudia* (s-dinosaur)
31	500f	*Ornitholestes* (s-dinosaur)
		Set of 6 stamps
MS32		One sheet 1000f *Anchiceratops* (o-dinosaur)
		Set of 1 sheet

1998

MS33 Two stamps in one sheet (a) 2000f Dromaeosaurid (s-dinosaur); (b) 2000f *Allosaurus* (s-dinosaur)
       Set of 1 sheet

34	750f	*Dicraeosaurus* (s-dinosaur)
35	750f	*Parasaurolophus* (o-dinosaur)
36	750f	*Saurornithoides* (s-dinosaur)
37	750f	*Dilophosaurus* (s-dinosaur)
38	750f	*Titanosaurus* (s-dinosaur) and *Bagaceratops* (o-dinosaur)
39	750f	*Iguanodon* (o-dinosaur)
40	750f	*Tenontosaurus* (o-dinosaur)
41	750f	*Dryosaurus* (o-dinosaur)
42	750f	*Ceratosaurus* (s-dinosaur)

Set of 9 stamps

MS43 One sheet 1500f *Ceratosaurus* [wrongly inscr *Yangchuanosaurus*] (s-dinosaur) and *Brachiosaurus* (s-dinosaur)
       Set of 1 sheet

1999

44	300f	*Ouranosaurus* (o-dinosaur)
45	450f	*Dilophosaurus* (s-dinosaur)
46	450f	*Centrosaurus* (o-dinosaur)
47	450f	*Saltasaurus* (s-dinosaur)
48	450f	*Corythosaurus* (o-dinosaur)
49	450f	*Protoceratops* (o-dinosaur)
50	450f	*Baryonyx* (s-dinosaur)
51	450f	*Pachycephalosaurus* (o-dinosaur)
52	450f	*Maiasaura* [wrongly inscr *Malasaurus*] (o-dinosaur)
53	450f	*Spinosaurus* (s-dinosaur)
54	450f	*Lambeosaurus* (o-dinosaur)

Set of 11 stamps

MS55 Two sheets (a) 3000f *Parasaurolophus* (o-dinosaur); (b) 3000f *Utahraptor* (s-dinosaur)
       Set of 2 sheets

56	350f	*Cymbospondylus* (ichthyosaur)
57	350f	*Kronosaurus* (plesiosaur)
58	350f	*Ichthyosaurus* (ichthyosaur)
59	350f	*Eurhinosaurus* (ichthyosaur)
60	350f	*Stenopterygius* (ichthyosaur)
61	350f	*Ophthalmosaurus* (ichthyosaur)
62	350f	*Shonisaurus* (ichthyosaur)
63	350f	*Temnodontosaurus* (ichthyosaur)
64	350f	*Mixosaurus* (ichthyosaur)
65	450f	*Eudimorphodon* (pterosaur)
66	450f	*Sordes* (pterosaur)
67	450f	*Dimorphodon* (pterosaur)
68	450f	*Albertosaurus* (s-dinosaur)
69	450f	*Triceratops* (o-dinosaur)
70	450f	*Alioramus* (s-dinosaur)
71	450	*Mesosaurus* (early reptile)

Dinosaurs and other Prehistoric Animals on Stamps

72	450f	*Labidosaurus* (turtle)
73	450f	*Struthiomimus* (s-dinosaur)
		Set of 18 stamps
MS74	Two sheets (a) 2500f *Elasmosaurus* (plesiosaur); (b) 3000f *Tyrannosaurus* (s-dinosaur)
		Set of 2 sheets

2002

75	200f	*Spinosaurus* (s-dinosaur)
76	300f	*Ouranosaurus* (o-dinosaur)
77	5000f	*Kentrosaurus* (o-dinosaur)
		Set of 3 stamps
MS78	Three sheets *Nos.* 75/77 *Spinosaurus* (s-dinosaur), *Ouranosaurus* (o-dinosaur), *Kentrosaurus* (o-dinosaur)
		Set of 3 sheets

2006

79†	2000f	*Giganotosaurus* (s-dinosaur)
80†	7500f	*Carcharodontosaurus* (s-dinosaur)
MS81†	Includes two sheets (a) 25000f *Giganotosaurus* (s-dinosaur); (b) 25000f *Carcharodontosaurus* (s-dinosaur)

82†	3500f	Trilobite
83†	4000f	*Liopleurodon* (plesiosaur)
84†	6000f	*Archelon* (turtle)
MS85†	Includes *Nos.* 82/84 Trilobite, *Liopleurodon* (plesiosaur), *Archelon* (turtle)

GUINEA-BISSAU
West Africa
100 centavos = 1 peso
1997. 100 centimes = 1 West African CFA franc

1989

1	50p	*Trachodon* [=*Anatotitan*] (o-dinosaur)
2	100p	*Edaphosaurus* (pelycosaur)
3	200p	*Mesosaurus* (early reptile)
4	350p	*Elephas* [=*Mammuthus*] *primigenius* woolly mammoth (mammal)
5	500p	*Tyrannosaurus* (s-dinosaur)
6	800p	*Stegosaurus* (o-dinosaur)
7	1000p	*Cervus megaceros* [=*Megaloceros giganteus*] (mammal)
		Set of 7 stamps

2001

8	275f	Theropod (s-dinosaur)
9	275f	*Avimimus* (?) (s-dinosaur)
10	275f	Theropod (s-dinosaur)
11	275f	*Archaeopteryx* (bird)
12	275f	*Shunosaurus* (s-dinosaur)
13	275f	Theropod (s-dinosaur)

14	275f	Theropod (s-dinosaur)
15	275f	*Centrosaurus* (?) (o-dinosaur)
16	275f	Theropod (s-dinosaur)
		Set of 9 stamps
MS17	Two sheets (a) 2000f *Ornitholestes* (s-dinosaur) and *Avimimus* (s-dinosaur); (b) 2000f Theropod (s-dinosaur) and *Anchisaurus* (s-dinosaur)	
		Set of 2 sheets

2003

18†	450f	Ornithopod (o-dinosaur)
MS19†	3000f	Ornithopod (o-dinosaur)
20	500f	*Phorusrhacus* (bird)
21	500f	Dinosaur
22	500f	*Platybelodon* (mammal)
23	500f	*Archaeopteryx* (bird)
24	500f	Ground sloth (mammal)
25	500f	Theropod (s-dinosaur)
		Set of 6 stamps
MS26	One sheet 3000f *Quetzalcoatlus* (pterosaur)	
		Set of 1 sheet

2005

DID YOU KNOW? *Quetzalcoatlus* (named for the Aztec feathered serpent god Quetzalcoatl), as depicted on the 2003 issue from Guinea-Bissau, was a pterodactyloid pterosaur known from the Late Cretaceous of North America (Campanian–Maastrichtian stages, 84–65 ma), and one of the largest known flying animals of all time. It was a member of the Azhdarchidae, a family of advanced toothless pterosaurs with unusually long, stiffened necks.

27	500f	Theropod (s-dinosaur)
28	500f	*Velociraptor* (?) (s-dinosaur)
29	500f	*Ceratosaurus* (s-dinosaur)
30	500f	*Deinonychus* (s-dinosaur)
31	500f	Theropod (s-dinosaur)
32	500f	*Brachiosaurus* (s-dinosaur)
		Set of 6 stamps
MS33	One sheet 3000f Pterosaur	
		Set of 1 sheet
34	500f	Hominids (mammal)
35	500f	Hominids (mammal)
36	500f	Hominids (mammal)
37	500f	Hominids (mammal)
38	500f	Hominids (mammal)
		Set of 5 stamps
MS39	One sheet 3000f Hominids (mammal)	
		Set of 1 sheet

GUYANA

South America
100 cents = 1 dollar

1991

1†	$12.80	*Palaelodus* (bird)
2†	$12.80	*Archaeotrogon* (bird)
3†	$12.80	*Teratornis mirabilis* (bird)
4†	$12.80	*Natalus stramineus* (mammal)
5†	$12.80	*Cuvieronius* (mammal)
6†	$12.80	*Phororhacos* [=*Phorusrhacus*] (bird)
7†	$12.80	*Smilodectes* (mammal)
8†	$12.80	*Megatherium* ground sloth (mammal)
9†	$12.80	*Titanotylopus* (mammal)
10†	$12.80	*Teleoceras* (mammal)
11†	$12.80	*Macrauchenia* (mammal)
12†	$12.80	*Mylodon* ground sloth (mammal)
13†	$12.80	*Smilodon* sabre-tooth tiger (mammal)
14†	$12.80	*Glyptodon* (mammal)
15†	$12.80	*Protohydrochoerus* (mammal)
16†	$12.80	*Archaeohyrax* (mammal)
17†	$12.80	*Pyrotherium* (mammal)
18†	$12.80	*Platypittamys* (mammal)

1992

19†	$50	Oligocene mastodon (mammal)
20†	$50	Mid-Miocene stegodon (mammal)
21†	$50	Pliocene mammoth (mammal)

1993

22	$30	*Pteranodon* (pterosaur)
23	$30	*Cearadactylus* (pterosaur)
24	$30	*Eudimorphodon* (pterosaur)
25	$30	*Pterodactylus* (pterosaur)
26	$30	*Staurikosaurus* (s-dinosaur)
27	$30	*Euoplocephalus* (o-dinosaur)
28	$30	*Tuojiangosaurus* (o-dinosaur)
29	$30	*Oviraptor* (s-dinosaur)
30	$30	*Protoceratops* (o-dinosaur)
31	$30	*Panoplosaurus* (o-dinosaur)
32	$30	*Psittacosaurus* (o-dinosaur)
33	$30	*Corythosaurus* (o-dinosaur)
34	$30	*Sordes* (pterosaur)
35	$30	*Quetzalcoatlus* (pterosaur)
36	$30	*Archaeopteryx* (bird)
37	$30	*Rhamphorhynchus* (pterosaur)
38	$30	*Spinosaurus* (s-dinosaur)
39	$30	*Anchisaurus* (s-dinosaur)
40	$30	*Stegosaurus* (o-dinosaur)

41	$30	*Leaellynasaura* (o-dinosaur)
42	$30	*Minmi* (o-dinosaur)
43	$30	*Heterodontosaurus* (o-dinosaur)
44	$30	*Lesothosaurus* (o-dinosaur)
45	$30	*Deinonychus* (s-dinosaur)
46	$30	*Archaeopteryx* (bird)
47	$30	*Pteranodon* (pterosaur)
48	$30	*Quetzalcoatlus* (pterosaur)
49	$30	*Protoavis* (bird)
50	$30	*Dicraeosaurus* (s-dinosaur)
51	$30	*Moschops* (therapsid)
52	$30	*Lystrosaurus* (therapsid)
53	$30	*Dimetrodon* (pelycosaur)
54	$30	*Staurikosaurus* (s-dinosaur)
55	$30	*Cacops* (amphibian)
56	$30	*Diarthrognathus* (therapsid)
57	$30	*Estemmenosuchus* (therapsid)
		Set of 36 stamps
58†	$25	*Archaeopteryx* (bird)
59†	$25	*Mammuthus* woolly mammoth (mammal)
60†	$25	Unspecified cynodont (therapsid)
61†	$25	*Proconsul* (?) (mammal)
62†	$25	Unspecified plesiosaur
63†	$25	Unspecified sauropod (s-dinosaur)

MS64 Six sheets (a) $250 *Styracosaurus* (o-dinosaur); (b) $250 *Tyrannosaurus* (s-dinosaur); (c) $250 *Plateosaurus* (s-dinosaur); (d) $250 *Diplodocus* (s-dinosaur); (e) $250 *Stegosaurus* (o-dinosaur); (f) $250 *Allosaurus* (s-dinosaur)
Set of 6 sheets

65† $50 Louis Leakey and prehistoric hominid skull (mammal)

1996

66	$35	*Apatosaurus* (s-dinosaur)
67	$35	*Archaeopteryx* (bird)
68	$35	*Dimorphodon* (pterosaur)
69	$35	*Deinonychus* (s-dinosaur)
70	$35	*Coelophysis* (s-dinosaur)
71	$35	*Tyrannosaurus* (s-dinosaur)
72	$35	*Triceratops* (o-dinosaur)
73	$35	*Anatosaurus* [=*Anatotitan*] (o-dinosaur)
74	$35	*Saltasaurus* (s-dinosaur)
75	$35	*Allosaurus* (s-dinosaur)
76	$35	*Oviraptor* (s-dinosaur)
77	$35	*Stegosaurus* (o-dinosaur)
78	$35	*Ornithomimus* (s-dinosaur)
79	$35	*Pteranodon* (pterosaur)
80	$35	*Rhamphorhynchus* (pterosaur)
81	$35	*Ornitholestes* (s-dinosaur)

Dinosaurs and other Prehistoric Animals on Stamps

82	$35	*Brachiosaurus* (s-dinosaur)
83	$35	*Parasaurolophus* (o-dinosaur)
84	$35	*Ceratosaurus* (s-dinosaur)
85	$35	*Camarasaurus* (s-dinosaur)
86	$35	*Euoplocephalus* (o-dinosaur)
87	$35	*Scutellosaurus* (o-dinosaur)
88	$35	*Compsognathus* (s-dinosaur)
89	$35	*Stegoceras* (o-dinosaur)
90	$35	*Criorhynchus* [wrongly inscr *Eudimorphodon*] (pterosaur)
91	$35	*Eudimorphodon* [wrongly inscr *Criorhynchus*] (pterosaur)
92	$35	*Elasmosaurus* (plesiosaur)
93	$35	*Rhomaleosaurus* (plesiosaur)
94	$35	*Ceresiosaurus* (nothosaur)
95	$35	*Mesosaurus* (early reptile)
96	$35	*Grendelius* (ichthyosaur)
97	$35	*Nothosaurus* (nothosaur)
98	$35	*Mixosaurus* (ichthyosaur)
99	$35	*Placodus* (placodont)
100	$35	Prehistoric coelacanth (fish)
101	$35	*Mosasaurus* (lizard)
102	$35	*Tarbosaurus* (s-dinosaur)
103	$35	*Hadrosaurus* (o-dinosaur)
104	$35	*Polacanthus* (o-dinosaur)
105	$35	*Psittacosaurus* (o-dinosaur)
106	$35	*Ornitholestes* (s-dinosaur)
107	$35	*Yangchuanosaurus* (s-dinosaur)
108	$35	*Scelidosaurus* (o-dinosaur)
109	$35	*Kentrosaurus* (o-dinosaur)
110	$35	*Coelophysis* (s-dinosaur)
111	$35	*Lesothosaurus* (o-dinosaur)
112	$35	*Plateosaurus* (s-dinosaur)
113	$35	*Staurikosaurus* (s-dinosaur)
		Set of 48 stamps

MS114 Two sheets (a) $60 *Saurolophus* (o-dinosaur), *Muttaburrasaurus* (o-dinosaur), *Dicraeosaurus* (s-dinosaur); (b) $60 *Heterodontosaurus* (o-dinosaur), *Compsognathus* (s-dinosaur), and *Ornithomimosaurus* (s-dinosaur)
Set of 2 sheets

MS115 Five sheets (a) $300 *Struthiomimus* (s-dinosaur); (b) $300 *Tyrannosaurus rex* (s-dinosaur); (c) $300 *Apatosaurus* (s-dinosaur) and *Allosaurus* (s-dinosaur); (d) $300 *Quetzalcoatlus* (pterosaur); (e) $300 *Lagosuchus* (thecodontian)
Set of 5 sheets

1998

116	$25	*Kentrosaurus* (o-dinosaur)
117	$30	*Lesothosaurus* (o-dinosaur)
118	$35	*Stegoceras* (o-dinosaur)
119	$55	*Ceresiosaurus* (nothosaur)
120	$55	*Nothosaurus* (nothosaur)
121	$55	*Rhomaleosaurus* (plesiosaur)
122	$55	*Grendelius* (ichthyosaur)

123	$55	*Mixosaurus* (ichthyosaur)
124	$55	*Mesosaurus* (early reptile)
125	$55	*Placodus* (placodont)
126	$55	*Stethacanthus* (shark)
127	$55	Prehistoric coelacanth (fish)
128	$55	*Quetzalcoatlus* (pterosaur)
129	$55	*Pteranodon* (pterosaur)
130	$55	*Peteinosaurus* (pterosaur)
131	$55	*Criorhynchus* (pterosaur)
132	$55	*Pterodaustro* (pterosaur)
133	$55	*Eudimorphodon* (pterosaur)
134	$55	*Archaeopteryx* (bird)
135	$55	*Dimorphodon* (pterosaur)
136	$55	*Sharovipteryx* (pterosaur)
137	$60	*Lagosuchus* (thecodontian)
138	$100	*Herrerasaurus* (s-dinosaur)
139	$200	*Iguanodon* (o-dinosaur)

Set of 24 stamps

MS140 Two sheets (a) $300 *Yangchuanosaurus* (s-dinosaur); (b) $300 *Styracosaurus* (o-dinosaur)
Set of 2 sheets

2001

141	$20	*Allosaurus* (s-dinosaur)
142	$30	*Spinosaurus* (s-dinosaur)
143	$35	*Pteranodon* (pterosaur)
144	$60	*Cetiosaurus* (s-dinosaur)
145	$100	*Alamosaurus* (s-dinosaur)
146	$100	*Archaeopteryx* (bird)
147	$100	*Pachycephalosaurus* (o-dinosaur)
148	$100	*Parasaurolophus* (o-dinosaur)
149	$100	*Edmontosaurus* (o-dinosaur)
150	$100	*Triceratops* (o-dinosaur)
151	$100	*Brachiosaurus* (s-dinosaur)
152	$100	*Dimorphodon* (pelycosaur)
153	$100	*Coelophysis* (s-dinosaur)
154	$100	*Velociraptor* (s-dinosaur)
155	$100	*Antrodemus* [=*Allosaurus*] (s-dinosaur)
156	$100	*Euparkeria* (thecodontian)
157	$100	*Brachiosaurus* (s-dinosaur)
158	$100	*Pteranodon* (pterosaur)
159	$100	*Compsognathus* (s-dinosaur)
160	$100	*Corythosaurus* (o-dinosaur)
161	$100	*Allosaurus* (s-dinosaur)
162	$100	*Torosaurus* (o-dinosaur)
163	$100	*Ichthyostega* (amphibian)
164	$100	*Eryops* (amphibian)
165	$100	Ichthyosaur
166	$100	Pliosaur (plesiosaur)
167	$100	*Dunkleosteus* (placoderm)
168	$100	*Eogyrinus* (amphibian)

169 $200 *Archaeopteryx* (bird)
170 $300 *Parasaurolophus* (o-dinosaur)
　　　　　Set of 30 stamps
MS171 Four sheets (a) $400 *Pteranodon* (pterosaur); (b) $400 Ichthyosaur;
　　　　　(c) $400 *Torosaurus* (o-dinosaur); $400 *Brachiosaurus* (s-dinosaur)
　　　　　Set of 4 sheets

2005

172 $150 *Moeritherium* (mammal)
173 $150 *Deinonychus* (s-dinosaur)
174 $150 *Ophthalmosaurus* (ichthyosaur)
175 $150 *Grendelius* (ichthyosaur)
176 $150 *Eustreptospondylus* (s-dinosaur)
177 $150 *Rhamphorhynchus* (pterosaur)
178 $150 *Utahraptor* (s-dinosaur)
179 $150 *Entelodon* (mammal)
180 $150 *Spinosaurus* (s-dinosaur)
181 $150 *Tarbosaurus* (s-dinosaur)
182 $150 *Coelophysis* (s-dinosaur)
183 $150 *Sinosauropteryx* (s-dinosaur)
　　　　　Set of 12 stamps
MS184 Three sheets (a) $400 *Ophthalmosaurus* (ichthyosaur);
　　　　　(b) $400 *Anatotitan* [wrongly inscr *Iguanodon*] (o-dinosaur);
　　　　　(c) $400 *Velociraptor* (s-dinosaur)
　　　　　Set of 3 sheets

HONG KONG
Eastern Asia
100 cents = 1 Hong Kong dollar

1994

MS1 $10 *Allosaurus* (s-dinosaur)
　　　　　Set of 1 sheet

HUNGARY
Central Europe
100 filler = 1 forint

1969

1† 1fo *Clupea hungarica* (fish)
2† 2fo *Reineckia crassicostata* (ammonite)
3† 4fo *Placochelys placodonta* (placodont)
　　　　　(in perforate and imperforate versions)

1986

4† 2fo Sauropod (s-dinosaur)

(in perforate and imperforate versions)

1990

5	3fo	*Tarbosaurus* (s-dinosaur)
6	5fo	*Brontosaurus* [=*Apatosaurus*] (s-dinosaur)
7	5fo	*Dimorphodon* (pterosaur)
8	5fo	*Stegosaurus* (o-dinosaur)
9	8fo	*Platybelodon* (mammal)
10	10fo	*Mammuthus* woolly mammoth (mammal)

Set of 6 stamps (in perforate and imperforate versions)

1993

11†	17f	*Homo neanderthalensis* Neanderthal man (mammal)

INDIA
Southern Asia
1862. 12 pies = 1 anna; 16 annas = 1 rupee
1957. 100 naye paise = 1 rupee
1964. 100 paisa = 1 rupee

1951

1	2a	*Stegodon ganesa* (mammal)

Set of 1 stamp

DID YOU KNOW? The stegodont, which featured on the first prehistoric stamp ever, (India, 1951, 2a) was a prehistoric elephant. Expeditions to a remote part of Nepal in the 1990s, led by the famous explorer Colonel John Blashford-Snell, found two enormous bull elephants with peculiar domed heads. Although - sadly - these elephants turned out to be just peculiar, and rather old Asian elephants, for some years many scientists within the cryptozoological community hoped that a surviving colony of stegodonts had been found.

INDONESIA
South-east Asia
100 cents (or sen) = 1 gulden (or rupiah)

1989

1	100r	'Sangiran 17' *Homo erectus* (mammal)
2	150r	'Perning 1' *Homo erectus* (mammal)
3	200r	'Sangiran 10' *Homo erectus* (mammal)
4	250r	'Wajak 1' *Homo erectus* (mammal)
5	300r	'Sambungmacan 1' *Homo erectus* (mammal)
6	350r	'Ngandong 7' *Homo erectus* (mammal)

Set of 6 stamps

2004

7†	1500r	*Hippopotamus simplex* (mammal)

IRELAND (REPUBLIC OF)
North-west Europe
100 pence = 1 pound (punt)
2002. 100 cents = 1 euro

1999

1†	30p	*Mammuthus primigenius* woolly mammoth (mammal)
2†	30p	*Megaloceros giganteus* (mammal)
MS3†		Includes *Nos.* 1-2 *Mammuthus primigenius* woolly mammoth (mammal), *Megaloceros giganteus* (mammal)
		Set of 1 sheet
4†	30p	*Mammuthus primigenius* woolly mammoth (mammal)
5†	30p	*Megaloceros giganteus* (mammal)

2007

6	55c	*Megaloceros giganteus* (mammal)
		Set of 1 stamp

ISLE OF MAN
North-west Europe
100 pence = 1 pound

1979

1†	6p	*Nassa* [=*Nassarius*] *kermodei* (gastropod)

1986

2†	22p	*Megaloceros giganteus* (mammal)

1994

3†	30p	*Solaster moretonis* (echinoderm)

2006

4†	97p	*Prolecanites* (ammonite)

ISRAEL
Western Asia
100 agorot = 1 shekel

2000

1	2s.20	*Struthiomimus* (s-dinosaur)
2	2s.20	*Struthiomimus* (s-dinosaur)
3	2s.20	*Struthiomimus* (s-dinosaur)
		Set of 3 stamps

2002

MS4† Three stamps, including (a) 2s.20 *Aipichthyoides galeatus* (fish);

(c) 4s.40 *Proeucalycoceras* (ammonite)
Set of 1 sheet

ITALY
Southern Europe
100 centesimi = 1 lira
2002. 100 cents = 1 euro

1988
1   500l   *Homo aeserniensis* [=*erectus*] (mammal)
Set of 1 stamp

1998
2   800l   *Hildoceras* (ammonite), *Hemihaploceras* (ammonite), and *Calliphylloceras* (ammonite)
Set of 1 stamp

JAPAN
Eastern Asia
100 sen = 1 yen

1977
1   50y   *Wellesiosaurus suzukii* (plesiosaur)
Set of 1 stamp

1992
2   62y   Ammonite
Set of 1 stamp

PREFECTURE STAMPS
1999
Fukui.
3   80y   *Iguanodon* (?) (o-dinosaur), 80y *Dromaeosaurus* (?) (s-dinosaur)

2005
4   80y   *Mammuthus primigenius* woolly mammoth (mammal)
5   80y   *Mammuthus primigenius* woolly mammoth (mammal)

JERSEY
North-west Europe
100 pence = 1 pound

1994
1†   23p   *Mammuthus primigenius* woolly mammoth (mammal)
2†   23p   *Mammuthus primigenius* woolly mammoth (mammal)

KAMPUCHEA
South-east Asia
100 cents = 1 riel

1986

1	20c	*Edaphosaurus* (pelycosaur)
2	50c	*Sauroctonus* (therapsid)
3	80c	*Mastodonsaurus giganteus* (amphibian)
4	1r	*Rhamphorhynchus* (pterosaur)
5	1r50	*Brachiosaurus brancai* (s-dinosaur)
6	2r	*Tarbosaurus bataar* (s-dinosaur)
7	3r	*Indricotherium* (mammal)
		Set of 7 stamps

KAZAKHSTAN
Central Asia
100 tyin (ty) = 1 tenge (t)

1994

1	1t	*Entelodon* (mammal)
2	1t20	*Saurolophus* (o-dinosaur)
3	2t	*Plesiosaurus* (plesiosaur)
4	3t	*Sordes pilosus* (pterosaur)
5	5t	*Mosasaurus* (lizard)
6	7t	*Megaloceros giganteus* (mammal)
		Set of 6 stamps
MS7		One sheet 10t *Coelodonta antiquitatis* woolly rhinoceros (mammal)
		Set of 1 sheet

KENYA
East Africa
100 cents = 1 shillings

1977

1†	3s	Prehistoric human (mammal)
MS2†		Includes *No.* 1 Prehistoric human (mammal)
		Set of 1 sheet

1982

3	50c	*Paranthropus boisei* (mammal)
4	2s	*Homo erectus* (mammal)
5	3s	*Homo habilis* (mammal)
6	5s	*Proconsul africanus* (mammal)
		Set of 4 stamps

KENYA, UGANDA AND TANGANYIKA (TANZANIA)
East Africa
100 cents = 1 shilling

1967

1†   2s50   *Proconsul* (mammal)

1975

2†   3s   Prehistoric human (mammal)

KIRIBATI
Pacific
100 cents = 1 dollar

2006

1	25c	*Ultrasaurus* (s-dinosaur)
2	50c	*Rhamphorhynchus* (pterosaur)
3	60c	*Dilophosaurus* (s-dinosaur)
4	75c	*Brachiosaurus* (s-dinosaur)
5	$1	*Eoraptor* (s-dinosaur)
6	$1	*Minmi* (o-dinosaur)
7	$1.25	*Stegosaurus* (o-dinosaur)
8	$1.50	*Giganotosaurus* (s-dinosaur)

Set of 8 stamps

KUWAIT
Arabian Peninsula
1000 fils = 1 dinar

1982

1   30f   *Plateosaurus* (?) (s-dinosaur)
2   80f   *Plateosaurus* (?) (s-dinosaur)
Set of 2 stamps

1997

3†   50f   Dinosaur

KYRGYZSTAN
Central Asia
100 tyin = 1 som

1998

1   10s   *Tyrannosaurus* (s-dinosaur)
2   10s   *Saurolophus* (o-dinosaur)

3	10s	*Gallimimus* (s-dinosaur)
4	10s	*Euoplocephalus* (o-dinosaur)
5	10s	*Protoceratops* (o-dinosaur)
6	10s	*Velociraptor* (s-dinosaur)
		Set of 6 stamps

DID YOU KNOW? *Gallimimus* is a genus of ornithomimosaurid dinosaur from the late Cretaceous Period of Mongolia. With a maximum length of 4 to 6 metres (13-20 feet) and weighing as much as 440 kilograms (970 pounds), it was one of the largest ornithomimosaurs. *Gallimimus* is known from multiple individuals, ranging from juvenile (about 0.5 metre tall at the hip) to adult (about 2 metres tall at the hip).

LAOS
South-east Asia
100 cents = 1 kip

1988

1	3k	*Tyrannosaurus* [wrongly inscr *Trachodon*] (s-dinosaur)
2	7k	*Ceratosaurus nasicornis* (s-dinosaur)
3	39k	*Iguanodon bernissartensis* (o-dinosaur)
4	44k	*Scolosaurus* [=*Euoplocephalus*] (o-dinosaur)
5	47k	*Phororhacus* [=*Phorusrhacus*] (bird)
6	50k	*Anatosaurus* [=*Anatotitan*] [wrongly inscr *Tyrannosaurus*] (o-dinosaur)
		Set of 6 stamps
MS7	One sheet 95k *Pteranodon* (pterosaur)	
		Set of 1 sheet

1994

8†	10k	*Hesperornis* (bird)
9†	150k	*Archaeopteryx* (bird)
10†	600k	*Phorusrhacus* (bird)
11†	700k	*Dinornis maximus* giant moa (bird)
MS12	One sheet 700k *Teratornis* (bird)	
		Set of 1 sheet
13	50k	*Segnosaurus* (s-dinosaur)
14	380k	*Muttaburrasaurus* (o-dinosaur)
15	420k	*Saltasaurus* (s-dinosaur)
		Set of 3 stamps

1995

16	50k	*Trachodon* [=*Anatotitan*] (o-dinosaur)
17	70k	*Protoceratops* (o-dinosaur)
18	300k	*Brontosaurus* [=*Apatosaurus*] (s-dinosaur)
19	400k	*Stegosaurus* (o-dinosaur)
20	600k	*Tyrannosaurus* (s-dinosaur)
		Set of 5 stamps

LEBANON
Middle East
100 centimes = 1 piastre;
100 piastres = 1 Lebanese pound

2002
1		L£5000 *Libanobythus milki* (insect) in amber
2		L£10000 *Nematonotus longispinus* (fish)
		Set of 2 stamps

LESOTHO
Southern Africa
100 cents = 1 rand
1979. 100 lisente = 1 (ma)loti

1970
1	3c	Dinosaur footprints
2	5c	*Gryponyx* [=*Massospondylus*] (s-dinosaur) and footprints
3	10c	*Plateosauravus* [=*Euskelosaurus*] (s-dinosaur) and footprints
4	15c	*Tritylodon* (therapsid) and footprints
5	25c	*Massospondylus* (s-dinosaur) and footprints
		Set of 5 stamps

1984
6	10s	Sauropodomorph (s-dinosaur) footprints
7	30s	*Lesothosaurus* (o-dinosaur) footprints
8	50s	Theropod (s-dinosaur) footprints
		Set of 3 stamps (in perforate and imperforate versions)

1992
9	20s	*Kentrosaurus* [wrongly inscr *Stegosaurus*] (o-dinosaur)
10	30s	*Ceratosaurus* (s-dinosaur)
11	40s	*Procompsognathus* (s-dinosaur)
12	50s	*Lesothosaurus* (o-dinosaur)
13	70s	*Plateosaurus* (s-dinosaur)
14	1m	*Gasosaurus* (s-dinosaur)
15	2m	*Massospondylus* (s-dinosaur)
16	3m	*Archaeopteryx* (bird)
		Set of 8 stamps
MS17		Two sheets (a) 5m *Lesothosaurus* (o-dinosaur); (b) 5m *Archaeopteryx* (bird)
		Set of 2 sheets

1998
18†	2m	*Ceresiosaurus* (nothosaur)
19†	2m	*Rhomaleosaurus* (plesiosaur)
20†	2m	*Anomalocaris* (early invertebrate)
21†	2m	*Mixosaurus* (ichthyosaur)

22†	2m	*Stethacanthus* (shark)
23†	2m	*Dunkleosteus* (placoderm)
24†	2m	*Tommotia* (cephalopod)
25†	2m	*Sanctacaris* (early invertebrate)
26†	2m	Belemnites [wrongly inscr ammonites]
27†	2m	*Rhamphorhynchus* (pterosaur)
28†	2m	*Brachiosaurus* (s-dinosaur)
29†	2m	*Mamenchisaurus hochuanensis* (s-dinosaur)
30†	2m	*Ceratosaurus nasicornis* (s-dinosaur)
31†	2m	*Archaeopteryx* (bird)
32†	2m	*Leaellynasaura amicagraphica* (o-dinosaur)
33†	2m	*Chasmosaurus belli* (o-dinosaur)
34†	2m	*Deinonychus* (s-dinosaur) and *Pachyrhinosaurus* (o-dinosaur)
35†	2m	*Deinonychus* (s-dinosaur)
36†	2m	*Nyctosaurus* (pterosaur)
37†	2m	*Eudimorphodon* (pterosaur)
38†	2m	*Apatosaurus* (s-dinosaur)
39†	2m	*Peteinosaurus* (pterosaur)
40†	2m	*Tropeognathus* (pterosaur)
41†	2m	*Pteranodon ingens* (pterosaur)
42†	2m	*Ornithodesmus* (pterosaur)
43†	2m	*Wuerhosaurus* (o-dinosaur)
MS44		Three sheets (a) 10m *Coelophysis* (s-dinosaur); (b) 10m *Tyrannosaurus* (s-dinosaur); (c) 10m *Coelodonta* woolly rhinoceros (mammal) Set of 3 sheets

2005

45†	8m	Plesiosaur

LIBERIA
West Africa
100 cents = 1 dollar

1999

1	40c	*Camarasaurus* (s-dinosaur)
2	40c	*Albertosaurus* (s-dinosaur)
3	40c	*Eudimorphodon* (pterosaur)
4	40c	*Dimorphodon* (pterosaur)
5	40c	*Compsognathus* (s-dinosaur)
6	40c	*Torosaurus* (o-dinosaur)
7	40c	*Nodosaurus* (o-dinosaur)
8	40c	*Probactrosaurus* (o-dinosaur)
9	40c	*Baryonyx* (s-dinosaur)
10	40c	*Pachycephalosaurus* (o-dinosaur)
11	40c	*Homalocephale* (o-dinosaur)
12	40c	*Pterodaustro* (pterosaur)
13	40c	*Pycnosteroides* (fish)
14	40c	Giant nautiloid

15	40c	*Kronosaurus* (plesiosaur)
16	40c	Giant nautiloid
17	50c	*Pachyrhinosaurus* (o-dinosaur)
18	50c	*Centrosaurus* (o-dinosaur)
19	70c	*Chasmosaurus* [wrongly inscr *Pentaceratops*] (o-dinosaur)
20	70c	*Oviraptor* (s-dinosaur)
21	1$	*Corythosaurus* (o-dinosaur)
22	1$50	*Stegosaurus* (o-dinosaur)
		Set of 22 stamps
MS23	\multicolumn{2}{l}{Two sheets (a) 2$ *Shunosaurus* (s-dinosaur); (b) 2$ *Tarbosaurus* (s-dinosaur)}
		Set of 2 sheets
24	50c	*Albertosaurus* (s-dinosaur)
25	50c	*Parasaurolophus* (o-dinosaur)
26	50c	*Styracosaurus* (o-dinosaur)
27	50c	*Struthiomimus* (s-dinosaur)
28	50c	*Ankylosaurus* (o-dinosaur)
29	50c	*Chasmosaurus* (o-dinosaur)
30	50c	*Brachiosaurus* (s-dinosaur)
31	70c	*Tyrannosaurus* (s-dinosaur)
32	1$	*Mosasaurus* (lizard) and ammonite
33	1$50	*Triceratops* (o-dinosaur)
		Set of 10 stamps
MS34	\multicolumn{2}{l}{Two sheets (a) 2$ *Stegosaurus* (o-dinosaur); (b) 2$ *Deinonychus* (s-dinosaur)}
		Set of 2 sheets
35†	10$	*Pterodactylus* (pterosaur)
36†	10$	*Archaeopteryx* (bird)
37†	10$	*Brachiosaurus* (s-dinosaur)
38†	10$	*Apatosaurus* (s-dinosaur)
39†	10$	*Scelidosaurus* (o-dinosaur)
40†	10$	*Dromiceiomimus* (s-dinosaur)
41†	10$	*Psittacosaurus* (o-dinosaur)
42†	10$	*Protoceratops* (o-dinosaur)
43†	10$	*Allosaurus* (s-dinosaur)
44†	10$	*Torosaurus* (o-dinosaur)
45†	10$	*Parasaurolophus* (o-dinosaur)
46†	10$	*Diplodocus* (s-dinosaur)
47†	10$	*Rhamphorhynchus* (pterosaur)
48†	10$	*Pteranodon* (pterosaur)
49†	10$	*Opisthocoelicaudia* (s-dinosaur)
50†	10$	*Tyrannosaurus* (s-dinosaur)
51†	10$	*Ouranosaurus* (o-dinosaur)
52†	10$	*Dryosaurus* (o-dinosaur)
53†	10$	*Pachycephalosaurus* (o-dinosaur)
54†	10$	*Anchiceratops* (o-dinosaur)
55†	10$	*Edmontosaurus* (o-dinosaur)
56†	10$	*Stegosaurus* (o-dinosaur)
57†	10$	*Dromaeosaurus* (s-dinosaur)
58†	15$	*Velociraptor* (s-dinosaur)

59†	20$	*Pinacosaurus* (o-dinosaur)
60†	25$	*Stegosaurus* (o-dinosaur)
61†	30$	*Shantungosaurus* (o-dinosaur)
MS62	\multicolumn{2}{l}{Two sheets (a) 100$ *Tyrannosaurus* (s-dinosaur); (b) 100$ *Spinosaurus* (s-dinosaur)}
		Set of 2 sheets
63†	10$	*Archaeopteryx* (bird)
64†	10$	*Quetzalcoatlus* (pterosaur)
65†	10$	*Eudimorphodon* (pterosaur)
66†	10$	*Dryosaurus* (o-dinosaur)
67†	10$	*Elasmosaurus* (plesiosaur)
68†	10$	*Ichthyostega* [wrongly inscr *Acanthostega*] (amphibian)
69†	10$	*Cacops* (amphibian)
70†	10$	Pliosaur (plesiosaur)
71†	10$	*Dunkleosteus* (placoderm)
72†	10$	*Nothosaurus* (plesiosaur)
73†	10$	Ichthyosaur
74†	10$	*Archaeopteryx* (bird)
75†	10$	*Saltasaurus* (s-dinosaur)
76†	10$	*Brachiosaurus* (s-dinosaur)
77†	10$	*Apatosaurus* (s-dinosaur)
78†	10$	*Compsognathus* (s-dinosaur)
79†	10$	*Dromaeosaurus* (s-dinosaur)
80†	10$	*Parasaurolophus* (o-dinosaur)
81†	10$	*Torosaurus* (o-dinosaur)
82†	10$	*Triceratops* (o-dinosaur)
83†	10$	*Allosaurus* (s-dinosaur)
84†	10$	*Tyrannosaurus* (s-dinosaur)
MS85	\multicolumn{2}{l}{Two sheets (a) 100$ *Pteranodon* (pterosaur); (b) 100$ *Velociraptor* (s-dinosaur)}
		Set of 2 sheets

2001

86	25$	*Ornithocheirus* (pterosaur)
87	25$	*Tyrannosaurus* (s-dinosaur)
88	25$	*Barosaurus* (s-dinosaur)
89	25$	*Centrosaurus* [wrongly inscr *Styracosaurus*] (o-dinosaur)
90	25$	*Deinonychus* (s-dinosaur)
91	25$	*Coelophysis* (s-dinosaur)
92	25$	*Allosaurus* (s-dinosaur)
93	25$	*Pteranodon* (pterosaur)
94	25$	*Brachiosaurus* (s-dinosaur) and *Pteranodon* (pterosaur)
95	25$	*Iguanodon* (o-dinosaur)
96	25$	*Supersaurus* (s-dinosaur)
97	25$	*Tyrannosaurus* (s-dinosaur)
		Set of 12 stamps
MS98	\multicolumn{2}{l}{Two sheets (a) 100$ *Stegosaurus* (o-dinosaur); (b) 100$ *Parasaurolophus* (o-dinosaur)}

2005

99	50$	*Cymbospondylus* (ichthyosaur)
100	50$	*Archelon* (turtle)

PREHISTORIC ANIMALS « DINOSAURUS »

101	50$	*Xiphactinus* (fish)
102	50$	*Dunkleosteus* (placoderm)
103	50$	*Smilodon* sabre-tooth tiger (mammal)
104	50$	*Brontotherium* (mammal)
105	50$	*Moeritherium* (mammal)
106	50$	*Ancyclotherium* (mammal)
107	50$	*Torosaurus* (o-dinosaur)
108	50$	*Tyrannosaurus* (s-dinosaur)
109	50$	*Polacanthus* (o-dinosaur)
110	50$	*Stegosaurus* (o-dinosaur)
		Set of 12 stamps

MS111 Three sheets (a) 120$ *Odobenocetops* (mammal); (b) 120$ *Stegosaurus* (o-dinosaur); (c) 120$ *Coelodonta* (mammal)
Set of 3 sheets

LIBYA
North Africa
1000 dirhams = 1 dinar

1976

1†	40d	*Tetralophodon longirostris* (mammal)

1985

2	150dh	Fossil fish
3	150dh	*Xenopus hasaunus* (amphibian)
4	150dh	*Titanohyrax palaeotheroides* (mammal)
		Set of 3 stamps

1995

5	100dh	*Baryonyx* (s-dinosaur)
6	100dh	*Oviraptor* (s-dinosaur)
7	100dh	*Stenonychosaurus* [=*Troodon*] (s-dinosaur)
8	100dh	*Tenontosaurus* (o-dinosaur)
9	100dh	*Yangchuanosaurus* (s-dinosaur)
10	100dh	*Stegotetrabelodon* (mammal)
11	100dh	*Stegotetrabelodon* (mammal)
12	100dh	*Psittacosaurus* (o-dinosaur)
13	100dh	*Heterodontosaurus* (o-dinosaur)
14	100dh	*Loxodonta atlantica* (mammal)
15	100dh	*Mammuthus africanavus* (mammal)
16	100dh	*Erlikosaurus* (s-dinosaur)
17	100dh	*Cynognathus* (therapsid)
18	100dh	*Plateosaurus* (s-dinosaur)
19	100dh	*Staurikosaurus* (s-dinosaur)
20	100dh	*Lystrosaurus* (therapsid)
		Set of 16 stamps

MS21 One sheet 500dh *Stegotetrabelodon* (mammal)
Set of 1 sheet

1996

22	200dh	*Mene rhombus* (fish)
23	200dh	*Mesodon macrocephalus* (fish)
24	200dh	*Eryon arctiformis* (crustacean)
25	200dh	*Stegosaurus* (o-dinosaur)
26	200dh	*Pteranodon* (pterosaur)
27	200dh	*Allosaurus* (s-dinosaur)
		Set of 6 stamps

LIECHTENSTEIN
Central Europe
100 rappen = 1 franc (Swiss)

2003

1†	1f20	*Hypacanthoplites milletianus* (ammonite)

2004

2	1f20	Ammonite
3	1f30	Fossil sea urchin (echinoderm)
4	2f20	Fossil shark's tooth (shark)
		Set of 3 stamps

LUXEMBOURG
Western Europe
100 centimes = 1 franc (Belgian)
2002. 100 cents = 1 euro

1984

1	4f	Fossil *Pecten* (bivalve)
2	7f	*Gryphaea arcuata* devil's toe-nail (bivalve)
3	10f	*Coeloceras raquinianum* (ammonite)
4	16f	*Dapedius* (fish)
		Set of 4 stamps

MACEDONIA
South-east Europe
100 deni (de) = 1 denar (d)

1998

1	4d	*Ursus spelaeus* cave bear (mammal)
2	8d	*Mesopithecus pentelici* (mammal)
3	18d	*Tragocerus* (mammal)
4	30d	*Aceratherium incisivum* (mammal)
		Set of 4 stamps

MADAGASCAR
(see also MALAGASY REPUBLIC)
Indian Ocean off East Africa
100 centimes = 1 franc

1994

1	35f	*Dinornis maximus* giant moa (bird)
2	40f	*Ceratosaurus* (s-dinosaur)
3	140f	*Mosasaurus* (lizard)
4	525f	*Protoceratops* (o-dinosaur)
5	640f	*Styracosaurus* (o-dinosaur)
6	755f	*Smilodon* sabre-tooth tiger (mammal)
7	1800f	*Uintatherium* (mammal)
		Set of 7 stamps
MS8		One sheet 2000f *Mammuthus* woolly mammoth (mammal)
		Set of 1 sheet

1998

9	1350f	*Herrerasaurus* (s-dinosaur) and *Archaeopteryx* (bird)
10	1350f	*Segnosaurus* (s-dinosaur) and *Dimorphodon* (pterosaur)
11	1350f	*Sauropelta* (o-dinosaur) and *Proavis* (bird)
12	5000f	*Eudimorphodon* (pterosaur) and *Eustreptospondylus* (s-dinosaur)
13	5000f	*Triceratops* (o-dinosaur) and *Rhamphorhynchus* (pterosaur)
14	5000f	*Segnosaurus* (s-dinosaur) and *Pteranodon* (pterosaur)
		Set of 6 stamps
MS15		One sheet 12500f *Tenontosaurus* (o-dinosaur) and *Deinonychus* (s-dinosaur)
		Set of 1 sheet
16	500f	*Plateosaurus* (s-dinosaur)
17	500f	*Iguanodon* (o-dinosaur)
18	500f	*Stenonychosaurus* [=*Troodon*] (s-dinosaur)
19	500f	*Staurikosaurus* (s-dinosaur)
20	1800f	*Psittacosaurus* (o-dinosaur)
21	1800f	*Allosaurus* (s-dinosaur)
22	1800f	*Stegosaurus* (o-dinosaur)
23	1800f	*Hypsilophodon* (o-dinosaur)
24	1800f	*Triceratops* (o-dinosaur)
25	1800f	*Camptosaurus* (o-dinosaur)
26	1800f	*Compsognathus* (s-dinosaur)
27	1800f	*Carnotaurus* (s-dinosaur)
		Set of 12 stamps
MS28		Two sheets (a) 1200f *Brachiosaurus* (s-dinosaur); (b) 1200f *Tyrannosaurus* (s-dinosaur)
		Set of 2 sheets

1999

29	300f	*Smilodon* [No. 6 surch 300f on 755f] sabre-tooth tiger (mammal)
30	500f	*Protoceratops* [No. 4 surch 500f on 525f] (o-dinosaur)
31	500f	*Uintatherium* [No. 7 surch 500f on 1800f] (mammal)

Set of 3 stamps

32	500f	*Lambeosaurus* (o-dinosaur)
33	500f	*Corythosaurus* (o-dinosaur)
34	500f	*Stegosaurus* (o-dinosaur)
35	500f	*Hypsilophodon* (o-dinosaur)
36	500f	*Antrodemus* [=*Allosaurus*] (s-dinosaur)
37	1950f	*Brachiosaurus* (s-dinosaur)
38	1950f	*Tyrannosaurus* (s-dinosaur)
39	1950f	*Plateosaurus* (s-dinosaur)
40	1959f	*Hadrosaurus* (o-dinosaur)
41	1950f	*Triceratops* (o-dinosaur)
42	1950f	*Iguanodon* (o-dinosaur)

Set of 11 stamps
MS43 One sheet 12500f *Styracosaurus* (o-dinosaur)
Set of 1 sheet

2001

44† 400f *Bothriolepis* (placoderm)

MALAGASY REPUBLIC
(see also MADAGASCAR)
Indian Ocean off East Africa
100 centimes = 1 franc

1970

1† 20f Ammonite

1989

2	20f	*Tyrannosaurus* (s-dinosaur)
3	80f	*Stegosaurus* (o-dinosaur)
4	250f	*Arsinotherium* (mammal)
5	450f	*Triceratops* (o-dinosaur)

Set of 4 stamps
MS6 One sheet 600f *Saurolophus* (o-dinosaur)
Set of 1 sheet

MALAWI
Central Africa
100 tambalas = 1 kwacha

1993

1	20t	*Kentrosaurus* (o-dinosaur)
2	75t	*Stegosaurus* (o-dinosaur)
3	95t	Sauropod (s-dinosaur)

Dinosaurs and other Prehistoric Animals on Stamps

		Set of 3 stamps
MS4		Six sheets (a) 2k *Tyrannosaurus rex* (s-dinosaur); (b) 2k *Dilophosaurus* (s-dinosaur); (c) 2k *Brachiosaurus* (s-dinosaur); (d) 2k *Gallimimus* (s-dinosaur); (e) 2k *Triceratops* (o-dinosaur); (f) 2k *Velociraptor* (s-dinosaur)
		Set of 1 sheet

MALDIVE ISLANDS
Indian Ocean
100 larees = 1 rupee

1972

1	2l	*Stegosaurus* (o-dinosaur)
2	7l	*Dimetrodon* [wrongly inscr *Edaphosaurus*] (pelycosaur)
3	25l	*Diplodocus* (s-dinosaur)
4	50l	*Triceratops* (o-dinosaur)
5	2r	*Pteranodon* (pterosaur)
6	5r	*Tyrannosaurus* (s-dinosaur)

Set of 6 stamps (in perforate and imperforate versions)

1992

7	5l	*Deinonychus* (s-dinosaur)
8	10l	*Styracosaurus* (o-dinosaur)
9	25l	*Mamenchisaurus* (s-dinosaur)
10	50l	*Stenonychosaurus* [=*Troodon*] (s-dinosaur)
11	1r	*Parasaurolophus* (o-dinosaur)
12	1r25	*Scelidosaurus* (o-dinosaur)
13	1r75	*Tyrannosaurus* (s-dinosaur)
14	2r	*Stegosaurus* (o-dinosaur)
15	3r50	*Iguanodon* (o-dinosaur)
16	4r	*Anatosaurus* [=*Anatotitan*] (o-dinosaur)
17	5r	*Monoclonius* (o-dinosaur)
18	7r	*Tenontosaurus* (o-dinosaur)
19	8r	*Brachiosaurus* (s-dinosaur)
20	10r	*Euoplocephalus* (o-dinosaur)
21	25r	*Triceratops* (o-dinosaur)
22	50r	*Apatosaurus* (s-dinosaur)

Set of 16 stamps

MS23 Four sheets (a) 25r Hadrosaur (o-dinosaur); (b) 25r *Iguanodon* (o-dinosaur) and *Allosaurus* (s-dinosaur); (c) 25r *Tyrannosaurus* (s-dinosaur) and *Triceratops* (o-dinosaur); (d) 25r *Brachiosaurus* (s-dinosaur) and *Iguanodon* (o-dinosaur)
Set of 4 sheets

MS24† Includes (b) 25r *Nessiteras rhombopteryx* Loch Ness monster (depicted here as plesiosaur)
Set of 16 sheets

1994

25	25l	*Elasmosaurus* (plesiosaur)

26	50l	*Dilophosaurus* (s-dinosaur)
27	1r	*Avimimus* (s-dinosaur)
28	3r	*Dimorphodon* (pterosaur)
29	3r	*Megalosaurus* (s-dinosaur)
30	3r	*Kuehneosaurus* (lizard)
31	3r	*Dryosaurus* (o-dinosaur)
32	3r	*Kentrosaurus* (o-dinosaur)
33	3r	*Barapasaurus* (s-dinosaur)
34	3r	*Tenontosaurus* (o-dinosaur)
35	3r	*Elaphrosaurus* (s-dinosaur)
36	3r	*Maiasaura* (o-dinosaur)
37	3r	*Huayangosaurus* (o-dinosaur)
38	3r	*Rutiodon* (thecodontian)
39	3r	*Piatnitzkysaurus* (s-dinosaur)
40	3r	*Quetzalcoatlus* (pterosaur)
41	3r	*Daspletosaurus* (s-dinosaur)
42	3r	*Pleurocoelus* (s-dinosaur)
43	3r	*Baryonyx* (s-dinosaur)
44	3r	*Pentaceratops* (o-dinosaur)
45	3r	*Kritosaurus* [=*Gryposaurus*] (o-dinosaur)
46	3r	*Microvenator* (s-dinosaur)
47	3r	*Nodosaurus* (o-dinosaur)
48	3r	*Montanoceratops* (o-dinosaur)
49	3r	*Dromiceiomimus* (s-dinosaur)
50	3r	*Dryptosaurus* (s-dinosaur)
51	3r	*Parksosaurus* (o-dinosaur)
52	5r	*Chasmosaurus* (o-dinosaur)
53	8r	*Edmontonia* (o-dinosaur)
54	10r	*Anatosaurus* [=*Anatotitan*] (o-dinosaur)
55	15r	*Velociraptor* (s-dinosaur)
56	20r	*Spinosaurus* (s-dinosaur)
		Set of 32 stamps
MS57		Two sheets (a) 25r *Gallimimus* (s-dinosaur); (b) 25r *Plateosaurus* (s-dinosaur)
		Set of 2 sheets

1997

58	5r	*Archaeopteryx* (bird)
59	7r	*Diplodocus* (s-dinosaur)
60	7r	*Tyrannosaurus rex* (s-dinosaur)
61	7r	*Pteranodon* (pterosaur)
62	7r	*Montanoceratops* (o-dinosaur)
63	7r	*Dromaeosaurus* (s-dinosaur)
64	7r	*Oviraptor* (s-dinosaur)
65	8r	*Mosasaurus* (lizard)
66	12r	*Deinonychus* (s-dinosaur)
67	15r	*Triceratops* (o-dinosaur)
68	7r	*Troodon* (s-dinosaur)
69	7r	*Brachiosaurus* (s-dinosaur)
70	7r	*Saltasaurus* (s-dinosaur)
71	7r	*Oviraptor* (s-dinosaur)

72	7r	*Parasaurolophus* (o-dinosaur)
73	7r	*Psittacosaurus* (o-dinosaur)
74	7r	*Triceratops* (o-dinosaur)
75	7r	*Pachycephalosaurus* (o-dinosaur)
76	7r	*Iguanodon* (o-dinosaur)
77	7r	*Tyrannosaurus rex* (s-dinosaur)
78	7r	*Corythosaurus* (o-dinosaur)
79	7r	*Stegosaurus* (o-dinosaur)
80	7r	*Euoplocephalus* (o-dinosaur)
81	7r	*Compsognathus* (s-dinosaur)
82	7r	*Herrerasaurus* (s-dinosaur)
83	7r	*Styracosaurus* (o-dinosaur)
84	7r	*Baryonyx* (s-dinosaur)
85	7r	*Lesothosaurus* (o-dinosaur)
		Set of 28 stamps
MS86		Two sheets (a) 25r *Tyrannosaurus rex* (s-dinosaur); (b) 25r *Archaeopteryx* (bird)
		Set of 2 sheets

1999

87	1r	*Scelidosaurus* (o-dinosaur)
88	3r	*Yandusaurus* (o-dinosaur)
89	5r	*Ornitholestes* (s-dinosaur)
90	7r	*Dimorphodon* (pterosaur)
91	7r	*Rhamphorhynchus* (pterosaur)
92	7r	*Allosaurus* (s-dinosaur)
93	7r	*Leaellynasaura* (o-dinosaur)
94	7r	*Troodon* (s-dinosaur)
95	7r	*Syntarsus* [=*Megapnosaurus*] (s-dinosaur)
96	7r	*Anchisaurus* (s-dinosaur)
97	7r	*Pteranodon* (pterosaur)
98	7r	*Barosaurus* (s-dinosaur)
99	7r	*Iguanodon* (o-dinosaur)
100	7r	*Archaeopteryx* (bird)
101	7r	*Ceratosaurus* (s-dinosaur)
102	7r	*Stegosaurus* (o-dinosaur)
103	7r	*Corythosaurus* (o-dinosaur)
104	7r	*Cetiosaurus* (s-dinosaur)
105	7r	*Avimimus* (s-dinosaur)
106	7r	*Styracosaurus* (o-dinosaur)
107	7r	*Massospondylus* (s-dinosaur)
108	8r	*Astrodon* [=*Pleurocoelus*] (s-dinosaur)
		Set of 22 stamps
MS109		Two sheets (a) 25r *Megalosaurus* (s-dinosaur); (b) 25r *Brachiosaurus* (s-dinosaur)
		Set of 2 sheets

2002

110	7r	*Sivatherium* (mammal)
111	7r	*Platygonus* flat-headed peccary (mammal)
112	7r	*Nothotheriops* Shasta ground sloth (mammal)
113	7r	*Glossotherium* Harlan's ground sloth (mammal)

114	7r	*Coelodonta* woolly rhinoceros (mammal)
115	7r	*Capromeryx* dwarf pronghorn (mammal)
116	7r	*Macrauchenia* (mammal)
117	7r	*Glyptodon* glyptodont (mammal)
118	7r	*Nesodon* (mammal)
119	7r	*Tapirus* imperial tapir (mammal)
120	7r	*Arctodus* short-faced bear (mammal)
121	7r	Mastodon [wrongly inscr Mammoth] (mammal)

Set of 12 stamps

MS122 Two sheets (a) 25r *Smilodon* sabre-tooth tiger (mammal); (b) 25r *Mammuthus* woolly mammoth (mammal)
Set of 2 sheets

2005

123	10r	*Macroplata* (plesiosaur)
124	10r	*Ichthyosaurus* (ichthyosaur)
125	10r	*Shonisaurus* (ichthyosaur)
126	10r	*Archelon* (turtle)
127	10r	*Deinonychus* (s-dinosaur)
128	10r	*Styracosaurus* (o-dinosaur)
129	10r	*Ornitholestes* (s-dinosaur)
130	10r	*Euoplocephalus* (o-dinosaur)
131	10r	*Pterodactylus* (pterosaur)
132	10r	*Cearadactylus* (pterosaur)
133	10r	Pterosaur
134	10r	*Sordes* (pterosaur)
135	10r	*Albertosaurus* (s-dinosaur)
136	10r	*Iguanodon* (o-dinosaur)
137	10r	*Deinonychus* (s-dinosaur)
138	10r	*Baryonyx* (s-dinosaur)

Set of 16 stamps

MS139 Four sheets (a) 25r *Muraenosaurus* (plesiosaur); (b) 25r *Leptoceratops* (o-dinosaur); (c) 25r *Archaeopteryx* (bird); (d) 25r *Styracosaurus* (o-dinosaur)
Set of 4 sheets

MALI
West Africa
100 centimes = 1 franc

1984

1	10f	*Dimetrodon* (pelycosaur)
2	25f	*Iguanodon* (o-dinosaur)
3	30f	*Archaeopteryx* (bird)
4	120f	*Dimetrodon* (pelycosaur)
5	175f	*Iguanodon* (o-dinosaur)
6	350f	*Archaeopteryx* (bird)
7	470f	*Triceratops* (o-dinosaur)

Set of 7 stamps

1992

8†	25f	*Triceratops* [*No. 7 surch* 25f] (o-dinosaur)	
9†	240f	*Archaeopteryx* [*No. 6 surch* 240f] (bird)	

1994

10	5f	*Scaphonyx* (rhynchosaur)
11	10f	*Cynognathus* (therapsid)
12	15f	*Lesothosaurus* (o-dinosaur)
13	20f	*Scutellosaurus* (o-dinosaur)
14	25f	*Ceratosaurus* (s-dinosaur)
15	30f	*Dilophosaurus* (s-dinosaur)
16	40f	*Dryosaurus* (o-dinosaur)
17	50f	*Heterodontosaurus* (o-dinosaur)
18	60f	*Anatosaurus* [=*Anatotitan*] (o-dinosaur)
19	70f	*Saurornithoides* (s-dinosaur)
20	80f	*Avimimus* (s-dinosaur)
21	90f	*Saltasaurus* (s-dinosaur)
22	300f	*Dromaeosaurus* (s-dinosaur)
23	400f	*Tsintaosaurus* (o-dinosaur)
24	600f	*Velociraptor* (s-dinosaur)
25	700f	*Ouranosaurus* (o-dinosaur)

Set of 16 stamps (in perforate and imperforate versions)

MS26 One sheet 2000f *Daspletosaurus* (s-dinosaur) and *Iguanodon* (o-dinosaur)

Set of 1 sheet (in perforate and imperforate versions)

1999

27	250f	*Edmontonia* (o-dinosaur)
28	250f	*Iguanodon* (o-dinosaur)
29	250f	*Allosaurus* (s-dinosaur)
30	250f	*Troodon* (s-dinosaur)
31	250f	*Lesothosaurus* (o-dinosaur)
32	250f	*Carnotaurus* (s-dinosaur)
33	250f	*Deinonychus* (s-dinosaur)
34	250f	*Dilophosaurus* (s-dinosaur)
35	250f	*Psittacosaurus* (o-dinosaur)

Set of 9 stamps (in perforate and imperforate versions)

2001

36	460f	*Psittacosaurus* (o-dinosaur)
37	460f	*Phororhacos* [=*Phorusrhacus*] (bird)
38	460f	*Coelophysis* (s-dinosaur)
39	460f	*Saurornithoides* (s-dinosaur)
40	460f	*Acantholis* (o-dinosaur)
41	460f	*Varanosaurus* (pelycosaur)
42	490f	*Dromiceiomimus* (s-dinosaur)
43	490f	*Placodus* (placodont)
44	490f	*Ceratosaurus* (s-dinosaur)
45	490f	*Heterodontosaurus* (o-dinosaur)

46	490f	*Diatryma* [=*Gastornis*] (bird)
47	490f	*Ouranosaurus* (o-dinosaur)
		Set of 12 stamps

MANAMA **
Arabian peninsula
100 dirhams = 1 riyal

1971

1	15d	*Uintatherium* (mammal)
2	20d	*Stegosaurus* (o-dinosaur)
3	25d	*Mammut* [wrongly inscr *Mastodon*] (mammal)
4	30d	*Plateosaurus* (s-dinosaur)
5	50d	*Styracosaurus* (o-dinosaur)
6	60d	*Allosaurus* (s-dinosaur)
7	1r	*Diatryma* [=*Gastornis*] (bird)
8	2r	*Brontosaurus* [=*Apatosaurus*] (s-dinosaur)
		Set of 8 stamps (in perforate and imperforate versions)
MS9		One sheet 10r *Elephas* [=*Mammuthus*] *primigenius* woolly mammoth (mammal)
		Set of 1 sheet (in perforate and imperforate versions)

DID YOU KNOW? There have been occasional claims that the woolly mammoth, as depicted on the 1971 Miniature Sheet from Manama, is not actually extinct, and that small isolated herds might survive in the vast and sparsely inhabited tundra of the northern hemisphere. In the late nineteenth century, there were persistent rumors about surviving mammoths hiding in Alaska. In October 1899, a story about a man named Henry Tukeman detailed his having killed a mammoth in Alaska and that he subsequently donated the specimen to the Smithsonian Institution in Washington, D.C. However, the museum denied the existence of any mammoth corpse and the story turned out to be a hoax.

MAURITANIA
West Africa
100 centimes = 1 franc
1973. 100 cents = 1 ouguiya (um)

1972

1	25f	Fossil brachiopod
2	75f	Trilobite
		Set of 2 stamps (in perforate and imperforate versions)

EDITOR'S NOTE: Manama is the capital of Bahrain, but it has also been a free port since 1958, and has issued stamps in its own right.

3†	5um	Fossil brachiopod [*No. 1 surch* 5um on 25f]
4†	15um	Trilobite [*No. 2 surch* 15um on 75f]

MAURITIUS
Indian Ocean
100 cents = 1 rupee

1982

1	25c	Charles Darwin issue, with trilobite, pterosaur, ammonite, prehistoric fish, and plesiosaur (?) in margins of stamp
2	2r	Charles Darwin issue, with ditto prehistoric animals in margins of stamp
3	2r50	Charles Darwin issue, with ditto prehistoric animals in margins of stamp
4	10r	Charles Darwin issue, with ditto prehistoric animals in margins of stamp
		Set of 4 stamps

MEXICO
Central America
8 reales = 100 centavos = 1 peso

2006

1	$6.50	*Muzquizopteryx* (pterosaur)
2	$7.50	*Sabinosaurus* (o-dinosaur)
3	$10.50	'Aramberri monster' [=*Liopleurodon*?] (plesiosaur)
		Set of 3 stamps

MICRONESIA (FEDERATED STATES OF)
Western Pacific
100 cents = 1 dollar

1994

1	29c	*Iguanodon* (o-dinosaur)
2	52c	*Iguanodon* (o-dinosaur), coelosaur (s-dinosaur), and *Ichthyornis* (bird)
3	$1	*Camarasaurus* (s-dinosaur)
		Set of 3 stamps

1999

4†	33c	*Megaladapis* (?) giant lemur (mammal)
5†	33c	*Pteranodon* (pterosaur)
6†	33c	*Shonisaurus* (ichthyosaur)
7†	33c	*Stegosaurus* (o-dinosaur)
8†	33c	*Gallimimus* (s-dinosaur)
9†	33c	*Tyrannosaurus* (s-dinosaur)
10†	33c	*Archelon* (turtle)
11†	33c	*Brachiosaurus* (s-dinosaur)

12†   33c   *Triceratops* (o-dinosaur)
MS13   One sheet $2 *Suchomimus* (s-dinosaur)
         Set of 1 sheet

2001

14   60c   *Triceratops* (o-dinosaur)
15   60c   *Psittacosaurus* (o-dinosaur) and *Archaeopteryx* (bird)
16   60c   *Archaeopteryx* (bird)
17   60c   *Allosaurus* (s-dinosaur)
         Set of 4 stamps
MS18   Four sheets (a) 60c x 6: *Tyrannosaurus* (s-dinosaur), *Pteranodon* (pterosaur), *Brachiosaurus* (s-dinosaur) and pterosaur, *Spinosaurus* (s-dinosaur), *Deinonychus* (s-dinosaur), *Teratosaurus* (thecodontian);
         (b) 6oc x 6: *Parasaurolophus* (o-dinosaur), *Plateosaurus* (s-dinosaur), *Archaeopteryx* (bird), *Allosaurus* (s-dinosaur), *Torosaurus* (o-dinosaur), *Tyrannosaurus* [wrongly inscr *Euoplocephalus*] (s-dinosaur);
         (c) $2 *Tyrannosaurus* (s-dinosaur); (d) $2 *Parasaurolophus* (o-dinosaur).
         Set of 4 sheets

2004

19   80c   *Allosaurus* (s-dinosaur)
20   80c   *Tyrannosaurus* (s-dinosaur)
21   80c   *Troodon* (s-dinosaur)
22   80c   *Carnotaurus* (s-dinosaur)
23   80c   *Apatosaurus* (s-dinosaur)
24   80c   *Pachyrhinosaurus* (o-dinosaur)
25   80c   *Kentrosaurus* (o-dinosaur)
26   80c   *Saltasaurus* (s-dinosaur)
27   80c   *Indricotherium* (mammal)
28   80c   *Hyaenodon* (mammal)
29   80c   *Deinotherium* (mammal)
30   80c   *Chalicotherium* (mammal)
         Set of 12 stamps
MS31   Three sheets (a) $2 *Deinonychus* (s-dinosaur); (b) $2 *Coelophysis* (s-dinosaur); (c) $2 *Moeritherium* (mammal)
         Set of 3 sheets

MOLDOVA
Eastern Europe
100 bani = 1 leu

1995

1†   10b+2b *Deinotherium gigantissimum* (mammal)

DID YOU KNOW? *Deinotherium* as depicted on the 10b+2b stamps from Moldova in 1995 was an ancient relative of the elephants which had strange downward curving tusks. Deinothere fossils found in Greece may have helped generate myths of archaic giant beings.

MONACO
Southern Europe
100 centimes = 1 French franc
2002. 100 cents = 1 euro

1955

1†	10f	Plesiosaur and ichthyosaur

1985

2	3f	*Mene rhombea* (fish)
		Set of 1 stamp

2000

3	5f20	*Ursus spelaeus* cave bear (mammal)
		Set of 1 stamp

MONGOLIA
Central Asia
100 mung = 1 tugrik

1966

1	5m	*Tarbosaurus* (s-dinosaur)
2	10m	*Talarurus* (o-dinosaur)
3	15m	*Protoceratops* (o-dinosaur)
4	20m	*Indricotherium* (mammal)
5	30m	*Parasaurolophus* [wrongly inscr *Saurolophus*] (o-dinosaur)
6	60m	Mastodon (mammal)
7	80m	*Mongolotherium* (mammal)
8	1t	*Mammuthus* woolly mammoth (mammal)
		Set of 8 stamps

1977

9†	10m	*Mongolemys elegans* (tortoise)
10†	20m	*Embolotherium ergilense* (mammal)
11†	30m	*Psittacosaurus mongoliensis* (o-dinosaur)
12†	40m	*Entelodon* (mammal)
13†	60m	*Spirocerus kiakhtensis* (mammal)
14†	80m	*Hipparion* (mammal)

1990

15	20m	*Chasmosaurus* (o-dinosaur)
16	30m	*Stegosaurus* (o-dinosaur)
17	40m	*Probactrosaurus* (o-dinosaur)
18	50m	*Opisthocoelicaudia* (s-dinosaur)
19	60m	*Iguanodon* (o-dinosaur)
20	80m	*Tarbosaurus* (s-dinosaur)
21	1t20	*Mamenchisaurus* (s-dinosaur)

Set of 7 stamps
MS22   One sheet 4t *Allosaurus* (s-dinosaur) and *Brachiosaurus* (s-dinosaur)
Set of 1 sheet

1991

MS23† Four sheets, including (b) 30t Sauropods (s-dinosaur)

1994

24	60t	*Mammuthus* woolly mammoth (mammal)
25	80t	*Stegosaurus* (o-dinosaur)
26	100t	*Talarurus* (o-dinosaur)
27	120t	*Corythosaurus* (o-dinosaur)
28	200t	*Tyrannosaurus* (s-dinosaur) and *Pteranodon* (pterosaur)

Set of 5 stamps (in perforate and imperforate versions)
MS29   One sheet 400t *Triceratops* (o-dinosaur)
Set of 1 sheet (in perforate and imperforate versions)

2000

30†   400t   Theropod (s-dinosaur)

2001

31	500t	*Tarbosaurus* (s-dinosaur)
32	500t	*Iguanodon* (o-dinosaur)
33	500t	*Triceratops* (o-dinosaur)

Set of 3 stamps

34†   400t   Theropod (s-dinosaur)

2006

35†   200t   Theropod (s-dinosaur)

MONTSERRAT
West Indies
100 cents = 1 West Indian dollar

1992

1	$1	*Tyrannosaurus* (s-dinosaur)
2	$1.15	*Diplodocus* (s-dinosaur)
3	$1.50	*Apatosaurus* (s-dinosaur)
4	$3.45	*Dimetrodon* (pelycosaur)

Set of 4 stamps
MS5   One sheet $4.60 Dinosaur bone
Set of 1 sheet

1994

6	$1	*Elasmosaurus* (plesiosaur)
7	$1.15	*Plesiosaurus* (plesiosaur)
8	$1.50	*Nothosaurus* (nothosaur)

9	$3.45	*Mosasaurus* (lizard)
		Set of 4 stamps

MOROCCO
North-west Africa
100 centimes = 1 peseta

1988

1	2d	*Cetiosaurus mogrebiensis* (s-dinosaur)
		Set of 1 stamp

2004

2	6d50	*Tazoudasaurus* (s-dinosaur)
		Set of 1 stamp

MOZAMBIQUE
South-east Africa
100 centavos = 1 escudo
1980. 100 centavos = 1 metical

1971

1†	50c	*Lytodiscoides conduciensis* (ammonite)
2†	2e	*Endothiodon* (therapsid)

1999

MS3 Six sheets (a) 9000m *Hylaeosaurus* (s-dinosaur); (b) 9000m
  Stegosaurus (o-dinosaur); (c) 9000m *Baryonyx* (s-dinosaur);
  (d) 900m *Tyrannosaurus* (s-dinosaur); (e) 9000m *Ornitholestes* (s-dinosaur);
  (f) 35000m *Velociraptor* (s-dinosaur)
  Set of 6 sheets

2000

MS4 Nine stamps 3000m *Pteranodon* (pterosaur); 3000m *Bothriospondylus* (s-dinosaur);
  3000m *Iguanodon* (o-dinosaur); 3000m *Stegosaurus* (o-dinosaur);
  3000m *Nodosaurus* (o-dinosaur); 3000m *Elaphrosaurus* (s-dinosaur);
  3000m *Petrolacosaurus* (early reptile); 3000m *Procompsognathus* (s-dinosaur);
  3000m *Dimetrodon* (pelycosaur)
  Set of 1 sheet

MS5 Nine stamps 3000m *Plesiosaurus* (plesiosaur); 3000m *Ceresiosaurus* (nothosaur);
  3000m *Cryptoclidus* (plesiosaur); 3000m *Placochelys* (placodont);
  3000m *Plotosaurus* (lizard); 3000m *Ichthyosaurus* (ichthyosaur);
  3000m *Platecarpus* (lizard); 3000m *Archelon* (turtle); 3000m Mosasaur (lizard)
  Set of 1 sheet

MS6 Two sheets (a) 20000m *Tyrannosaurus rex* (s-dinosaur);

Dinosaurs and other Prehistoric Animals on Stamps

        (b) 20000m *Henodus* [wrongly inscr *Honodus*] (placodont)
        Set of 2 sheets

2002

7	5000m	*Protoceratops* [wrongly inscr *Protosaurus*] (o-dinosaur)
8	10000	*Psittacosaurus* (o-dinosaur)
9	17000	*Torosaurus* (o-dinosaur)
10	28000	*Triceratops* (o-dinosaur)

        Set of 4 stamps

MS11 Two sheets (a) 10000m *Diplodocus* (s-dinosaur), 10000m Pterosaurs,
        10000m *Diplodocus* (s-dinosaur), 10000m *Afrovenator* (s-dinosaur),
        10000m *Parasaurolophus* (o-dinosaur), 10000m *Rhamphorhynchus* (pterosaur),
        10000m *Lambeosaurus* (o-dinosaur), 10000m *Euoplocephalus* (o-dinosaur),
        10000m Cynodont (therapsid); (b) 10000m *Brachiosaurus* (s-dinosaur),
        10000m *Monoclonius* (o-dinosaur), 10000m *Homalocephale* (o-dinosaur),
        10000m Pterodactyl (pterosaur), 10000m *Deinonychus* (s-dinosaur),
        10000m *Archaeopteryx* (bird), 10000m Cretaceous fauna,
        10000m *Hypsilophodon* (o-dinosaur), 10000m *Lystrosaurus* (therapsid)
        Set of 2 sheets

MS12 Two sheets (a) 50000m *Baryonyx* (s-dinosaur); (b) 50000m *Styracosaurus* (o-dinosaur)
        Set of 2 sheets

MS13 One sheet 33000m Charles Darwin and *Byronosaurus* (s-dinosaur),
        33000m Charles Darwin and *Irritator* (s-dinosaur)
        Set of 1 sheet

MS14 Two sheets (a) 25000m *Scipionyx* (s-dinosaur); (b) 25000m *Beipiaosaurus* (s-dinosaur)
        Set of 2 sheets

DID YOU KNOW? *Scipionyx* as pictured on the Mozambique MS14 is a genus of theropod dinosaur from the Early Cretaceous of Italy. There has been only one skeleton discovered, which is notable for the preservation of soft tissue and internal organs. It is the fossil of a juvenile only a few inches long.

NAMIBIA
Southern Africa
100 cents = 1 Namibia dollar

1995

1	40c	*Geochelone stromeri* (tortoise)
2	80c	*Diamantornis wardi* (bird)
3	90c	*Prohyrax hendeyi* (mammal)
4	$1.20	*Crocodylus lloydi* (crocodilian)

        Set of 4 stamps

1997

MS5 One sheet $5 *Triceratops* (o-dinosaur)
        Set of 1 sheet

NAURU
West Pacific
100 cents = 1 Australian dollar

2006

1	10c	*Parasaurolophus* (o-dinosaur)
2	25c	*Quetzalcoatlus* (pterosaur)
3	50c	*Spinosaurus* (s-dinosaur)
4	75c	*Triceratops* (o-dinosaur)
5	$1	*Tyrannosaurus* (s-dinosaur)
6	$1.50	*Euoplocephalus* (o-dinosaur)
7	$2	*Velociraptor* (s-dinosaur)
8	$2.50	*Protoceratops* (o-dinosaur)

Set of 8 stamps

NETHERLANDS
North-west Europe
100 cents = 1 gulden (florin)
2002. 100 cents = 1 euro

1962

1†   6c+4c   *Platypleuroceras spinatus* (ammonite)

NEVIS
West Indies
100 cents = 1 dollar

1999

1	30c	*Kritosaurus* [=*Gryposaurus*] (o-dinosaur)
2	60c	*Oviraptor* (s-dinosaur)
3	80c	*Eustreptospondylus* (s-dinosaur)
4	$1.20	*Tenontosaurus* (o-dinosaur)
5	$1.20	*Edmontosaurus* (o-dinosaur)
6	$1.20	*Avimimus* (s-dinosaur)
7	$1.20	*Minmi* (o-dinosaur)
8	$1.20	*Segnosaurus* (s-dinosaur)
9	$1.20	*Kentrosaurus* (o-dinosaur)
10	$1.20	*Deinonychus* (s-dinosaur)
11	$1.20	*Saltasaurus* (s-dinosaur)
12	$1.20	*Compsognathus* (s-dinosaur)
13	$1.20	*Hadrosaurus* (o-dinosaur)
14	$1.20	*Tuojiangosaurus* (o-dinosaur)
15	$1.20	*Euoplocephalus* (o-dinosaur)
16	$1.20	*Anchisaurus* (s-dinosaur)
17	$2	*Ouranosaurus* (o-dinosaur)

18	$3	*Muttaburrasaurus* (o-dinosaur)
		Set of 18 stamps
MS19		Two sheets (a) $5 *Triceratops* (o-dinosaur); (b) $5 *Stegosaurus* (o-dinosaur)
		Set of 2 sheets

2005

20	30c	*Tyrannosaurus* (s-dinosaur)
21	$1.20	*Deinotherium* (mammal)
22	$1.20	*Platybelodon* (mammal)
23	$1.20	*Loxodonta* [wrongly inscr *Palaeoloxodon*] (mammal)
24	$1.20	*Arsinotherium* (mammal)
25	$1.20	*Procoptodon* (mammal)
26	$1.20	*Macrauchenia* (mammal)
27	$1.20	*Apatosaurus* (s-dinosaur)
28	$1.20	*Camarasaurus* (s-dinosaur)
29	$1.20	*Iguanodon* (o-dinosaur)
30	$1.20	*Edmontosaurus* (o-dinosaur)
31	$1.20	*Centrosaurus* (o-dinosaur)
32	$1.20	*Euoplocephalus* (o-dinosaur)
33	$1.20	*Ouranosaurus* (o-dinosaur)
34	$1.20	*Parasaurolophus* (o-dinosaur)
35	$1.20	*Psittacosaurus* (o-dinosaur)
36	$1.20	*Stegosaurus* (o-dinosaur)
37	$1.20	*Scelidosaurus* (o-dinosaur)
38	$1.20	*Hypsilophodon* (o-dinosaur)
39	$5	*Hadrosaurus* (o-dinosaur)
		Set of 20 stamps
MS40		Three sheets (a) $5 *Pliosaurus* (plesiosaur); (b) $5 *Daspletosaurus* (s-dinosaur); (c) $5 *Brontotherium* (mammal)
		Set of 3 sheets

NEW CALEDONIA
South Pacific
100 centimes = 1 franc

1995

1	60f	*Sylviornis neocaledoniae* (bird)
		Set of 1 stamp
2	125f	*Mekosuchus inexpectatus* (crocodilian)
		Set of 1 stamp

1997

3	95f	*Meiolania mackayi* (tortoise)
		Set of 1 stamp

1999

4	100f	*Carcharodon* [=*Carcharocles*] *megalodon* (shark)
		Set of 1 stamp

MS5 Three stamps (a) 70f *Carcharodon* [=*Carcharocles*] *megalodon* (shark);
(b) 70f *Carcharodon* [=*Carcharocles*] *megalodon* (shark) and human diver;
(c) 70f *Carcharodon* [=*Carcharocles*] *megalodon* tooth (shark)
Set of 1 sheet

NEW ZEALAND
Australasia
100 cents = 1 dollar

1993

1	45c	Sauropod (s-dinosaur)
2	45c	Carnosaur (s-dinosaur) and sauropod (s-dinosaur)
3	80c	Pterosaur
4	$1	Ankylosaur (o-dinosaur)
5	$1.20	*Mauisaurus* (plesiosaur)
6	$1.50	Carnosaur (s-dinosaur)

Set of 6 stamps

MS7 One sheet $1.50 Carnosaur (s-dinosaur)
Set of 1 sheet

MS8 *overprinted* **BANGKOK '93**
Set of 1 sheet

MS9 One sheet $1.50 Carnosaur (s-dinosaur)
Set of 1 sheet

1996

10†	40c	*Aptornis* adzebill (bird)
11†	$1.50	*Harpagornis* New Zealand giant eagle (bird)
12†	$1.80	*Dinornis* giant moa (bird)

MS13 One sheet $1.80 *Dinornis* giant moa (bird)
Set of 1 sheet

14† 40c *Pachyplichas* stout-legged wren (bird)

MS15 One sheet $1.80 *Dinornis* giant moa (bird) *overprinted* **TAIPEI '96**
Set of 1 sheet

MS16 One sheet $1.80 *Dinornis* giant moa (bird)
Set of 1 sheet

NICARAGUA
Central America
100 centavos = 1 cordoba

1978

1† 3c Plesiosaur and ichthyosaur

1987

2	10cor	*Mammuthus columbi* (mammal)
3	10cor	*Triceratops* (o-dinosaur)

4	10cor	*Dimetrodon* (pelycosaur)
5	15cor	*Uintatherium* (mammal) (air)
6	15cor	*Dinichthys* (placoderm)
7	30cor	*Pteranodon* (pterosaur)
8	40cor	*Tylosaurus* (lizard) and *Pteranodon* (pterosaur)
		Set of 7 stamps

1994

9†	1cor50	*Tyrannosaurus rex* (s-dinosaur)
10†	1cor50	*Plateosaurus* (s-dinosaur)
11†	1cor50	*Pteranodon* (pterosaur)
12†	1cor50	*Camarasaurus* (s-dinosaur)
13†	1cor50	*Euoplocephalus* (o-dinosaur)
14†	1cor50	*Deinonychus* (s-dinosaur)
15†	1cor50	*Chasmosaurus* (o-dinosaur)
16†	1cor50	*Dimorphodon* (pterosaur)
17†	1cor50	*Metriorhynchus* (crocodilian)
18†	1cor50	*Ichthyosaurus* (ichthyosaur)
19†	1cor50	*Pteraspis* (agnathan) and *Compsognathus* (s-dinosaur)
20†	1cor50	Ammonite
21†	1cor50	*Archelon* (turtle)
22†	1cor50	*Griphognathus* (fish) and *Gyroptychius* (fish)
23†	1cor50	Plesiosaur and nautiloid

1999

24	5cor	*Sordes* (pterosaur)
25	5cor	*Dimorphodon* (pterosaur)
26	5cor	*Anurognathus* (pterosaur)
27	5cor	*Rhamphorhynchus* (pterosaur)
28	5cor	*Pterodaustro* (pterosaur)
29	5cor	*Pteranodon* (pterosaur)
30	6cor	*Macroplata* (plesiosaur)
31	6cor	*Mesosaurus* [wrongly inscr *Coelurus*] (early reptile)
32	6cor	*Liopleurodon* [wrongly inscr *Stegosaurus*] (plesiosaur)
33	6cor	*Shonisaurus* [wrongly inscr *Corythosaurus*] (ichthyosaur)
34	6cor	*Crassigyrinus* [wrongly inscr *Thadeosaurus*] (amphibian)
35	6cor	*Placochelys* [wrongly inscr *Brachiosaurus*] (placodont)
		Set of 12 stamps
MS36		Two sheets (a) 12cor *Pterodactylus* (pterosaur); (b) 12cor *Platecarpus* (lizard), *Xenacanthus* (shark), and *Bothriolepis* (placoderm)
		Set of 2 sheets

NIGER
West Africa
100 centimes = 1 franc

1976

1†	60f	*Ouranosaurus* (o-dinosaur)

1977

2†   50f   *Sarcosuchus imperator* (crocodilian)

1996

3   300f   *Iguanodon* [wrongly inscr *Ouranosaurus*] (o-dinosaur)
4   300f   *Spinosaurus* (s-dinosaur)
5   300f   *Polacanthus* (o-dinosaur)
6   300f   *Deinonychus* (s-dinosaur)
7   450f   *Camptosaurus* (o-dinosaur)
8   450f   *Allosaurus* (s-dinosaur)
9   450f   *Nodosaurus* (o-dinosaur)
10   450f   *Kritosaurus* [=*Gryposaurus*] (o-dinosaur)
                 Set of 8 stamps
MS11   One sheet 2000f *Protoceratops* (o-dinosaur) and *Oviraptor* (s-dinosaur)
                 Set of 1 sheet

1999

12†   1000f   *Ouranosaurus* (?) (o-dinosaur)

2000

13†   225f   *Sordes* (pterosaur)
14†   225f   *Quetalcoatlus* (pterosaur)
15†   225f   *Dimorphodon* (pterosaur)
16†   225f   *Podopteryx* [=*Sharovipteryx*] (pterosaur)
17†   225f   *Archaeopteryx* (bird)
18†   225f   *Pteranodon* (pterosaur)
19†   450f   *Hipparion* (mammal)
20†   450f   *Moeritherium* (mammal)
21†   450f   *Proconsul* (mammal)
22†   450f   *Metamynodon* (mammal)
23†   450f   *Hipparion* (mammal)
24†   475f   *Palaeobatrachus* (amphibian)
25†   475f   *Metoposaurus* (amphibian)
26†   475f   *Tylosaurus* (lizard)
27†   475f   *Basilosaurus* (mammal)
28†   475f   *Mesosaurus* (early reptile)
29†   475f   *Sarcosuchus* (crocodilian)

NIUAFO'OU

South Pacific
100 seniti = 1 pa'anga

1989

1†   15s   Prehistoric fishes
2†   45s   Prehistoric sponges, and jellyfishes (cnidarians)
3†   50s   Trilobites and Cambrian crustaceans
4†   60s   Ornithopod (o-dinosaur), sauropod (s-dinosaur), pterosaur
5†   80s   *Tyrannosaurus* (s-dinosaur) and *Triceratops* (o-dinosaur)

Dinosaurs and other Prehistoric Animals on Stamps

6†	1p	*Meganeura* giant dragonfly (insect), *Eusthenopteron* (fish), *Ichthyostega* (amphibian)
7†	1p50	*Stegosaurus* (o-dinosaur) and *Pteranodon* (pterosaur)
8†	2p	*Archaeopteryx* (bird) and early mammals
9†	10p	*Mammuthus primigenius* woolly mammoth (mammal) and sabre-tooth tiger (mammal)

MS10 One sheet 32s x 5 stamps, includes *No.* 1 prehistoric fishes; 42s x 5 stamps, includes *No.* 3 trilobites and Cambrian crustaceans; 57s x 5 stamps, includes *Nos.* 6-8 *Meganeura* giant dragonfly (insect) and *Eusthenopteron* (fish) and *Ichthyostega* (amphibian), *Stegosaurus* (o-dinosaur) and *Pteranodon* (pterosaur), *Archaeopteryx* (bird) and early mammals
Set of 1 sheet

1995

11	45s	Ornithopod (o-dinosaur), sauropod (s-dinosaur), pterosaur (as *No.* 126a)
12	60s	*Tyrannosaurus* (s-dinosaur) and *Triceratops* (o-dinosaur) (as *No.* 126b)
		Set of 2 stamps
MS13		One sheet 2p *Plesiosaurus* (plesiosaur)
		Set of 1 sheet

1996

14†	1p	*Mammuthus primigenius* woolly mammoth (mammal), sabre-tooth tiger (mammal), prehistoric deer (mammal)

NORTH KOREA
Eastern Asia
100 cheun = 1 won

1980

1†	30ch	*Stegosaurus* (o-dinosaur), *Ankylosaurus* (?) (o-dinosaur), and *Pteranodon* (pterosaur)
2†	40ch	*Tyrannosaurus* (?) (s-dinosaur)

1991

3	10ch	*Cynognathus* (therapsid) and *Dimetrodon* (pelycosaur)
4	20ch	*Brontosaurus* [=*Apatosaurus*] (s-dinosaur)
5	30ch	*Stegosaurus* (o-dinosaur) and *Allosaurus* (s-dinosaur)
6	40ch	Pterosaur
7	50ch	*Ichthyosaurus* (ichthyosaur)
		Set of 5 stamps

1994

8†	40ch	Fossil onsong fish (fish)
9†	40ch	Mammoth teeth (mammal)
10†	80ch	*Archaeopteryx* (bird)

EDITOR'S NOTE: Niuafo'ou (meaning: new coconut) is the most northerly island in the kingdom of Tonga. In earlier times, mail was delivered and picked up by strong swimmers who would retrieve packages sealed up in a biscuit tin and thrown overboard from passing ships. An early trader, named Walter George Quensell, acted as postmaster at that time and stamped the mail with colourful marks, which have become a collector's item. The Tongan government took over this tradition with special Niuafo'ou stamps since 1983.

1995
11†   50ch   Fossil *Ostrea* (bivalve)

1997
12   50ch   *Redlichia chinensis* (trilobite)
13   1wn   *Ptychoparia coreanica* (trilobite)
               Set of 2 stamps

1998
14   10ch   Prehistoric humans (mammal)
15   2wn50   Prehistoric humans (mammal)
               Set of 2 stamps

2000
16†   2wn   *Corythosaurus* (o-dinosaur)
17†   2wn   *Psittacosaurus* (o-dinosaur)
18†   2wn   *Megalosaurus* (s-dinosaur)
19†   2wn   *Muttaburrasaurus* (o-dinosaur)

MS20   Three sheets (a) 1wn *Styracosaurus* (o-dinosaur); (b) 1 wn *Saltasaurus* (s-dinosaur); (c) 1 wn *Tyrannosaurus* (s-dinosaur)
         Set of 3 sheets (in perforate and imperforate versions)

MS21   *Overprinted* **Exposicion Mundial de Filatelia**
         Three sheets (a) 1wn *Styracosaurus* (o-dinosaur); (b) 1 wn *Saltasaurus* (s-dinosaur); (c) 1 wn *Tyrannosaurus* (s-dinosaur)
         Set of 3 sheets

2004
22†   3w   *Calcinoplanx* (crustacean)
23†   140w   *Clinocardium* (bivalve) (in perforate and imperforate versions)

2006
24†   140w   *Australopithecus afarensis* (mammal)

2007
25†   15w   Fossil coral (cnidarian)
26†   70w   Fossil mollusc
27†   200w   Fossil rhinoceros (mammal)

PALAU
North Pacific
100 cents = 1 dollar

1988
MS1†   5 stamps, including (a) 25c Ammonite

This extremely eyecatching sheet deftly combines palaeontology with cryptozoology. For in addition to depicting such prehistoric stalwarts as a long-necked plesiosaur (elasmosaur) and a short-necked long-jawed pliosaur, it also portrays the giant squid, and a very striking lake monster - made even more unusual by virtue of the fact that it does not match the description of any lake monster ever reported, but does bear more than a passing resemblance to the oarfish, a crested elongate species of marine fish deemed responsible for certain sea serpent reports.

1993

2†	29c	*Rhamphorhynchus* (pterosaur)
3†	29c	Head of plesiosaur
4†	29c	*Rhamphorhynchus* (pterosaur) and neck of plesiosaur
5†	29c	*Rhamphorhynchus* (pterosaur)
6†	29c	Neck of plesiosaur
7†	29c	Neck of plesiosaur
8†	29c	Body of plesiosaur
9†	29c	Body of plesiosaur
10†	29c	Body of plesiosaur
11†	29c	Flipper of plesiosaur
12†	29c	Flipper of plesiosaur
13†	29c	Body of kronosaur (plesiosaur)
14†	29c	Tail of plesiosaur
15†	29c	Flipper of plesiosaur
16†	29c	Head of kronosaur (plesiosaur)
17†	29c	Body of kronosaur (plesiosaur)

Nos. 2-17 were issued together, se-tenant, forming a composite design, in which the same plesiosaur individual occupies all or part of several different stamps, as does the same kronosaur individual

1995

18	32c	*Pteranodon sternbergi* (pterosaur)
19	32c	*Pteranodon ingens* (pterosaur)
20	32c	Pterodactyl (pterosaur)
21	32c	*Dorygnathus* (pterosaur)
22	32c	*Dimorphodon* (pterosaur)
23	32c	*Nyctosaurus* (pterosaur)
24	32c	*Pterodactylus kochi* (pterosaur)
25	32c	*Ornithodesmus* (pterosaur)
26	32c	*Tyrannosaurus* (s-dinosaur) and *Diatryma* [=*Gastornis*] (bird)
27	32c	*Archaeopteryx* (bird)
28	32c	*Campylognathus* (pterosaur)
29	32c	*Gallodactylus* (pterosaur)
30	32c	*Batrachognathus* (pterosaur)
31	32c	*Scaphognathus* (pterosaur)
32	32c	*Peteinosaurus* (pterosaur)
33	32c	*Ichthyornis* (bird)
34	32c	*Ctenochasma* (pterosaur)
35	32c	*Rhamphorhynchus* (pterosaur)
		Set of 18 stamps

2000

36†	20c	Australopithecine (mammal)
37†	20c	Australopithecine (mammal)
38†	20c	*Homo habilis* (mammal)
39†	20c	*Homo habilis* (mammal)
40†	20c	'Lucy' *Australopithecus afarensis* (mammal)
41†	20c	Diapithecine (mammal)
42†	20c	*Homo erectus* (mammal)
43†	20c	Australopithecine (mammal)

44†	20c	*Australopithecus africanus* Taung Baby (mammal)
45†	20c	*Homo ergaster* (mammal)
46†	20c	*Homo neanderthalensis* Neanderthal man (mammal)
47†	20c	*Homo neanderthalensis* Neanderthal man (mammal)
48	33c	*Rhamphorhynchus* (pterosaur)
49	33c	*Ceratosaurus* (s-dinosaur)
50	33c	*Apatosaurus* (s-dinosaur)
51	33c	*Stegosaurus* (o-dinosaur)
52	33c	*Archaeopteryx* (bird)
53	33c	*Allosaurus* (s-dinosaur)
54	33c	*Parasaurolophus* (o-dinosaur)
55	33c	*Pteranodon* (pterosaur)
56	33c	*Tyrannosaurus* (s-dinosaur)
57	33c	*Triceratops* (o-dinosaur)
58	33c	*Ankylosaurus* (o-dinosaur)
59	33c	*Velociraptor* (s-dinosaur)
		Set of 12 stamps
MS60		Two sheets (a) $2 Jurassic dinosaurs; (b) $2 Cretaceous dinosaurs
		Set of 2 sheets

2004

61	26c	*Kritosaurus* [=*Gryposaurus*] (o-dinosaur)
62	26c	*Triceratops* (o-dinosaur)
63	26c	*Hypselosaurus* (s-dinosaur)
64	26c	*Yingshanosaurus* (o-dinosaur)
65	80c	*Hadrosaurus* (o-dinosaur)
66	80c	*Pterodaustro* (pterosaur)
67	80c	*Agilisaurus* (o-dinosaur)
68	80c	*Amargasaurus* (s-dinosaur)
69	80c	*Corythosaurus* (o-dinosaur)
70	80c	*Dryosaurus* (o-dinosaur)
71	80c	*Euoplocephalus* (o-dinosaur)
72	80c	*Compsognathus* (s-dinosaur)
		Set of 12 stamps
MS73		Three sheets (a) $2 *Archaeopteryx* (bird); (b) $2 *Deinonychus* (s-dinosaur); (c) $2 *Ornithomimus* (s-dinosaur)
		Set of 3 sheets

2005

74†	$1	Plesiosaur and ichthyosaur

PAPUA NEW GUINEA
```
        Australasia
   100 toea = 1 kina
```

2004

1	70t	*Ankylosaurus* (o-dinosaur)

2	1k	*Oviraptor* (s-dinosaur)
3	2k	*Tyrannosaurus* (s-dinosaur)
4	2k65	*Giganotosaurus* (s-dinosaur)
5	2k70	*Centrosaurus* (o-dinosaur)
6	4k60	*Carcharodontosaurus* (s-dinosaur)
		Set of 6 stamps
MS7		Six stamps (a) 1k50 *Edmontonia* (o-dinosaur); (b) 1k50 *Struthiomimus* (s-dinosaur); (c) 1k50 *Psittacosaurus* (o-dinosaur); (d) 1k50 *Gastonia* (o-dinosaur); (e) 1k50 *Shunosaurus* (s-dinosaur); (f) 1k50 *Iguanodon* (o-dinosaur)
		Set of 1 sheet
MS8		One sheet 7k *Afrovenator* (s-dinosaur)
		Set of 1 sheet

PERU

South America
100 centimos = 1 sol

1999

1†	5s	*Virgotrigonia peterseni* (bivalve)

2004

2	1s80	*Smilodon* sabre-tooth tiger (mammal) and *Toxodon* (mammal)
3	3s20	*Smilodon* sabre-tooth tiger (mammal) and *Toxodon* (mammal)
		Set of 2 stamps

2005

4†	5s	*Roemoceras* (ammonite)

2006

MS5		One sheet 8s50 *Purussaurus* (crocodilian)
		Set of 1 sheet

POLAND

Eastern Europe
100 groszy = 1 zloty

1965

1	20g	*Edaphosaurus* (pelycosaur)
2	30g	*Cryptoclidus* (plesiosaur)
3	40g	*Brontosaurus* [=*Apatosaurus*] (s-dinosaur)
4	60g	*Mesosaurus* (early reptile)
5	90g	*Stegosaurus* (o-dinosaur)
6	1z15	*Brachiosaurus* (s-dinosaur)
7	1z35	*Styracosaurus* (o-dinosaur)
8	3z40	*Corythosaurus* (o-dinosaur)
9	5z60	*Rhamphorhynchus* (pterosaur)

10	6z50	*Tyrannosaurus* (s-dinosaur)
		Set of 10 stamps

1966

11	20g	*Dinichthys* (placoderm)
12	30g	*Eusthenopteron* (fish)
13	40g	*Ichthyostega* (amphibian)
14	50g	*Mastodonsaurus* (amphibian)
15	60g	*Cynognathus* (therapsid)
16	2z50	*Archaeopteryx* (bird)
17	3z40	*Brontotherium* (mammal)
18	6z50	*Machairodus* sabre-tooth tiger (mammal)
19	7z10	*Mammuthus* woolly mammoth (mammal)
		Set of 9 stamps

1980

20†	8z40	Carnosaur [*Tarbosaurus*?] (s-dinosaur)

1993

21†	3000z	Amber containing prehistoric wasp (insect)

2000

22	70g	*Saurolophus* (o-dinosaur)
23	70g	*Gallimimus* (s-dinosaur)
24	80g	*Saichania* (o-dinosaur)
25	80g	*Protoceratops* (o-dinosaur)
26	1z55	*Prenocephale* (o-dinosaur)
27	1z55	*Velociraptor* (s-dinosaur)
		Set of 6 stamps

2002

28†	2z	*Coelodonta* woolly rhinoceros (mammal)

2004

29†	1z25	Sauropods (s-dinosaur), *Pteranodon* (pterosaur), and theropods (s-dinosaur)

ROMANIA

South-east Europe
100 bani = 1 leu

1966

1	5b	*Ursus spelaeus* cave bear (mammal)
2	10b	*Mammuthus trogontherii* (mammal)
3	15b	*Bison priscus* (mammal)
4	55b	*Archidiskodon* (mammal)
5	1l55	*Megaceros* [=*Megaloceros*] *eurycerus* (mammal)
6	4l	*Deinotherium gigantissimum* (mammal)
		Set of 6 stamps

1967

7	40b	*Deinotherium* (mammal)
		Set of 1 stamp

1993

8	29l	*Brontosaurus* [=*Apatosaurus*] (s-dinosaur)
9	46l	*Plesiosaurus* (plesiosaur)
10	85l	*Triceratops* (o-dinosaur)
11	171l	*Stegosaurus* (o-dinosaur)
12	216l	*Tyrannosaurus* (s-dinosaur)
13	319l	*Archaeopteryx* (bird)
		Set of 6 stamps

1994

14	90l	*Struthiosaurus* (o-dinosaur)
15	130l	*Megalosaurus* (s-dinosaur)
16	150l	*Parasaurolophus* (o-dinosaur)
17	380l	*Stenonychosaurus* [=*Troodon*] (s-dinosaur)
18	500l	*Camarasaurus* (s-dinosaur)
19	635l	*Gallimimus* (s-dinosaur)
		Set of 6 stamps

1999

An insect stamp [SG 5799 in Stanley Gibbons catalogue] *surch*, with the old value cancelled by a dinosaur emblem

20	100l on 70l	*Brontosaurus* [=*Apatosaurus*] (s-dinosaur) emblem
21	200l on 70l	*Iguanodon* (o-dinosaur) emblem
22	200l on 70l	*Allosaurus* (s-dinosaur) emblem
23	1500l on 70l	*Diplodocus* (s-dinosaur) emblem
24	1600l on 70l	*Tyrannosaurus* (s-dinosaur) emblem
25	3200l on 70l	*Stegosaurus* (o-dinosaur) emblem
26	6000l on 70l	*Plateosaurus* (s-dinosaur) emblem
		Set of 7 stamps

2001

27†	300l	*Struthiosaurus* [*No. 14 surch* 300l on 90l] (o-dinosaur)

2005

28	21000l	*Elopteryx* (s-dinosaur)
29	31000l	*Telmatosaurus* (o-dinosaur)
30	35000l	*Struthiosaurus* (o-dinosaur)
31	47000l	*Hatzegopteryx* (pterosaur)
		Set of 4 stamps
MS32		Nos. 28-31 *Elopteryx* (s-dinosaur), *Telmatosaurus* (o-dinosaur), *Struthiosaurus* (o-dinosaur), and *Hatzegopteryx* (pterosaur)
		Set of 1 sheet

2007

33†	7120	*Ursus spelaeus* cave bear (mammal)

MS34† One sheet, includes *No. 33 Ursus spelaeus* cave bear (mammal)

RUSSIA
Eastern Europe and Northern Asia
100 kopeks = 1 rouble

1990

1	1k	*Sordes* (pterosaur)
2	3k	*Chalicotherium* (mammal)
3	5k	*Indricotherium (*mammal)
4	10k	*Saurolophus* (o-dinosaur)
5	20k	*Thyestes* cephalaspid ostracoderm (agnathan)

Set of 5 stamps

ST HELENA
South Atlantic
100 pence = 1 pound

1982

1	7p	Charles Darwin issue, with trilobite, pterosaur, ammonite, prehistoric fish,
2		and plesiosaur (?) in the margins of the stamp
2	14p	Charles Darwin issue, with ditto prehistoric animals in margins of stamp
3	25p	Charles Darwin issue, with ditto prehistoric animals in margins of stamp
4	29p	Charles Darwin issue, with ditto prehistoric animals in margins of stamp

Set of 4 stamps

ST KITTS
West Indies
100 cents = 1 West Indian dollar

1994

1	$1.20	*Mesosaurus* (early reptile)
2	$1.20	*Placodus* (placodont)
3	$1.20	*Liopleurodon* (plesiosaur)
4	$1.20	*Hydrotherosaurus* (plesiosaur)
5	$1.20	*Caretta* (turtle)

Set of 5 stamps

Nos. 1-5 *overprinted* **HONG KONG '94** and emblem

6	$1.20	*Mesosaurus* (early reptile)
7	$1.20	*Placodus* (placodont)
8	$1.20	*Liopleurodon* (plesiosaur)
9	$1.20	*Hydrotherosaurus* (plesiosaur)
10	$1.20	*Caretta* (turtle)

Set of 5 stamps

2005

11	$3	*Triceratops* (o-dinosaur)
12	$3	*Deinonychus* (s-dinosaur)
13	$3	*Apatosaurus* (s-dinosaur)
14	$3	*Dimetrodon* (pelycosaur)
15	$3	*Homalocephale* (o-dinosaur)
16	$3	*Stegosaurus* (o-dinosaur)
17	$3	*Smilodon* sabre-tooth tiger (mammal)
18	$3	*Edmontosaurus* (o-dinosaur)
19	$3	*Tyrannosaurus* (s-dinosaur)
		Set of 9 stamps
MS20	Three sheets (a) $5 *Brontosaurus* [=*Apatosaurus*] (s-dinosaur); (b) $5 *Mammuthus* woolly mammoth (mammal) and *Parasaurolophus* (o-dinosaur); (c) $5 *Andrewsarchus* (mammal)	
	Set of 3 sheets	

ST VINCENT
West Indies
100 cents = 1 West Indian dollar

1994

1	75c	*Dimorphodon* (pterosaur)
2	75c	*Camarasaurus* (s-dinosaur)
3	75c	*Spinosaurus* (s-dinosaur)
4	75c	*Allosaurus* (s-dinosaur)
5	75c	*Rhamphorhynchus* (pterosaur)
6	75c	*Pteranodon* (pterosaur)
7	75c	*Eudimorphodon* (pterosaur)
8	75c	*Ornithomimus* (s-dinosaur)
9	75c	*Protoavis* (bird)
10	75c	*Pteranodon* (pterosaur)
11	75c	*Quetzalcoatlus* (pterosaur)
12	75c	*Lesothosaurus* (o-dinosaur)
13	75c	*Heterodontosaurus* (o-dinosaur)
14	75c	*Archaeopteryx* (bird)
15	75c	*Cearadactylus* (pterosaur)
16	75c	*Anchisaurus* (s-dinosaur)
		Set of 16 stamps
MS17	Four stamps (a) $1.50 *Triceratops* (o-dinosaur); (b) $1.50 *Tyrannosaurus rex* (s-dinosaur); (c) $1.50 *Diplodocus* (s-dinosaur); (d) $1.50 *Stegosaurus* (o-dinosaur)	
	Set of 1 sheet	
18	75c	*Albertosaurus* (s-dinosaur)
19	75c	*Chasmosaurus* (o-dinosaur)
20	75c	*Brachiosaurus* (s-dinosaur)
21	75c	*Coelophysis* (s-dinosaur)
22	75c	*Deinonychus* (s-dinosaur)
23	75c	*Anatosaurus* [=*Anatotitan*] (o-dinosaur)

PREHISTORIC ANIMALS OF THE WORLD

Struthiomimus
Ornithomimosaur
Late Cretaceous 110-64 million years ago
Omnivorous Bipedal
Height 3-4m
W. North America, China

Indricotherium
Mammal
Oligocene 20-35 million years ago
Herbivorous Browser
Height more than 9m, Weight 20-30 tons
Largest Ever Land Mammal
C. Asia, Mongolia, China

Giant Moa
Flightless Bird
Terciary 65 million years ago
Extinct 1,000 years ago
Forest Dwelling Grazer
Height 3.5m
New Zealand

Deinonychus
Dromaeosaur
Late Cretaceous 110-64 million years ago
Carnivorous Predator
Height 3.3m
W. North America

Sabre Tooth Cat
Mammal
Pleistocene 1-6 million years ago
8,000 years extinct
Carnivorous Hunter
Length 1.5m
North and South America

Dawn Horse
Mammal
Eocene 50-55 million years ago
Herbivorous Grazer
Height 30-45cm
Asia, Europe, North America

Psittacosaurus
Parrot Beak Dinosaur
Late Cretaceous 110-64 million years ago
Herbivorous Grazer
Height 2m
S.E. Asia

Giant Ground Sloth
Mammal
Miocene 12-7 million years ago
Herbivorous Forest Grazer
Length 6m, Weight 3 tons
W. South America

Wooly Rhinoceros
Mammal
Miocene 12 million years ago
Extinct 10,000 years ago
Herbivorous Grazer
Length up to 4m
Central Asia

Mosasaur
Marine Reptile
Late Cretaceous 110-64 million years ago
Open Sea Predator
Length up to 9m
North America

Mastodon
Mammal
Miocene 12-7 million years ago
Herbivorous Plains Grazer
Height 2m
Asia, North America

Syndyoceras
Lower Miocene 12 million years ago
Woodland Grazer
Height 1m
North America

24	75c	*Iguanodon* (o-dinosaur)
25	75c	*Baryonyx* (s-dinosaur)
26	75c	*Steneosaurus* (crocodilian)
27	75c	*Nanotyrannus* (s-dinosaur)
28	75c	*Camptosaurus* (o-dinosaur)
29	75c	*Camarasaurus* (s-dinosaur)
30	75c	*Hesperornis* (bird)
31	75c	*Mesosaurus* (early reptile)
32	75c	*Dolichorhynchops* (plesiosaur)
33	75c	*Squalicorax* (shark)
34	75c	*Tylosaurus* (lizard)
35	75c	*Plesiosaurus* (plesiosaur)
36	75c	*Stenopterygius* (ichthyosaur)
37	75c	*Steneosaurus* (crocodilian)
38	75c	*Eurhinosaurus longirostris* (ichthyosaur)
39	75c	*Cryptoclidus oxoniensis* (plesiosaur)
40	75c	*Caturus* (fish)
41	75c	*Protostega* (turtle)
42	75c	*Dimorphodon* (pterosaur)
43	75c	*Pterodactylus* (pterosaur)
44	75c	*Rhamphorhynchus* (pterosaur)
45	75c	*Pterodactylus* [wrongly inscr *Pteranodon*] (pterosaur)
46	75c	*Gallimimus* (s-dinosaur)
47	75c	*Stegosaurus* (o-dinosaur)
48	75c	*Acanthopholis* (o-dinosaur)
49	75c	*Trachodon* [=*Anatotitan*] (o-dinosaur)
50	75c	Thecodontian
51	75c	*Ankylosaurus* (o-dinosaur)
52	75c	*Compsognathus* (s-dinosaur)
53	75c	*Protoceratops* (o-dinosaur)
54	75c	*Quetzalcoatlus* (pterosaur)
55	75c	*Diplodocus* (s-dinosaur)
56	75c	*Spinosaurus* (s-dinosaur)
57	75c	*Apatosaurus* (s-dinosaur)
58	75c	*Ornitholestes* (s-dinosaur)
59	75c	*Lesothosaurus* (o-dinosaur)
60	75c	*Trachodon* [=*Anatotitan*] (o-dinosaur)
61	75c	*Protoavis* (bird)
62	75c	*Oviraptor* (s-dinosaur)
63	75c	*Coelophysis* (s-dinosaur)
64	75c	*Ornitholestes* (s-dinosaur)
65	75c	*Archaeopteryx* (bird)
		Set of 48 stamps
MS66		Four sheets (a) $6 *Tyrannosaurus rex* (s-dinosaur); (b) $6 *Triceratops* (o-dinosaur); (c) $6 *Pteranodon* (pterosaur) and *Diplodocus carnegii* (s-dinosaur); (d) $6 *Styracosaurus* (o-dinosaur)
		Set of 4 sheets

1999

67	70c	*Plateosaurus* (s-dinosaur)
68	70c	*Struthiomimus* (s-dinosaur)
69	70c	*Indricotherium* (mammal)
70	70c	*Dinornis* giant moa (bird)
71	70c	*Deinonychus* (s-dinosaur)
72	70c	Sabre-tooth tiger (mammal)
73	70c	*Eohippus* [=*Hyracotherium*] dawn horse (mammal)
74	70c	*Psittacosaurus* (o-dinosaur)
75	70c	Giant ground sloth (mammal)
76	70c	*Coelodonta* woolly rhinoceros (mammal)
77	70c	Mosasaur (lizard)
78	70c	Mastodon (mammal)
79	70c	*Syndyoceras* (mammal)
80	90c	*Euoplocephalus* (o-dinosaur)
81	90c	*Rhamphorhynchus* (pterosaur)
82	90c	*Pteranodon* (pterosaur)
83	90c	*Archaeopteryx* (bird)
84	90c	*Dimetrodon* (pelycosaur)
85	90c	*Stegosaurus* (o-dinosaur)
86	90c	*Parasaurolophus* (o-dinosaur)
87	90c	*Iguanodon* (o-dinosaur)
88	90c	*Triceratops* (o-dinosaur)
89	90c	*Tyrannosaurus* (s-dinosaur)
90	90c	*Ichthyosaurus* (ichthyosaur)
91	90c	*Plesiosaurus* (plesiosaur)
92	90c	*Hesperornis* (bird)
93	$1.10	*Pachycephalosaurus* (o-dinosaur)
94	$1.40	*Dilophosaurus* (s-dinosaur)
		Set of 28 stamps
MS95		Two sheets (a) $5 *Diplodocus* (s-dinosaur); (b) $5 *Coelodonta* woolly rhinoceros (mammal)
		Set of 2 sheets

2001

96	10c	*Mammuthus* woolly mammoth (mammal)
97	20c	*Pinacosaurus* (o-dinosaur)
98	90c	*Oviraptor* (s-dinosaur)
99	90c	*Saltasaurus* (s-dinosaur)
100	90c	*Apatosaurus* (s-dinosaur)
101	90c	*Brachiosaurus* (s-dinosaur)
102	90c	*Troodon* (s-dinosaur)
103	90c	*Deinonychus* (s-dinosaur)
104	90c	*Segnosaurus* (s-dinosaur)
105	90c	*Iguanodon* (o-dinosaur)
106	90c	*Hypacrosaurus* (o-dinosaur)
107	90c	*Ceratosaurus* (s-dinosaur)
108	90c	*Hypsilophodon* (o-dinosaur)
109	90c	*Herrerasaurus* (s-dinosaur)
110	90c	*Velociraptor* (s-dinosaur)
111	$1	*Centrosaurus* (o-dinosaur)

112	$1.40	*Protoceratops* (o-dinosaur)
113	$1.40	*Pteranodon* (pterosaur)
114	$1.40	*Archaeopteryx* (bird)
115	$1.40	*Eudimorphodon* (pterosaur)
116	$1.40	*Shonisaurus* (ichthyosaur)
117	$1.40	*Elasmosaurus* (plesiosaur)
118	$1.40	*Kronosaurus* (plesiosaur)
119	$1.40	*Allosaurus* (s-dinosaur)
120	$1.40	*Dilophosaurus* (s-dinosaur)
121	$1.40	*Lambeosaurus* (o-dinosaur)
122	$1.40	*Coelophysis* (s-dinosaur)
123	$1.40	*Ornitholestes* (s-dinosaur)
124	$1.40	*Eustreptospondylus* (s-dinosaur)
125	$2	*Batrachosaurus* (early reptile)
		Set of 30 stamps

MS126 Four sheets (a) $5 *Stegosaurus* (o-dinosaur); (b) $5 *Parasaurolophus* (o-dinosaur); (c) $5 *Tyrannosaurus* (s-dinosaur); (d) $5 *Triceratops* (o-dinosaur);
Set of 4 sheets

2003

MS127 Four stamps (a) $2 *Daspletosaurus* (s-dinosaur); (b) $2 *Utahraptor* (s-dinosaur); (c) $2 *Scutellosaurus* (o-dinosaur); (d) *Scelidosaurus* (o-dinosaur)
Set of 1 sheet

MS128 Four stamps (a) $2 *Syntarsus* [=*Megapnosaurus*] (s-dinosaur); (b) $2 *Velociraptor* (s-dinosaur); (c) $2 *Mononykus* (bird); (d) $2 *Massospondylus* (s-dinosaur)
Set of 1 sheet

MS129 Two sheets (a) $5 *Giganotosaurus* (s-dinosaur); (b) $5 *Pterodactylus* (pterosaur)
Set of 2 sheets

2005

130	$1.50	*Mammuthus* woolly mammoth (mammal)
131	$1.50	*Mammuthus* woolly mammoth (mammal)
132	$1.50	*Mammuthus* woolly mammoth (mammal)
		Set of 3 stamps

SAN MARINO
Southern Europe
100 centesimi = 1 lira
2002. 100 cents = 1 euro

1965

1	1l	*Brontosaurus* [=*Apatosaurus*] (s-dinosaur)
2	2l	*Brachiosaurus* (s-dinosaur)
3	3l	*Pteranodon* (pterosaur)
4	4l	*Elasmosaurus* (plesiosaur)
5	5l	*Tyrannosaurus* (s-dinosaur)
6	10l	*Stegosaurus* (o-dinosaur)
7	75l	*Thaumatosaurus* (plesiosaur)

8	1001	*Iguanodon* (o-dinosaur)
9	2001	*Triceratops* (o-dinosaur)
		Set of 9 stamps

SÃO TOMÉ E PRINCIPE
West Africa
100 cents = 1 dobra

1982

1	6d	*Parasaurolophus* (o-dinosaur)
2	16d	*Stegosaurus* (o-dinosaur)
3	16d	*Triceratops* (o-dinosaur)
4	16d	*Tyrannosaurus* (s-dinosaur)
5	16d	*Brontosaurus* [=*Apatosaurus*] (s-dinosaur)
6	50d	*Dimetrodon* (pelycosaur)
		Set of 6 stamps
MS7	Two sheets (a) 25d *Pteranodon* (pterosaur); (b) 50d *Stenopterygius* (ichthyosaur)	
		Set of 1 sheet

1993

8	500d	*Tyrannosaurus* (s-dinosaur) and *Pteranodon* (pterosaur)
9	500d	*Dicraeosaurus* (s-dinosaur)
10	500d	*Patagosaurus* (s-dinosaur)
11	500d	*Lystrosaurus* (therapsid)
12	500d	*Shonisaurus* (ichthyosaur)
13	500d	*Dilophosaurus* (s-dinosaur) and *Scutellosaurus* (o-dinosaur)
		Set of 6 stamps
MS14	Two sheets (a) 1000d *Brachiosaurus* (s-dinosaur), *Rhamphorhynchus* (pterosaur), and *Ceratosaurus* (s-dinosaur); (b) 1000d *Protoavis* (bird) and *Postosuchus* (thecodontian)	
		Set of 2 sheets

2003

15†	5000d	*Chasmosaurus* (o-dinosaur)
16	1000d	*Corythosaurus* (o-dinosaur)
17	2000d	*Archaeopteryx* [wrongly inscr *Compsognathus*] (bird)
18	3000d	*Edaphosaurus* (pelycosaur)
19	5000d	*Monoclonius* (o-dinosaur)
20	6000d	*Dimorphodon* [wrongly inscr *Rhamphorhynchus*] (pterosaur)
21	15000d	*Stegosaurus* (o-dinosaur)
		Set of 6 stamps
MS22	One sheet 38000d *Corythosaurus* (o-dinosaur)	
		Set of 1 sheet

2004

23	10000d	Pterosaur
24	10000d	Theropod (s-dinosaur)

25	10000d	Pterosaur
26	10000d	Sauropod (s-dinosaur)
27	10000d	Theropod (s-dinosaur)
28	10000d	Theropod (s-dinosaur)
29	10000d	Ornithischian (o-dinosaur)
30	10000d	*Pteranodon* (pterosaur)
31	10000d	*Pachyrhinosaurus* (o-dinosaur)
		Set of 9 stamps
32	5000d	*Iguanodon* (o-dinosaur)
33	7000d	Ankylosaur (o-dinosaur) and theropods (s-dinosaur)
34	10000d	*Suchomimus* (s-dinosaur), *Deinosuchus* (crocodilian), and pterosaurs
35	15000d	*Giganotosaurus* (s-dinosaur) and *Amargasaurus* (s-dinosaur)
		Set of 4 stamps
MS36	One sheet 43000d *Baryonyx* (s-dinosaur)	
		Set of 1 sheet

2005

37†	10000d	*Ichthyosaurus* (ichthyosaur) and *Plesiosaurus* (plesiosaur)

2006

38	7000d	*Pachycephalosaurus* (o-dinosaur)
39	9000d	*Psittacosaurus* (o-dinosaur)
40	10000d	*Troodon* (s-dinosaur)
41	14000d	*Struthiomimus* (s-dinosaur)
		Set of 4 stamps
MS42	One sheet 40000d *Stegosaurus* (o-dinosaur)	
		Set of 1 sheet

DID YOU KNOW? *Stegosaurus* as depicted on MS42 from São Tomé E Principe is a genus of stegosaurid armoured dinosaur from the Late Jurassic period (Kimmeridgian to Early Tithonian) in what is now western North America. In 2006, a specimen of *Stegosaurus* was announced from Portugal, suggesting that they were present in Europe as well.

SENEGAL
West Africa
100 centimes = 1 franc

1994

1	100f	*Diplodocus* (s-dinosaur)
2	175f	*Brontosaurus* [=*Apatosaurus*] (s-dinosaur)
3	215f	*Triceratops* (o-dinosaur)
4	290f	*Stegosaurus* (o-dinosaur)
5	300f	*Tyrannosaurus* (s-dinosaur)
		Set of 5 stamps

SIERRA LEONE
West Africa
100 cents = 1 leone

1992

1	50l	*Rhamphorhynchus* (pterosaur)
2	50l	*Pteranodon* (pterosaur)
3	50l	*Dimorphodon* (pterosaur)
4	50l	*Pterodactylus* (pterosaur)
5	50l	*Archaeopteryx* (bird)
6	50l	*Iguanodon* (o-dinosaur)
7	50l	*Hypsilophodon* (o-dinosaur)
8	50l	*Nothosaurus* (nothosaur)
9	50l	*Brachiosaurus* (s-dinosaur)
10	50l	*Kentrosaurus* (o-dinosaur)
11	50l	*Plesiosaurus* (plesiosaur)
12	50l	*Trachodon* [=*Anatotitan*] (o-dinosaur)
13	50l	*Hesperornis* (bird)
14	50l	*Henodus* (placodont)
15	50l	*Steneosaurus* (crocodilian)
16	50l	*Stenopterygius* (ichthyosaur)
17	50l	*Eurhinosaurus* (ichthyosaur)
18	50l	*Placodus* (placodont)
19	50l	*Mosasaurus* (lizard)
20	50l	*Mixosaurus* (ichthyosaur)
		Set of 20 stamps
MS21	One sheet 50l *Hesperornis* (bird)	
		Set of 1 sheet

1995

22	200l	*Ceratosaurus* (s-dinosaur)
23	200l	*Brachiosaurus* (s-dinosaur)
24	200l	*Pteranodon* (pterosaur)
25	200l	*Stegoceras* (o-dinosaur)
26	200l	*Saurolophus* (o-dinosaur)
27	200l	*Ornithomimus* (s-dinosaur)
28	200l	*Compsognathus* (s-dinosaur)
29	200l	*Deinonychus* (s-dinosaur)
30	200l	*Ornitholestes* (s-dinosaur)
31	200l	*Archaeopteryx* (bird)
32	200l	*Heterodontosaurus* (o-dinosaur)
33	200l	*Lesothosaurus* (o-dinosaur)
		Set of 12 stamps
MS34	Four stamps (a) 100l *Triceratops* (o-dinosaur); (b) 250l *Protoceratops* (o-dinosaur); (c) 400l *Monoclonius* (o-dinosaur); (d) 800l *Styracosaurus* (o-dinosaur)	
		Set of 1 sheet
MS35	Two sheets (a) 2500l *Rhamphorhynchus* (pterosaur); (b) 2500l *Deinonychus* (s-dinosaur)	
		Set of 2 sheets

1998

36	200l	*Hypsilophodon* (o-dinosaur)
37	400l	*Lambeosaurus* (o-dinosaur)
38	500l	*Corythosaurus* (o-dinosaur)
39	500l	*Tyrannosaurus* (s-dinosaur)
40	500l	*Tenontosaurus* (o-dinosaur)
41	500l	*Deinonychus* (s-dinosaur)
42	500l	*Triceratops* (o-dinosaur)
43	500l	*Maiasaura* (o-dinosaur)
44	500l	*Struthiomimus* (s-dinosaur)
45	500l	*Plateosaurus* (s-dinosaur)
46	500l	*Tyrannosaurus* (s-dinosaur)
47	500l	*Brachiosaurus* (s-dinosaur)
48	500l	*Iguanodon* (o-dinosaur)
49	500l	*Styracosaurus* (o-dinosaur)
50	500l	*Hadrosaurus* (o-dinosaur)
51	600l	*Stegosaurus* (o-dinosaur)
52	800l	*Antrodemus* [=*Allosaurus*] (s-dinosaur)
		Set of 17 stamps
MS53		Two sheets (a) 2000l *Triceratops* (o-dinosaur); (b) 2000l *Tyrannosaurus* (s-dinosaur)
		Set of 2 sheets

2001

54	1000l	*Acrocanthosaurus* (s-dinosaur)
55	1000l	*Edmontosaurus* (o-dinosaur)
56	1000l	*Archaeopteryx* (bird)
57	1000l	*Hadrosaurus* (o-dinosaur)
58	1000l	*Avimimus* (s-dinosaur)
59	1000l	*Pachyrhinosaurus* (o-dinosaur)
60	1000l	*Iguanodon* (o-dinosaur)
61	1000l	*Iguanodon* group (o-dinosaur)
62	1000l	*Albertosaurus* (s-dinosaur)
63	1000l	*Pteranodon ingens* (pterosaur)
64	1000l	*Iguanodon* (o-dinosaur)
65	1000l	*Sordes* (pterosaur)
66	1000l	*Coelophysis* (s-dinosaur)
67	1000l	*Saichania* (o-dinosaur)
68	1000l	*Bactrosaurus* (o-dinosaur)
69	1000l	*Triceratops* (o-dinosaur)
		Set of 16 stamps
MS70		Five sheets (a) 5000l *Rhamphorhynchus* [wrongly inscr *Dryosaurus*] (pterosaur) and *Brachiosaurus* (s-dinosaur); (b) 5000l *Diplodocus* (s-dinosaur); (c) 5000l *Allosaurus* (s-dinosaur); (d) 5000l *Stenonychosaurus* [=*Troodon*] (s-dinosaur); (e) 5000l *Corythosaurus* (o-dinosaur)
		Set of 5 sheets

2004

MS71	Four stamps 2000l *Camarasaurus* (s-dinosaur), 2000l *Lystrosaurus* (therapsid), 2000l *Ankylosaurus* (o-dinosaur), 2000l *Herrerasaurus* (s-dinosaur)

| | | Set of 1 sheet |

MS72 Four stamps 2000l *Apatosaurus* (s-dinosaur), 2000l *Styracosaurus* (o-dinosaur), 2000l *Plateosaurus* (s-dinosaur), 2000l *Pachyrhinosaurus* (o-dinosaur)
Set of 1 sheet

MS73 Two sheets (a) 5000l *Archaeopteryx* (bird); (b) 5000l *Dunkleosteus* (placoderm)
Set of 2 sheets

SINGAPORE
South-east Asia
100 cents = 1 dollar

1998

1	(22c)	*Pentaceratops* (o-dinosaur)
2	(22c)	*Apatosaurus* (s-dinosaur)
3	(22c)	*Albertosaurus* (s-dinosaur)
		Set of 3 stamps

Nos. 1-3 are inscr "For Local Addresses Only".

SLOVENIA
South-east Europe
100 stotinas = 1 tolar

1993

| 1 | 44t | *Schwagerina carniolica* (protozoan) |
| | | Set of 1 stamp |

1995

| 2 | 70t | *Karavankina schellwieni* (brachiopod) |
| | | Set of 1 stamp |

2000

| 3† | 80t | *Paladin* [=*Kaskia*] *bedici* (trilobite) |

2001

| 4 | 107t | Fossilised starfish (echinoderm) |
| | | Set of 1 stamp |

2002

| 5 | C (95t) | *Bibio* (insect) |
| | | Set of 1 stamp |

2004

| 6 | D (107t) Oligocene fossil bony fish (fish) |
| | Set of 1 stamp |

2006

7	D	Middle Miocene fossil gastropod
		Set of 1 stamp

SOLOMON ISLANDS
West Pacific
100 cents = 1 Australian dollar

2006

1	5c	*Baryonyx* (s-dinosaur)
2	10c	*Diplodocus* (s-dinosaur)
3	$1.50	*Pteranodon* (pterosaur)
4	$2.15	*Argentinosaurus* (s-dinosaur)
5	$2.40	*Centrosaurus* (o-dinosaur)
6	$3	*Allosaurus* (s-dinosaur)
7	$10	*Ankylosaurus* (o-dinosaur)
8	$20	*Iguanodon* (o-dinosaur)
		Set of 8 stamps

SOMALIA
East Africa
100 cents = 1 Somali shilling

1993

1	200s	*Brontosaurus* [=*Apatosaurus*] (s-dinosaur)
2	500s	*Pteranodon* (pterosaur)
3	1000s	*Stegosaurus* (o-dinosaur)
4	2000s	*Triceratops* (o-dinosaur)
		Set of 4 stamps
MS5	One sheet 2000s *Triceratops* (o-dinosaur)	
		Set of 1 sheet

1997

6†	200s	Fish and ichthyosaur
7†	300s	Trilobite and ammonite
8†	500s	Crinoid (echinoderm), brachiopod, and coral (cnidarian)

2000

9	100s	*Placodus* (placodont)
10	500s	*Mesosaurus* (early reptile)
11	3000s	*Nothosaurus* (nothosaur)
		Set of 3 stamps
MS12	One sheet 3300s *Mosasaurus* (lizard) and belemnite	
		Set of 1 sheet

SOUTH AFRICA
Southern Africa
100 cents = 1 rand

1982

1	8c	*Bradysaurus* (early reptile)
2	15c	*Lystrosaurus* (therapsid)
3	20c	*Euparkeria* (thecodontian)
4	25c	*Thrinaxodon* (therapsid)
		Set of 4 stamps
MS5		Nos. 1-4 *Bradysaurus* (early reptile), *Lystrosaurus* (therapsid), *Euparkeria* (thecodontian), *hrinaxodon* (therapsid)
		Set of 1 sheet

1991

6† 65c *Australopithecus africanus* (mammal)

1998

7† (1r10) *Australopithecus africanus* Taung skull (mammal)

Nos. 1-7 are inscr "standard postage".

2000

8† 1r30 Sterkfontein *Australopithecus* (mammal)

2006

9	APR	*Paranthropus robustus* (mammal)
10	APR	*Australopithecus africanus* (mammal)
11	APR	*Homo heidelbergensis* (mammal)
12	APR	*Homo ergaster* (mammal)

[APR = Airmail Postcard Rate]
Set of 4 stamps

DID YOU KNOW? *Australopithecus* is a long extinct genus of hominids closely related to humans. Some cryptozoologists believe that evolved descendants of australopithecines, like the one depicted on the 10 APR stamp from South Africa in 2006, may explain certain sightings of hairy dwarves that have been reported all over sub-Saharan Africa.

SOUTH KOREA
Eastern Asia
100 chon = 1 won

2006

1	220ch	*Megaraptor* (s-dinosaur)
2	220ch	*Iguanodon* (o-dinosaur)
		Set of 2 stamps

WORLD of the DINOSAURS

SRI LANKA
Indian Ocean
100 cents = 1 rupee

2006
1†   20r   Fossil rhinoceros (mammal) and fossil hippopotamus (mammal)

SWEDEN
Northern Europe
100 ore = 1 krona

1992
1   2k80   *Plateosaurus* (s-dinosaur)
2   2k80   *Thoracosaurus scanicus* (crocodilian) and *Pteranodon* (pterosaur)
3   2k80   *Coelodonta antiquitatis* woolly rhinoceros (mammal)
4   2k80   *Mammuthus primigenius* woolly mammoth (mammal)
                Set of 4 stamps

DID YOU KNOW? *Plateosaurus* as shown on the 2k80 1992 Swedish stamp was one of the first dinosaurs formally named, (in 1837), although not one of the three genera originally used to define Dinosauria, because at the time it was poorly known and impossible to identify as a dinosaur.

SWITZERLAND
Central Europe
100 rappen = 1 franken
100 centimes = 1 franc
100 centesimi = 1 franco

1958
1†   20c+10c *Lytoceras fimbriatus* (ammonite)

1959
2†   40c+10c *Andrias scheuchzeri* (amphibian)

1960
3†   20c+10c *Gryphaea arcuata* (bivalve)

1961
4†   20c+10c *Archaeoteuthis* (fish)

2004
5   100c   *Neusticosaurus* (plesiosaur)
                Set of 1 stamp

TAJIKISTAN
Western Asia
100 kopeks = 1 (Russian) rouble
1995. 100 tanga = 1 (Tajik) rouble

1994

1	500r	*Tyrannosaurus* (s-dinosaur)
2	500r	*Stegosaurus* (o-dinosaur)
3	500r	*Anatosaurus* [=*Anatotitan*] (o-dinosaur)
4	500r	*Parasaurolophus* (o-dinosaur)
5	500r	*Anchiceratops* [wrongly inscr *Triceratops*] (o-dinosaur)
6	500r	*Diatryma* [=*Gastornis*] (bird)
7	500r	*Polacanthus* [wrongly inscr *Tyrannosaurus*] (o-dinosaur)
8	500r	*Spinosaurus* (s-dinosaur)
		Set of 8 stamps

TANZANIA
East Africa
100 cents = 1 shilling

1965

1†	1s30	*Zinjanthropus* [=*Paranthropus*] *boisei* (mammal)

1988

2†	2s	*Plateosaurus* (s-dinosaur)
3†	3s	*Pteranodon* (pterosaur)
4†	5s	*Brontosaurus* [=*Apatosaurus*] (s-dinosaur)
5†	100s	*Stegosaurus* (o-dinosaur)

1991

6	10s	*Stegosaurus* (o-dinosaur)
7	15s	*Triceratops* (o-dinosaur)
8	25s	*Edmontosaurus* (o-dinosaur)
9	30s	*Plateosaurus* (s-dinosaur)
10	35s	*Diplodocus* (s-dinosaur)
11	100s	*Iguanodon* (o-dinosaur)
12	200s	*Silvisaurus* (o-dinosaur)
		Set of 7 stamps
MS13		One sheet 150s *Rhamphorhynchus* (pterosaur)
		Set of 1 sheet
MS14		One sheet 400s *Mammuthus primigenius* woolly mammoth (mammal) and *Deinotherium* (mammal)
		Set of 1 sheet

1992

15	100s	*Iguanodon* (o-dinosaur)

16	100s	*Saltasaurus* (s-dinosaur)
17	100s	*Cetiosaurus* (s-dinosaur)
18	100s	*Camarasaurus* (s-dinosaur)
19	100s	*Spinosaurus* (s-dinosaur)
20	100s	*Stegosaurus* (o-dinosaur)
21	100s	*Allosaurus* (s-dinosaur)
22	100s	*Ceratosaurus* (s-dinosaur)
23	100s	*Lesothosaurus* (o-dinosaur)
24	100s	*Anchisaurus* (s-dinosaur)
25	100s	*Ornithomimus* (s-dinosaur)
26	100s	*Baryonyx* (s-dinosaur)
27	100s	*Pachycephalosaurus* (o-dinosaur)
28	100s	*Heterodontosaurus* (o-dinosaur)
29	100s	*Dryosaurus* (o-dinosaur)
30	100s	*Coelophysis* (s-dinosaur)
		Set of 16 stamps

1994

31	40s	*Diatryma* [=*Gastornis*] (bird)
32	50s	*Tyrannosaurus rex* (s-dinosaur)
33	100s	*Uintatherium* [wrongly inscr *Uintaterius*] (mammal)
34	120s	*Styracosaurus* (o-dinosaur)
35	170s	*Diplodocus* (s-dinosaur)
36	250s	*Archaeopteryx* (bird)
37	300s	*Sordes* (pterosaur)
		Set of 7 stamps
MS38	One sheet 500s *Dimetrodon* (pelycosaur)	
		Set of 1 sheet

39	120s	*Deinonychus* (s-dinosaur)
40	120s	*Styracosaurus* (o-dinosaur)
41	120s	*Anatosaurus* [=*Anatotitan*] (o-dinosaur)
42	120s	*Plateosaurus* (s-dinosaur)
43	120s	*Iguanodon* (o-dinosaur)
44	120s	*Oviraptor* (s-dinosaur)
45	120s	*Dimorphodon* (pterosaur)
46	120s	*Ornithomimus* (s-dinosaur)
47	120s	*Lambeosaurus* (o-dinosaur)
48	120s	*Megalosaurus* (s-dinosaur)
49	120s	*Cetiosaurus* (s-dinosaur)
50	120s	*Hypsilophodon* (o-dinosaur)
51	120s	*Rhamphorhynchus* (pterosaur)
52	120s	*Scelidosaurus* (o-dinosaur)
53	120s	*Antrodemus* [=*Allosaurus*] (s-dinosaur)
54	120s	*Dimetrodon* (pelycosaur)
55	120s	*Brontosaurus* [=*Apatosaurus*] (s-dinosaur)
56	120s	*Albertosaurus* (s-dinosaur)
57	120s	*Parasaurolophus* (o-dinosaur)
58	120s	*Pteranodon* (pterosaur)
59	120s	*Stegosaurus* (o-dinosaur)

Dinosaurs and other Prehistoric Animals on Stamps

60	120s	*Tyrannosaurus* (s-dinosaur)
61	120s	*Triceratops* (o-dinosaur)
62	120s	*Ornitholestes* (s-dinosaur)
63	120s	*Camarasaurus* (s-dinosaur)
64	120s	*Ankylosaurus* (o-dinosaur)
65	120s	*Trachodon* [=*Anatotitan*] (o-dinosaur)
66	120s	*Allosaurus* (s-dinosaur)
67	120s	*Corythosaurus* (o-dinosaur)
68	120s	*Struthiomimus* (s-dinosaur)
69	120s	*Camptosaurus* (o-dinosaur)
70	120s	*Heterodontosaurus* (o-dinosaur)
		Set of 48 stamps
MS71	One sheet 1000s *Brachiosaurus* (s-dinosaur)	
		Set of 1 sheet

1996

72†	50s	*Tyrannosaurus rex* (s-dinosaur)
73†	170s	*Diplodocus* (o-dinosaur)
74†	250s	*Archaeopteryx* (bird)
75†	300s	*Sordes* (pterosaur) all embossed on gold foil
MS76	One sheet *Tyrannosaurus rex* (s-dinosaur), *Diplodocus* (s-dinosaur),	
	Archaeopteryx (bird), *Sordes* (pterosaur), *Dimetrodon* (pelycosaur)	
	Set of 1 sheet - all embossed on gold foil	

1999

77	400s	*Tyrannosaurus* (s-dinosaur)
78	400s	*Coelurus* (s-dinosaur)
79	400s	*Stegosaurus* (o-dinosaur)
80	400s	*Corythosaurus* (o-dinosaur) and *Leptictidium* (mammal)
81	400s	*Thadeosaurus* (early reptile)
82	400s	*Brachiosaurus* (s-dinosaur)
		Set of 6 stamps
MS83	One sheet 1500s *Ceratosaurus* (s-dinosaur)	
		Set of 1 sheet

84	200s	*Stegosaurus* [wrongly inscr *Edmontonia*] (o-dinosaur)
85	250s	*Archaeopteryx* (bird)
86	370s	*Stegosaurus* (o-dinosaur)
87	370s	*Dromiceiomimus* (s-dinosaur)
88	370s	*Saurolophus* (o-dinosaur)
89	370s	*Camarasaurus* (s-dinosaur)
90	370s	*Protoceratops* (o-dinosaur)
91	370s	*Psittacosaurus* (o-dinosaur)
92	370s	*Stegoceras* (o-dinosaur)
93	370s	*Gallimimus* (s-dinosaur)
94	370s	*Peteinosaurus* (pterosaur)
95	370s	*Lambeosaurus* (o-dinosaur)
96	370s	*Coelophysis* (s-dinosaur)
97	370s	*Parasaurolophus* (o-dinosaur)
98	370s	*Tyrannosaurus rex* (s-dinosaur)

99   410s   *Lagosuchus* (thecodontian)
                  Set of 16 stamps
MS100 Two sheets (a) 1500s *Quetzalcoatlus* (pterosaur),
                  (b) 1500s *Rhomaleosaurus* (plesiosaur)
                  Set of 2 sheets

THAILAND
South-east Asia
100 satangs = 1 baht

1992
1†   2b   Theropod (s-dinosaur) and sauropod (s-dinosaur)

1997
2   2b   *Phuwiangosaurus sirindhornae* (s-dinosaur)
3   3b   *Siamotyrannus isanensis* (s-dinosaur)
4   6b   *Siamosaurus* [=*Spinosaurus*] *suteethorni* (s-dinosaur)
5   9b   *Psittacosaurus sattayaraki* (o-dinosaur)
                  Set of 4 stamps
MS6   *Nos.* 2-5 2b *Phuwiangosaurus sirindhornae* (s-dinosaur),
                  3b *Siamotyrannus isanensis* (s-dinosaur),
                  6b *Siamosaurus* [=*Spinosaurus*] *suteethorni* (s-dinosaur),
                  9b *Psittacosaurus sattayaraki* (o-dinosaur)
                  Set of 1 sheet

2004
7†   3b   Sauropods (s-dinosaur)

TOGO
West Africa
100 centimes = 1 franc

1994
1   125f   *Polacanthus* (o-dinosaur)
2   180f   *Pachycephalosaurus* (o-dinosaur)
3   425f   *Coelophysis* (s-dinosaur)
4   480f   *Brachiosaurus* (s-dinosaur)
5   500f   *Dilophosaurus* (s-dinosaur)
6   1500f   *Scutellosaurus* (o-dinosaur)
                  Set of 6 stamps (in perforate and imperforate versions)
MS7   One sheet 1500f *Velociraptor* (s-dinosaur)
                  Set of 1 sheet (in perforate and imperforate versions)
MS8   *Nos.* 1-6 *Polacanthus* (o-dinosaur), *Pachycephalosaurus* (o-dinosaur),
                  Coelophysis (s-dinosaur), *Brachiosaurus* (s-dinosaur),
                  Dilophosaurus (s-dinosaur), and *Scutellosaurus* (o-dinosaur)
                  Set of 6 sheets (in perforate and imperforate versions)

1997

9	290f	*Brachiosaurus* (s-dinosaur)
10	290f	*Deinonychus* (s-dinosaur)
11	290f	*Dilophosaurus* (s-dinosaur)
12	290f	*Stegosaurus* (o-dinosaur)
13	290f	*Tyrannosaurus* (s-dinosaur)
14	290f	*Triceratops* (o-dinosaur)
15	290f	*Dilophosaurus* (s-dinosaur)
16	290f	*Pachycephalosaurus* (o-dinosaur)
17	290f	*Struthiomimus* (s-dinosaur)
		Set of 9 stamps
MS18	One sheet 2000f *Tyrannosaurus* (s-dinosaur)	
		Set of 1 sheet

TONGA
South Pacific
100 seniti = 1 pa'anga

1996

1†	1p	Prehistoric humans (mammal), *Ursus spelaeus* cave bear (mammal), and *Megaloceros* (mammal)

DID YOU KNOW? Geneticist Bryan Sykes from Oxford University has shown that nearly every person living in Europe today is descended from one of just seven prehistoric humans like the ones depicted on the 1p Tongan stamp from 1996.

TRANSKEI
Southern Africa
100 cents = 1 rand

1992

1	35c	*Pseudomelania sutherlandi* (gastropod)
2	70c	*Gaudryceras denseplicatum* (ammonite)
3	90c	*Neithea quinquecostata* (bivalve)
4	1r05	*Pugilina acuticarinatus* (gastropod)
		Set of 4 stamps

1993

5	45c	*Fabrosaurus* (o-dinosaur)
6	65c	*Diictodon* (therapsid)
7	85c	*Chasmatosaurus* (thecodontian)
8	1r05	*Rubidgea* (therapsid)
		Set of 4 stamps

TRISTAN DA CUNHA
South Atlantic
100 pence = 1 pound

1997
MS1   Four stamps (a) 35p *Archelon* (turtle); (b) 35p *Trinacromerum* (plesiosaur); (c) 35p *Platecarpus* (lizard); (d) 35p *Clidastes* (lizard)
       Set of 1 sheet

1998
MS2   Four stamps (a) 45p *Carcharodon* [=*Carcharocles*] *megalodon* (shark) and *Eurhinodelphis* (mammal); (b) 45p *Orycterocetus* (mammal); (c) 45p *Eurhinodelphis* (mammal); (d) 45p Miocene *Hexanchus* (shark) and *Myliobatis* ray (shark)
       Set of 1 sheet

TUNISIA
North Africa
100 milliemes = 1 dinar

1982
1	80m	*Pseudophillipsia azzouzi* (trilobite)	
2	200m	*Mediterraneotrigonia cherahilensis* (bivalve)	
3	280m	*Numidopleura enigmatica* (fish)	
4	300m	*Micreschara tunisiensis* (gastropod)	
5	500m	*Mantelliceras pervinquieri* (ammonite)	
6	1000m	*Elephas africanavus* (mammal)	

Set of 6 stamps

TURKISH (NORTHERN) CYPRUS
South-east Europe
100 kurus = 1 lira

1991
1†   250l   Elephant (mammal) and hippopotamus (mammal) fossils

TURKS AND CAICOS ISLANDS
West Indies
100 cents = 1 dollar

1991
1   5c   *Protohydrochoerus* (mammal)
2   10c   *Phororhacos* [=*Phorusrhacus*] (bird)
3   15c   *Prothylacynus* (mammal)

Dinosaurs and other Prehistoric Animals on Stamps

4	50c	*Borhyaena* (mammal)
5	75c	*Smilodon* sabre-tooth tiger (mammal)
6	$1	*Thoatherium* (mammal)
7	$1.25	*Cuvieronius* (mammal)
8	$1.50	*Toxodon* (mammal)
		Set of 8 stamps
MS9		Two sheets (a) $2 *Astrapotherium* (mammal); (b) $2 *Mesosaurus* (early reptile)
		Set of 2 sheets

1993

10	8c	*Omphalosaurus* (ichthyosaur)
11	15c	*Coelophysis* (s-dinosaur)
12	20c	*Triceratops* (o-dinosaur)
13	35c	*Dilophosaurus* (s-dinosaur)
14	50c	*Pterodactylus* (pterosaur)
15	65c	*Elasmosaurus* (plesiosaur)
16	80c	*Stegosaurus* (o-dinosaur)
17	$1.25	*Euoplocephalus* (o-dinosaur)
		Set of 8 stamps
MS18		Two sheets (a) $2 *Triceratops* (o-dinosaur); (b) $2 *Dilophosaurus* (s-dinosaur)
		Set of 2 sheets

1994

19	35c	*Elasmosaurus* (plesiosaur)
20	35c	*Plesiosaurus* (plesiosaur)
21	35c	*Ichthyosaurus* (ichthyosaur)
22	35c	*Archelon* (turtle)
23	35c	*Askeptosaurus* (early reptile)
24	35c	*Macroplata* (plesiosaur)
25	35c	*Ceresiosaurus* (nothosaur)
26	35c	*Liopleurodon* (plesiosaur)
27	35c	*Henodus* (placodont)
28	35c	*Muraenosaurus* (plesiosaur)
29	35c	*Placodus* (placodont)
30	35c	*Kronosaurus* (plesiosaur)
		Set of 12 stamps

UGANDA
East Africa
100 cents = 1 shilling

1992

1	50s	*Kentrosaurus* (o-dinosaur)
2	200s	*Iguanodon* (o-dinosaur)
3	250s	*Hypsilophodon* (o-dinosaur)
4	300s	*Brachiosaurus* (s-dinosaur)
5	400s	*Peloneustes* (plesiosaur)
6	500s	*Pteranodon* (pterosaur)

7	800s	*Tetralophodon* (mammal)
8	1000s	*Megalosaurus* (s-dinosaur)
		Set of 8 stamps
MS9	Two sheets (a) 2000s *Hypsilophodon* (o-dinosaur); (b) 2000s *Megalosaurus* (s-dinosaur)	
	Set of 2 sheets	

1995

10	150s	*Velociraptor* (s-dinosaur)
11	200s	*Psittacosaurus* (o-dinosaur)
12	300s	*Archaeopteryx* (bird)
13	300s	*Quetzalcoatlus* (pterosaur)
14	300s	*Pteranodon* (pterosaur)
15	300s	*Brachiosaurus* (s-dinosaur)
16	300s	*Tsintaosaurus* (o-dinosaur)
17	300s	*Allosaurus* (s-dinosaur)
18	300s	*Tyrannosaurus* (s-dinosaur)
19	300s	*Apatosaurus* (s-dinosaur)
20	300s	Prehistoric giant dragonfly (insect)
21	300s	*Dimorphodon* (pterosaur)
22	300s	*Triceratops* (o-dinosaur)
23	300s	*Compsognathus* (s-dinosaur)
24	350s	*Dilophosaurus* (s-dinosaur)
25	400s	*Kentrosaurus* (o-dinosaur)
26	500s	*Stegosaurus* (o-dinosaur)
27	1500s	*Pterodaustro* (pterosaur)
		Set of 18 stamps
MS28	Two sheets (a) 2000s *Parasaurolophus* (o-dinosaur); (b) 2000s *Shunosaurus* (s-dinosaur)	
	Set of 2 sheets	

1998

29	300s	*Pteranodon* (pterosaur)
30	400s	*Diplodocus* (s-dinosaur)
31	500s	*Lambeosaurus* (o-dinosaur)
32	600s	*Centrosaurus* (o-dinosaur)
33	600s	*Cetiosaurus* (s-dinosaur)
34	600s	*Brontosaurus* [=*Apatosaurus*] (s-dinosaur)
35	600s	*Brachiosaurus* (s-dinosaur)
36	600s	*Deinonychus* (s-dinosaur)
37	600s	*Dimetrodon* (pelycosaur)
38	600s	*Megalosaurus* (s-dinosaur)
39	700s	*Parasaurolophus* (o-dinosaur)
		Set of 11 stamps
MS40	Two sheets (a) 2500s *Tyrannosaurus* (s-dinosaur); (b) 2500s *Iguanodon* (o-dinosaur)	
	Set of 2 sheets	

2002

41	600s	*Cetiosaurus* (s-dinosaur)
42	600s	*Brontosaurus* [=*Apatosaurus*] (s-dinosaur)
43	600s	*Brachiosaurus* (s-dinosaur)
44	600s	*Deinonychus* (s-dinosaur)

Dinosaurs and other Prehistoric Animals on Stamps

45	600s	*Dimetrodon* (pelycosaur)
46	600s	*Megalosaurus* (s-dinosaur)
		Set of 6 stamps

UNITED STATES OF AMERICA
North America
100 cents = 1 dollar

1955

1	3c	*Mammut americanus* mastodon (mammal)
		Set of 1 stamp

1970

2†	6c	*Diplodocus* (s-dinosaur), *Apatosaurus* (s-dinosaur), *Stegosaurus* (o-dinosaur), *Allosaurus* (s-dinosaur), *Camptosaurus* (o-dinosaur), *Compsognathus* (s-dinosaur), *Archaeopteryx* (bird), and *Rhamphorhynchus* (pterosaur)

1982

3†	20c	Trilobite

1989

4	25c	*Tyrannosaurus rex* (s-dinosaur)
5	25c	*Pteranodon* (pterosaur)
6	25c	*Stegosaurus* (o-dinosaur)
7	25c	*Brontosaurus* [=*Apatosaurus*] (s-dinosaur)
		Set of 4 stamps

1996

8	32c	*Mammut* mastodon (mammal)
9	32c	*Smilodon* sabre-tooth tiger (mammal)
10	32c	*Eohippus* [=*Hyracotherium*] dawn horse (mammal)
11	32c	*Mammuthus primigenius* woolly mammoth (mammal)
		Set of 4 stamps

1997

12	32c	*Ceratosaurus* (s-dinosaur)
13	32c	*Camptosaurus* (o-dinosaur)
14	32c	*Camarasaurus* (s-dinosaur)
15	32c	*Brachiosaurus* (s-dinosaur)
16	32c	*Stegosaurus* (o-dinosaur)
17	32c	*Allosaurus* (s-dinosaur)
18	32c	*Goniopholis* (crocodilian)
19	32c	*Opisthias* (sphenodontian)
20	32c	*Parasaurolophus* (o-dinosaur)
21	32c	*Edmontonia* (o-dinosaur)
22	32c	*Einiosaurus* (o-dinosaur)
23	32c	*Daspletosaurus* (s-dinosaur)
24	32c	*Corythosaurus* (o-dinosaur)

25	32c	*Ornithomimus* (s-dinosaur)
26	32c	*Palaeosaniwa* (lizard)
		Set of 15 stamps

2000

27†	33c	*Tyrannosaurus rex* (s-dinosaur)

URUGUAY
South America
1000 milesimos = 100 centesimos = 1 peso

1988

1†	90p	*Toxodon platensis* (mammal)

1996

2	3p20	*Glyptodon claripes* glyptodont (mammal)
3	3p20	*Macrauchenia patachonica* (mammal)
4	3p20	*Toxodon platensis* (mammal)
5	3p20	*Glossotherium robustum* ground sloth (mammal)
6	3p20	*Titanosaurus* (s-dinosaur)
		Set of 5 stamps

1997

7	5p	*Devincenzia gallinali* (bird)
8	5p	*Smilodon populator* sabre-tooth tiger (mammal)
9	5p	*Mesosaurus tenuidens* (early reptile)
10	5p	*Doedicurus clavicaudatus* glyptodont (mammal)
11	5p	*Artigasia magna* (mammal)
		Set of 5 stamps

1998

12	6p	*Testudinites sellowi* (tortoise)
13	6p	*Proborhyaena gigantea* (mammal)
14	6p	*Propachyrucos schiaffinos* (mammal)
15	6p	*Stegomastodon platensis* (mammal)
		Set of 4 stamps

UZBEKISTAN
Central Asia
100 tyin = 1 sum

1999

1	28s	*Meganeura* (insect)
2	28s	*Mesosaurus* (early reptile)
3	36s	*Rhamphorhynchus* (pterosaur)
4	36s	*Styracosaurus* (o-dinosaur)

5	56s	*Trachodon* [=*Anatotitan*] (o-dinosaur)
6	56s	*Tarbosaurus* (s-dinosaur)
7	69s	*Arsinotherium* (mammal)
8	75s	*Phororhacos* [=*Phorusrhacus*] (bird)
		Set of 8 stamps

2002

MS9   Nine stamps in one sheet: 40s *Dryopithecus major* (mammal); 45s *Homo erectus* (mammal); 50s *Pithecanthropus* [=*Homo*] *erectus* (mammal); 60s *Australopithecus afarensis* (mammal); 70s *Zinjanthropus* [=*Paranthropus*] *boisei* (mammal); 85s *Homo neanderthalensis* (mammal); 90s *Sinanthropus pekinensis* [=*Homo erectus*] (mammal); 125s *Protanthropus* [=*Homo*] *heidelbergensis*; 160s *Homo sapiens* Cro-Magnon man (mammal)
      Set of 1 sheet

VIETNAM
```
South-east Asia
100 xu = 1 dong
```

1979

1	12x	*Plesiosaurus* (plesiosaur)
2	12x	*Brontosaurus* [=*Apatosaurus*] (s-dinosaur)
3	20x	*Iguanodon* (o-dinosaur)
4	30x	*Tyrannosaurus* (s-dinosaur)
5	40x	*Stegosaurus* (o-dinosaur)
6	50x	*Mosasaurus* (lizard)
7	60x	*Triceratops* (o-dinosaur)
8	1d	*Pteranodon* (pterosaur)
		Set of 8 stamps (in perforate and imperforate versions)

1984

9	50x	*Styracosaurus* (o-dinosaur)
10	50x	*Diplodocus* (s-dinosaur)
11	1d	*Rhamphorhynchus* (pterosaur)
12	1d	*Corythosaurus* (o-dinosaur)
13	2d	*Seymouria* (amphibian)
14	3d	*Allosaurus* (s-dinosaur)
15	5d	*Dimetrodon* (pelycosaur)
16	8d	*Brachiosaurus* (s-dinosaur)
		Set of 8 stamps

1990

17	100d	*Gorgosaurus* (s-dinosaur)
18	500d	*Ceratosaurus* (s-dinosaur)
19	1000d	*Ankylosaurus* (o-dinosaur)
20	2000d	*Euoplocephalus* [wrongly inscr *Ankylosaurus*] (o-dinosaur)

21	3000d	*Edaphosaurus* (pelycosaur)
		Set of 5 stamps

1991

22	200d	*Arsinotherium zitteli* (mammal)
23	500d	*Elephas* [=*Mammuthus*] *primigenius* woolly mammoth (mammal)
24	1000d	*Baluchitherium* [=*Indricotherium*] (mammal)
25	2000d	*Deinotherium giganteum* (mammal)
26	3000d	*Brontops* (mammal)
27	3000d	*Uintatherium* (mammal)
		Set of 6 stamps (in perforate and imperforate versions)

1996

28	400d	*Tsintaosaurus* (o-dinosaur)
29	1000d	*Archaeopteryx* (bird)
30	2000d	*Psittacosaurus* (o-dinosaur)
31	3000d	*Hypsilophodon* (o-dinosaur)
32	13000d	*Parasaurolophus* (o-dinosaur)
		Set of 5 stamps (in perforate and imperforate versions)

WALLIS AND FUTUNA ISLANDS
South Pacific
100 centimes = 1 franc

1990

1	48f	Fossil tortoise
		Set of 1 stamp

WEST BERLIN
Central Europe
100 pfennig = 1 Deutsche mark (West)

1977

1	20pf	*Iguanodon* (o-dinosaur) included in right-hand edge
2	30pf	*Iguanodon* (o-dinosaur) included in right-hand edge
3	40pf	*Iguanodon* (o-dinosaur) included in right-hand edge
4	50pf	*Iguanodon* (o-dinosaur) included in right-hand edge
		Set of 4 stamps

WEST GERMANY (GERMAN FEDERAL REPUBLIC)
Central Europe
100 pfennig = 1 Deutsche mark (West)

1978

1	80pf	*Palaeochiropteryx tupaiodon* bat (mammal)

2	200pf	*Propalaeotherium messelens* (mammal)
		Set of 2 stamps

1998

3	100pf	*Diplocynodon* or *Pristichampsus* (crocodilian)
		Set of 1 stamp

YEMEN REPUBLIC
Arabian peninsula
100 fils = 1 rial

1990

1	5f	*Protembolotherium* (mammal)
2	10f	*Diatryma* [=*Gastornis*] (bird)
3	35f	*Mammuthus* woolly mammoth (mammal)
4	40f	*Edaphosaurus* (pelycosaur)
5	55f	*Dimorphodon* (pterosaur)
6	75f	*Phororhacos* [=*Phorusrhacus*] (bird)
7	700f	*Ichthyosaurus* (ichthyosaur)
		Set of 7 stamps
MS8		One sheet 460f *Tyrannosaurus* (s-dinosaur)
		Set of 1 sheet

YUGOSLAVIA
South-east Europe
100 paras = 1 dinar

1985

1	5d	*Aturia aturi* (nautiloid)
2	6d	*Pachyophis woodwardi* (lizard)
3	33d	*Chaetodon hoeferi* (fish)
4	60d	*Homo neanderthalensis* Neanderthal man (mammal)
		Set of 4 stamps

ZAIRE
Central Africa
100 sengi = 1 (li)kuta; 100 (ma)kuta = 1 zaire

1996

1†	20000z	*Scutellosaurus* (o-dinosaur)
2†	20000z	*Compsognathus* (s-dinosaur)
3†	20000z	*Dryosaurus* (o-dinosaur)
4†	20000z	*Velociraptor* (s-dinosaur) (in perforate and imperforate versions)

MS5† Includes sheet (b) 105000z *Tyrannosaurus* (s-dinosaur) (in perforate and imperforate versions)

1997

MS6† *Overprinted* **HONG KONG '97** Includes sheet (b) 105000z *Tyrannosaurus* (s-dinosaur)

ZAMBIA
Central Africa
100 ngwee = 1 kwacha

1973

1†	4n	*Oudenodon* (therapsid) and *Rubidgea* (therapsid)
2†	10n	*Zambiasaurus* (therapsid)

DID YOU KNOW? *Dimetrodon*, as depicted on the 1973 50k stamp from Zambia, flourished during the Permian Period, living between 280–265 million years ago. Its huge sail is believed to have been thermoregulatory and/or used in mating displays.

Dimetrodon was not a dinosaur, despite being popularly grouped with them. Rather, it is classified as a pelycosaur. Fossils of *Dimetrodon* have been found in North America and Europe, as well as a significant discovery of *Dimetrodon* footprints in southern New Mexico by Jerry MacDonald.

3†	15n	*Luangwa drysdalli* (therapsid)
4	50k	*Dimetrodon* (pelycosaur)
5	100k	*Deinonychus* (s-dinosaur)
6	500k	*Protoceratops* (o-dinosaur)
7	900k	*Heterodontosaurus* (o-dinosaur)
8	900k	*Stegosaurus* (o-dinosaur)
9	900k	*Triceratops* (o-dinosaur)
10	900k	*Brontosaurus* [=*Apatosaurus*] (s-dinosaur)
11	900k	*Gallimimus* (s-dinosaur)
12	900k	*Saurolophus* (o-dinosaur)
13	900k	*Lambeosaurus* (o-dinosaur)
14	900k	*Centrosaurus* (o-dinosaur)
15	900k	*Edmontonia* (o-dinosaur)
16	900k	*Parasaurolophus* (o-dinosaur)
17	900k	*Ceratosaurus* (s-dinosaur)
18	900k	*Daspletosaurus* (s-dinosaur)
19	900k	*Baryonyx* (s-dinosaur)
20	900k	*Ornitholestes* (s-dinosaur)
21	900k	*Troodon* (s-dinosaur)
22	900k	*Coelophysis* (s-dinosaur)
23	900k	*Tyrannosaurus* (s-dinosaur)
24	900k	*Allosaurus* (s-dinosaur)
25	900k	*Compsognathus* (s-dinosaur)
26	1000k	*Oviraptor* (s-dinosaur)
27	1800k	*Psittacosaurus* (o-dinosaur).

Set of 24 stamps
MS28 Two sheets: (a) 4000k *Saltasaurus* (s-dinosaur); (b) 4000k *Stygimoloch* (o-dinosaur)
Set of 2 sheets

ZIMBABWE
Central Africa
100 cents = 1 dollar

1998

1† $1.20   Fossil fish
2† $5.60   *Allosaurus* (s-dinosaur)
3† $7.40   *Massospondylus* (s-dinosaur)

TAXONOMIC CROSS-REFERENCING BY GENUS

Unlike those of previous wildlife-based thematic stamp catalogues, the present catalogue's subjects span the entire spectrum of the zoological classification system, from the highest vertebrates to the lowest invertebrates. Consequently, in order to avoid this section of the catalogue becoming disproportionately long and unnecessarily complex, I have incorporated various simplifications where necessary. For example: reptiles belonging to certain very early, taxonomically-controversial/anomalous reptile orders and which are only represented in the main body of the catalogue by a handful or less of stamps have been listed together within the single non-taxonomic group 'Early Reptiles' for the sake of clarity and easy access (I have also adopted this policy with the invertebrates). In addition, I have adhered throughout this section of the catalogue to the traditional (i.e. non-cladistic) non-controversial system of zoological classification that will be familiar to the great majority of philatelists, thus retaining, for example, the thecodontians as a discrete (albeit recognisably polyphyletic, non-taxonomic) order, and birds as a separate taxonomic class (as opposed to submerging them within the saurischian dinosaurs).

Invertebrate animals are listed here within their respective phyla, and in the case of the mollusc phylum are sub-divided into its respective classes (with Cephalopoda further sub-divided into Ammonoidea and Other Cephalopoda). Vertebrates (which all belong to the phylum Chordata) are divided into classes, and in the case of the reptiles (comprising the vast majority of animals in this catalogue) are further sub-divided into orders (plus the afore-mentioned non-taxonomic groups the thecodontians and Early Reptiles). Equally, as the vast majority of animals contained in this catalogue are referred to on the stamps depicting them only by their generic name (genus), only genera (rather than species) are listed in the main portion of this section. Lastly, it will be noticed that the this section of the catalogue does not include a listing of animals by way of their English names. This omission is due very simply to the fact that unlike most sizeable living animals (especially vertebrates), dinosaurs and the vast majority of other prehistoric animals do not have English names, only zoological ones.

LISTING OF ZOOLOGICAL NAMES

This listing includes the generic names (genera) of all the animals contained in this catalogue alongside their respective taxa (zoological classification categories). Synonyms are included where these differ from the genus on the stamp, but spelling variations or errors are not listed. Names given below in square brackets are ones that are now deemed obsolete by scientists and are placed directly after the respective names that have replaced them. For cross-reference purposes, these obsolete names are also given their own headings below, followed immediately by 'see' and the respective names that have replaced them.

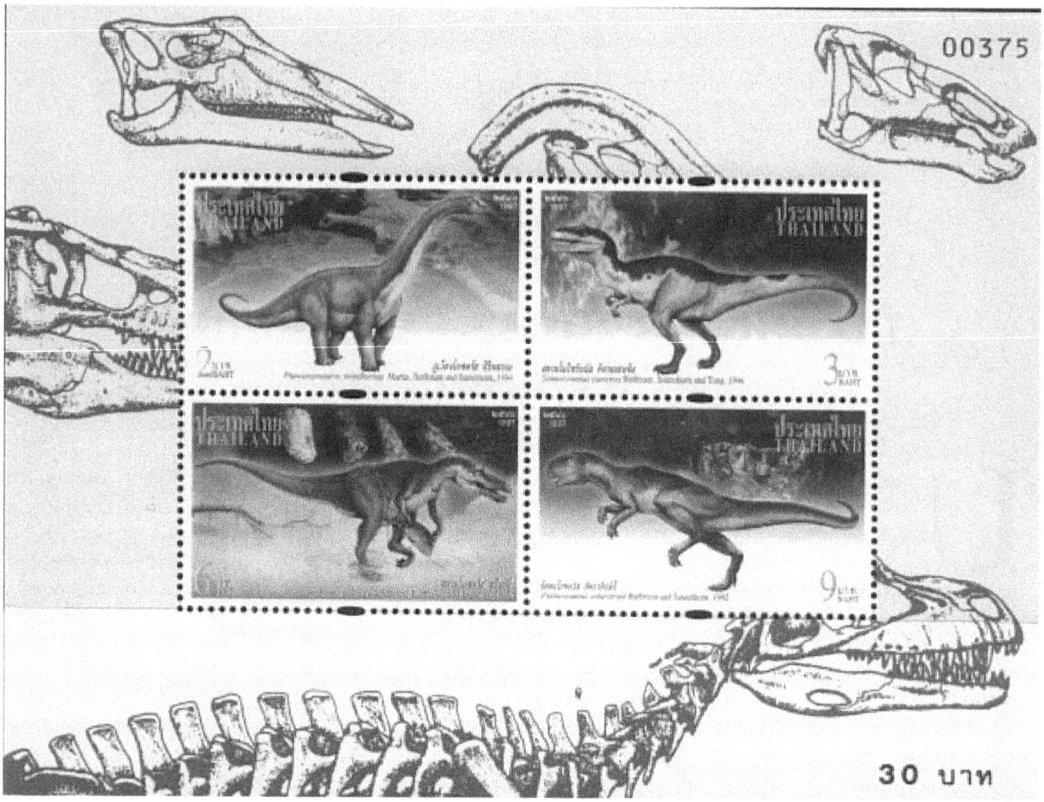
00375
ประเทศไทย
THAILAND
30 บาท

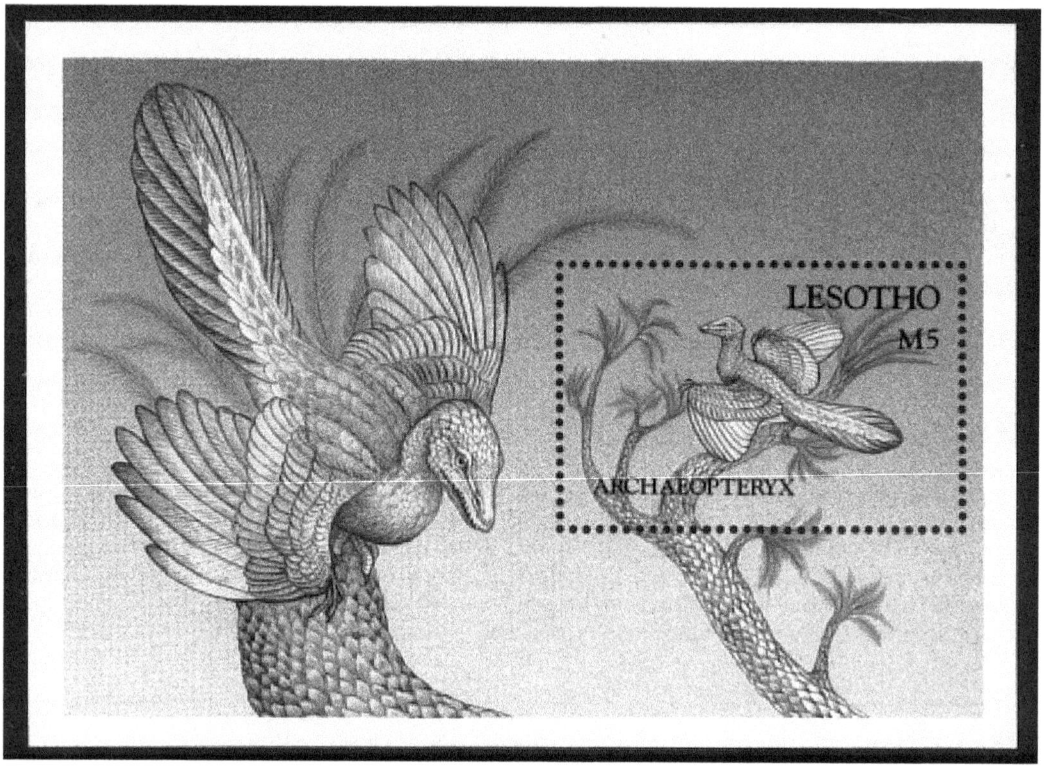
LESOTHO
M5
ARCHAEOPTERYX

A

Acanthopholis see 1-3-2 (Ornithischia)
Acanthostega see 1-4 (Amphibia)
Aceratherium see 1-1 (Mammalia)
Acrocanthosaurus see 1-3-1 (Saurischia)
Aellopos [=*Spathobathis*] see 1-5 (Osteichthyes)
Afrovenator see 1-3-1 (Saurischia)
Agathamas see 1-3-2 (Ornithischia)
Agilisaurus see 1-3-2 (Ornithischia)
Ainoceras see 2-7-1 (Ammonoidea)
Aipichthys see 1-5 (Osteichthyes)
Alamosaurus see 1-3-1 (Saurischia)
Albertosaurus see 1-3-1 (Saurischia)
Alioramus see 1-3-1 (Saurischia)
Alligator, unspecified giant prehistoric see 1-3-5 (Crocodylia)
Allosaurus [=*Antrodemus*] see 1-3-1 (Saurischia)
Amargasaurus see 1-3-1 (Saurischia)
Amebelodon see 1-1 (Mammalia)
Ammonite, unspecified see 2-7-1 (Ammonoidea)
Anatosaurus see *Anatotitan* see 1-3-2 (Ornithischia)
Anatotitan [=*Anatosaurus*] [=*Trachodon*] see 1-3-2 (Ornithischia)
Anchiceratops see 1-3-2 (Ornithischia)
Anchisaurus see 1-3-1 (Saurischia)
Ancyclotherium see 1-1 (Mammalia)
Andrewsarchus see 1-1 (Mammalia)
Andrias see 1-4 (Amphibia)
Angaturama see 1-3-1 (Saurischia)
Angolosaurus see 1-3-7 (Squamata)
Ankylosaur, unspecified see 1-3-2 (Ornithischia)
Ankyosaurus see 1-3-2 (Ornithischia)
Anolcites see 2-7-1 (Ammonoidea)
Anomalocaris see 2-12 (Early Invertebrata)
Antrodemus see *Allosaurus* see 1-3-1 (Saurischia)
Anurognathus see 1-3-4 (Pterosauria)
Apatosaurus [=*Brontosaurus*] see 1-3-1 (Saurischia)
Aptornis see 1-2 (Aves)
Aquila see 1-2 (Aves)
'Aramberri monster' see 1-3-12 (Sauropterygia)
Archaeohyrax see 1-1 (Mammalia)
Archaeopteryx see 1-2 (Aves)
Archaeoteuthis see 1-5 (Osteichthyes)
Archaeotrogon see 1-2 (Aves)
Archelon see 1-3-15 (Chelonia)
Archidiskodon see 1-1 (Mammalia)
Arctodus see 1-1 (Mammalia)
Argentinosaurus see 1-3-1 (Saurischia)
Argyrolagus see 1-1 (Mammalia)

Arrhinoceratops see 1-3-2 (Ornithischia)
Arsinotherium see 1-1 (Mammalia)
Artigasia see 1-1 (Mammalia)
Asaphus see 2-3 (Trilobita)
Ascocystites see 2-1 (Echinodermata)
Askeptosaurus see 1-3-16 (Early Reptiles)
Astrapotherium see 1-1 (Mammalia)
Astrodon see *Pleurocoelus* see 1-3-1 (Saurischia)
Atlascopcosaurus see 1-3-2 (Ornithischia)
Aturia see 2-7-2 (Other Cephalopoda)
Aucellina see 2-7-3 (Bivalvia)
Australopithecine, unspecified see 1-1 (Mammalia)
Australopithecus see 1-1 (Mammalia)
Avimimus see 1-3-1 (Saurischia)

B

Bactrosaurus see 1-3-2 (Ornithischia)
Bagaceratops see 1-3-2 (Ornithischia)
Baluchitherium see *Indricotherium* see 1-1 (Mammalia)
Barapasaurus see 1-3-1 (Saurischia)
Barosaurus see 1-3-1 (Saurischia)
Baryonyx see 1-3-1 (Saurischia)
Basilosaurus see 1-1 (Mammalia)
Batrachognathus see 1-3-4 (Pterosauria)
Batrachosaurus see 1-3-16 (Early Reptiles)
Beipiaosaurus see 1-3-1 (Saurischia)
Belemnopsis see 2-7-2 (Other Cephalopoda)
Belonostomus [=*Vinctifer*] see 1-5 (Osteichthyes)
Berbericeras see 2-7-1 (Ammonoidea)
Bibio see 2-6 (Uniramia)
Bison see 1-1 (Mammalia)
Borhyaena see 1-1 (Mammalia)
Borophagus see *Osteoborus* see 1-1 (Mammalia)
Bothriolepis see 1-7 (Placodermi)
Bothriospondylus see 1-3-1 (Saurischia)
Brachiopod, unspecified fossil see 2-2 (Brachiopoda)
Brachiosaurus see 1-3-1 (Saurischia)
Brachylophosaurus see 1-3-2 (Ornithischia)
Bradysaurus see 1-3-16 (Early Reptiles)
Brontops see 1-1 (Mammalia)
Brontosaurus see *Apatosaurus* see 1-3-1 (Saurischia)
Brontotherium see 1-1 (Mammalia)
Byronosaurus see 1-3-1 (Saurischia)

C

Cacops see 1-4 (Amphibia)
Calcinoplanx see 2-4 (Crustacea)

OLD FOURLEGS ON STAMPS

It is hardly surprising that the coelacanth has been depicted on so many stamps issued by a number of different countries, because this modern-day representative of a truly archaic group of prehistoric fishes is one of the most sensational and significant zoological discoveries of the past century.

Its astonishing story began on 22 December 1938, when Marjorie Courtenay-Latimer, curator of the small East London Museum in South Africa, visited her local docks to see if any fishes had been caught that were worth preserving as specimens for the museum. There only seemed to be a pile of sharks, but at the very bottom of the pile she noticed a strange fin sticking out. When its owner was extricated, it proved to be an extraordinary-looking fish, mauve-blue in colour and 5 ft long, with thick armour-like scales, a unique three-lobed tail, and two pairs of bizarre leg-like lobed fins (which later earned it the affectionate name Old Fourlegs) on its body. She was unable to identify it, so she sent a drawing of it to Prof. J.L.B. Smith, South Africa's leading ichthyologist, who recognised to his astonishment that it was a coelacanth – a member of a prehistoric group of fishes called crossopterygians, believed to have died out over 64 million years ago, along with the dinosaurs! In honour of its discoverer, Smith named its species *Latimeria chalumnae*.

No further modern-day coelacanths were found until 1952, when one (intriguingly, a freak specimen with a deformed two-lobed tail) was caught off the Comoro Islands (near Madagascar). Almost all of the other specimens recorded since have been found off these islands too. Ironically, although un-

This very attractive First Day Cover commemorates the discovery of the coelacanth in 1938. It depicts its discoverers, Marjorie Courtenay-Latimer (who signed this FDC), and Prof. J.L.B. Smith, as well as the East London Museum where the original specimen is still displayed.

known to science for so long, the coelacanth was so familiar to the Comoro natives, who call it kombessa, that they traditionally used its hard scales as sandpaper for roughening bicycle tyres when mending a puncture!

Moreover, during the late 1990s a second species of modern-day coelacanth, later christened *Latimeria menadoensis*, was discovered by science in the waters off Sulawesi, a large Indonesian island - where once again it was already familiar to the local people, who call it the ikan raja laut ('king of the sea').

Unlike its African relative, this species is golden in colour, not mauve-blue, and has been beautifully depicted in this Indonesian miniature sheet.

Calliphylloceras see 2-7-1 (Ammonoidea)
Camarasaurus see 1-3-1 (Saurischia)
Camptosaurus see 1-3-2 (Ornithischia)
Campylognathus see 1-3-4 (Pterosauria)
Canis see 1-1 (Mammalia)
Capromeryx see 1-1 (Mammalia)
Carcharocles [=*Carcharodon*] [=*Procarcharodon*] see 1-6 (Chondrichthyes)
Carcharodon see *Carcharocles* see 1-6 (Chondrichthyes)
Carcharodontosaurus see 1-3-1 (Saurischia)
Caretta see 1-3-15 (Chelonia)
Carnosaur, unspecified see 1-3-1 (Saurischia)
Carnotaurus see 1-3-1 (Saurischia)
Carolicrinus see 2-1 (Echinodermata)
Caturus see 1-5 (Osteichthyes)
Caudipteryx see 1-3-1 (Saurischia)
Cearadactylus see 1-3-4 (Pterosauria)
Centrosaurus see 1-3-2 (Ornithischia)
Cephalopod, unspecified see 2-7-2 (Other Cephalopoda)
Ceratosaurus see 1-3-1 (Saurischia)
Ceresiosaurus see 1-3-12 (Sauropterygia)
Cetiosaurus see 1-3-1 (Saurischia)
Cetotherium see 1-1 (Mammalia)
Chaetodon see 1-5 (Osteichthyes)
Chalicotherium see 1-1 (Mammalia)
Charnodiscus see 2-12 (Early Invertebrata)
Chasmatosaurus see 1-3-6 (Thecodontia)
Chasmosaurus see 1-3-2 (Ornithischia)
Cheirurus see 2-3 (Trilobita)
Chlamys see 2-7-3 (Bivalvia)
Chriacus see 1-1 (Mammalia)
Cladoselache see 1-6 (Chondrichthyes)
Clidastes see 1-3-7 (Squamata)
Clinocardium see 2-7-3 (Bivalvia)
Clupea see 1-5 (Osteichthyes)
Coelacanth, prehistoric see 1-5 (Osteichthyes)
Coeloceras see 2-7-1 (Ammonoidea)
Coelodonta see 1-1 (Mammalia)
Coelophysis see 1-3-1 (Saurischia)
Coelosaur, unspecified see 1-3-1 (Saurischia)
Coelurosaur, unspecified see 1-3-1 (Saurischia)
Coelurosauravus see 1-3-16 (Early Reptiles)
Coelurus see 1-3-1 (Saurischia)
Compsognathus see 1-3-1 (Saurischia)
Conodont, unspecified see 1-8 (Agnatha)
Coral, unspecified fossil see 2-8 (Cnidaria)
Coryphodon see 1-1 (Mammalia)
Corythosaurus see 1-3-2 (Ornithischia)
Crassigyrinus see 1-4 (Amphibia)
Crinoid, unspecified fossil see 2-1 (Echinodermata)
Criorhynchus see 1-3-4 (Pterosauria)

Crocodylus see 1-3-5 (Crocodylia)
Crustacean, prehistoric see 2-4 (Crustacea)
Cryolophosaurus see 1-3-1 (Saurischia)
Cryptoclidus see 1-3-12 (Sauropterygia)
Ctenochasma see 1-3-4 (Pterosauria)
Cucullaea see 2-7-3 (Bivalvia)
Cuvieronius see 1-1 (Mammalia)
Cymbospondylus see 1-3-13 (Ichthyosauria)
Cynodont, unspecified see 1-3-10 (Therapsida)
Cynognathus see 1-3-10 (Therapsida)

D

Dapedius see 1-5 (Osteichthyes)
Daspletosaurus see 1-3-1 (Saurischia)
Deer, prehistoric see 1-1 (Mammalia)
Deinonychus see 1-3-1 (Saurischia)
Deinosuchus [=*Phobosuchus*] see 1-3-5 (Crocodylia)
Deinotherium see 1-1 (Mammalia)
Deiphon see 2-3 (Trilobita)
Deltoptychius see 1-6 (Chondrichthyes)
Desmatosuchus see 1-3-6 (Thecodontia)
Devincenzia see 1-2 (Aves)
Diacodexis see 1-1 (Mammalia)
Diamantornis see 1-2 (Aves)
Diapithecine, unspecified see 1-1 (Mammalia)
Diarthrognathus see 1-3-10 (Therapsida)
Diatryma see *Gastornis* see 1-2 (Aves)
Dickinsonia see 2-12 (Early Invertebrata)
Dicraeosaurus see 1-3-1 (Saurischia)
Diictodon see 1-3-10 (Therapsida)
Dilophosaurus see 1-3-1 (Saurischia)
Dimetrodon see 1-3-11 (Pelycosauria)
Dimorphodon see 1-3-4 (Pterosauria)
Dinichthys see 1-7 (Placodermi)
Dinornis see 1-2 (Aves)
Dinosaur, unspecified see 1-3-3 (Unspecified Dinosaurs)
Diplocaulus see 1-4 (Amphibia)
Diplocynodon see 1-3-5 (Crocodylia)
Diplodocus see 1-3-1 (Saurischia)
Diplosaurus see 1-3-5 (Crocodylia)
Diprotodon see 1-1 (Mammalia)
Doedicurus see 1-1 (Mammalia)
Dolichorhynchops see 1-3-12 (Sauropterygia)
Dorygnathus see 1-3-4 (Pterosauria)
Dragonfly, prehistoric giant see 2-6 (Uniramia)
Dromaeosaurids, unspecified see 1-3-1 (Saurischia)
Dromaeosaurus see 1-3-1 (Saurischia)
Dromiceiomimus see 1-3-1 (Saurischia)
Dryopithecus see 1-1 (Mammalia)

Dryosaurus [=*Dysalotosaurus*] see 1-3-2 (Ornithischia)
Dryptosaurus see 1-3-1 (Saurischia)
Dsungaripterus see 1-3-4 (Pterosauria)
Duckbill see Hadrosaur, unspecified see 1-3-2 (Ornithischia)
Dunkleosteus see 1-7 (Placodermi)
Dysalotosaurus see *Dryosaurus* see 1-3-2 (Ornithischia)

E

Echinocorys see 2-1 (Echinodermata)
Echinoderm, unspecified fossil see 2-2 (Echinodermata)
Echioceras see 2-7-1 (Ammonoidea)
Edaphosaurus see 1-3-11 (Pelycosauria)
Edmontonia see 1-3-2 (Ornithischia)
Edmontosaurus see 1-3-2 (Ornithischia)
Einiosaurus see 1-3-2 (Ornithischia)
Elaphrosaurus see 1-3-1 (Saurischia)
Elasmosaurus see 1-3-12 (Sauropterygia)
Elephant, fossil see 1-1 (Mammalia)
Elephas see 1-1 (Mammalia)
Elopteryx see 1-3-1 (Saurischia)
Embolotherium see 1-1 (Mammalia)
Enchodus see 1-5 (Osteichthyes)
Endothiodon see 1-3-10 (Therapsida)
Entelodon see 1-1 (Mammalia)
Eogyrinus see 1-4 (Amphibia)
Eohippus see *Hyracotherium* see 1-1 (Mammalia)
Eoraptor see 1-3-1 (Saurischia)
Equus see 1-1 (Mammalia)
Eremotherium see 1-1 (Mammalia)
Erlikosaurus see 1-3-1 (Saurischia)
Eryon see 2-4 (Crustacea)
Eryops see 1-4 (Amphibia)
Erythrosuchus see 1-3-6 (Thecodontia)
Estemmenosuchus see 1-3-10 (Therapsida)
Euamophalus see 2-7-4 (Gastropoda)
Eudimorphodon see 1-3-4 (Pterosauria)
Euoplocephalus [=*Scolosaurus*] see 1-3-2 (Ornithischia)
Euparkeria see 1-3-6 (Thecodontia)
Eurhinodelphis see 1-1 (Mammalia)
Eurhinosaurus see 1-3-13 (Ichthyosauria)
Euryapteryx see 1-2 (Aves)
Eurypholis see 1-5 (Osteichthyes)
Eurypterus see 2-5 (Chelicerata)
Euskelosaurus see 1-3-1 (Saurischia)
Eusthenopteron see 1-5 (Osteichthyes)
Eustreptospondylus see 1-3-1 (Saurischia)

F

Fabrosaurus see 1-3-2 (Ornithischia)
Fish, unspecified fossil bony see 1-5 (Osteichthyes)
Fly, fossil see 2-6 (Uniramia)
Frog, fossil see 1-4 (Amphibia)
Fulgotherium see 1-3-2 (Ornithischia)

G

Gallimimus see 1-3-1 (Saurischia)
Gallodactylus see 1-3-4 (Pterosauria)
Garudimimus see 1-3-1 (Saurischia)
Gasosaurus see 1-3-1 (Saurischia)
Gasparinisaura see 1-3-2 (Saurischia)
Gastonia see 1-3-2 (Ornithischia)
Gastornis [=*Diatryma*] see 1-2 (Aves)
Gastropod, unspecified see 2-7-4 (Gastropoda)
Gaudryceras see 2-7-1 (Ammonoidea)
Genyornis see 1-2 (Aves)
Geocapromys see 1-1 (Mammalia)
Geochelone see 1-3-15 (Chelonia)
Geosaurus see 1-3-5 (Crocodylia)
Germanodactylus see 1-3-4 (Pterosauria)
Gerrothorax see 1-4 (Amphibia)
Giganotosaurus see 1-3-1 (Saurischia)
Giantoneris see *Cacops* see 1-4 (Amphibia)
Glossotherium see 1-1 (Mammalia)
Glyptodon see 1-1 (Mammalia)
Gomphotherium see 1-1 (Mammalia)
Goniopholis see 1-3-5 (Crocodylia)
Gorgosaurus see 1-3-1 (Saurischia)
Graciliceratops [=*Microceratops*] see 1-3-2 (Ornithischia)
Grendelius see 1-3-13 (Ichthyosauria)
Griphognathus see 1-5 (Osteichthyes)
Ground sloth, unspecified see 1-1 (Mammalia)
Gryphaea see 2-7-3 (Bivalvia)
Gryponyx see *Massospondylus* see 1-3-1 (Saurischia)
Gryposaurus [=*Kritosaurus*] see 1-3-2 (Ornithischia)
Gunnarites see 2-7-1 (Ammonoidea)
Gyroptychius see 1-5 (Osteichthyes)

H

Hadrosaur, unspecified see 1-3-2 (Ornithischia)
Hadrosaurus see 1-3-2 (Ornithischia)
Halticosaurus see 1-3-1 (Saurischia)
Harpagornis see 1-2 (Aves)

Hatzegopteryx see 1-3-4 (Pterosauria)
Hekatobatrachus see *Palaeobatrachus* see 1-4 (Amphibia)
Hemicyon see 1-1 (Mammalia)
Hemihaploceras see 2-7-1 (Ammonoidea)
Henodus see 1-3-14 (Placodontia)
Heraclites see 2-7-1 (Ammonoidea)
Herrerasaurus see 1-3-1 (Saurischia)
Hesperocyon see 1-1 (Mammalia)
Hesperornis see 1-2 (Aves)
Hesperosuchus see 1-3-6 (Thecodontia)
Heterodontosaurus see 1-3-2 (Ornithischia)
Hexanchus see 1-6 (Chondrichthyes)
Hildoceras see 2-7-1 (Ammonoidea)
Hipparion see 1-1 (Mammalia)
Hippopotamus see 1-1 (Mammalia)
Hippopotamus see 1-1 (Mammalia)
Homalocephale see 1-3-2 (Ornithischia)
Hominid, unspecified see 1-1 (Mammalia)
Homo see 1-1 (Mammalia)
Homotherium see 1-1 (Mammalia)
Hoploparia see 2-4 (Crustacea)
Huayangosaurus see 1-3-2 (Ornithischia)
Human, Gibraltar prehistoric see 1-1 (Mammalia)
Human, unspecified prehistoric see 1-1 (Mammalia)
Hyaenodon see 1-1 (Mammalia)
Hydrotherosaurus see 1-3-12 (Sauropterygia)
Hylaeosaurus see 1-3-1 (Saurischia)
Hylonomus see 1-3-16 (Early Reptiles)
Hypacanthoplites see 2-7-1 (Ammonoidea)
Hypacrosaurus see 1-3-2 (Ornithischia)
Hypophylloceras see 2-7-1 (Ammonoidea)
Hypselosaurus see 1-3-1 (Saurischia)
Hypsilophodon see 1-3-2 (Ornithischia)
Hypsognathus see 1-3-16 (Early Reptiles)
Hyrachyus see 1-1 (Mammalia)
Hyracotherium [=*Eohippus*] see 1-1 (Mammalia)

I

Iberomesornis see 1-2 (Aves)
Icaronycthris see 1-1 (Mammalia)
Ichthyornis see 1-2 (Aves)
Ichthyosaur, unspecified see 1-3-13 (Ichthyosauria)
Ichthyosaurus see 1-3-13 (Ichthyosauria)
Ichthyostega see 1-4 (Amphibia)
Ictitherium see 1-1 (Mammalia)
Iguanodon see 1-3-2 (Ornithischia)
Inaria see 2-12 (Early Invertebrata)

Indricotherium [=*Baluchitherium*] see 1-1 (Mammalia)
Insect, unspecified prehistoric see 2-6 (Uniramia)
Irritator see 1-3-1 (Saurischia)
Ischyodes see 1-6 (Chondrichthyes)

J

Jellyfish, prehistoric see 2-8 (Cnidaria)

K

Kannemeyeria see 1-3-10 (Therapsida)
Kanuites see 1-1 (Mammalia)
Kaolishania see 2-3 (Trilobita)
Karavankina see 2-2 (Brachiopoda)
Kaskia see 2-3 (Trilobita)
Keichousaurus see 1-3-12 (Sauropterygia)
Kentrosaurus [=*Kentrurosaurus*] see 1-3-2 (Ornithischia)
Kentrurosaurus see *Kentrosaurus* see 1-3-2 (Ornithischia)
Kimberella see 2-12 (Early Invertebrata)
Kritosaurus see *Gryposaurus* see 1-3-2 (Ornithischia)
Kronosaur, unspecified see 1-3-12 (Sauropterygia)
Kronosaurus see 1-3-12 (Sauropterygia)
Kuehneosaurus see 1-3-7 (Squamata)

L

Labidosaurus see 1-3-15 (Chelonia)
Lagosuchus see 1-3-6 (Thecodontia)
Lambeosaurus see 1-3-2 (Ornithischia)
Leaellynasaura see 1-3-2 (Ornithischia)
Lepisosteus see 1-5 (Osteichthyes)
Leptictidium see 1-1 (Mammalia)
Leptoceratops see 1-3-2 (Ornithischia)
Lesothosaurus see 1-3-2 (Ornithischia)
Lewesiceras see 2-7-1 (Ammonoidea)
Libanobythus see 2-6 (Uniramia)
Lingulella see 2-2 (Brachiopoda)
Liopleurodon see 1-3-12 (Sauropterygia)
Longisquama see 1-3-6 (Thecodontia)
Loxodonta see 1-1 (Mammalia)
Luamgwa see 1-3-10 (Therapsida)
Lufengosaurus see 1-3-1 (Saurischia)
Lyriaspis see 2-3 (Trilobita)
Lystrosaurus see 1-3-10 (Therapsida)
Lytoceras see 2-7-1 (Ammonoidea)
Lytodiscoides see 2-7-4 (Ammonoidea)

JAWS!!!

The megalodon was a giant shark that lived in prehistoric times, between about 18 million to 1.5 million years ago and was the apex predator of its time. The oldest *Caracharadon megalodon* teeth found are about 18 million years old

C. megalodon became extinct in the Pleistocene epoch probably about 1.5 million years ago. It is the largest carnivorous fish known to have existed and quite possibly the largest shark ever to have lived.

The South Atlantic had widened considerably by the Miocene Epoch of the Cenozoic Era (15 million years ago). The ocean animals were quite different from those of the earlier Cretaceous and included forms similar to those of today, as well as some which are now extinct. The bony fish swam together with squid, cuttlefish, sand sharks *(Odontaspis)* and *Nautilus* with the sea bottom colonised by clams and snails, ideal food for the rays such as *Myliobatis*. The dolphins included long snouted forms such as *Eurhinodelphis* which may have fallen prey to the fearsome *Carcharodon*, many times larger than today's great white shark. There were also large carnivorous sperm whales such as *Orycterocetus*, always ready to feed on a stray hammerhead shark such as *Sphyrna*.

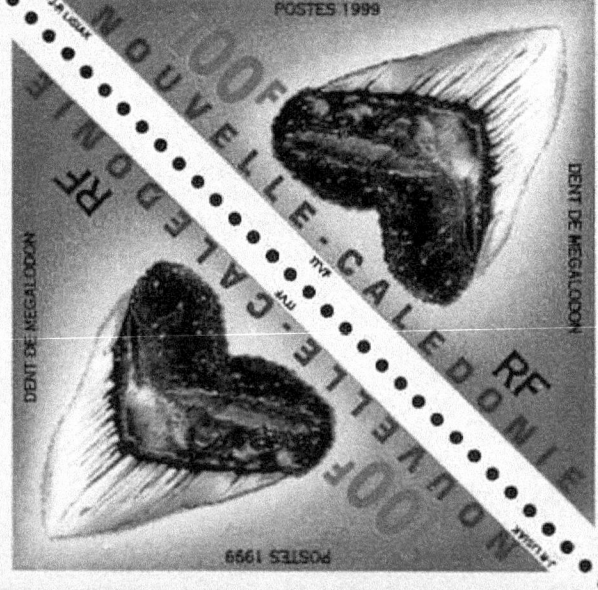

M

Machairodus see 1-1 (Mammalia)
Macrauchenia see 1-1 (Mammalia)
Macroplata see 1-3-12 (Sauropterygia)
Maiasaura see 1-3-2 (Ornithischia)
Mamenchisaurus see 1-3-1 (Saurischia)
Mammal, unspecified prehistoric see 1-1 (Mammalia)
Mammoth, unspecified see 1-1 (Mammalia)
Mammut see 1-1 (Mammalia)
Mammuthus see 1-1 (Mammalia)
Mantelliceras see 2-7-1 (Ammonoidea)
Marsupial, fossil see 1-1 (Mammalia)
Massospondylus see 1-3-1 (Saurischia)
Mastodon see 1-1 (Mammalia)
Mastodonsaurus see 1-4 (Amphibia)
Mastodont, unspecified see 1-1 (Mammalia)
Mauisaurus see 1-3-12 (Sauropterygia)
Mcnamaraspis see 1-7 (Placodermi)
Mediterraneotrigonia see 2-7-3 (Bivalvia)
Megacerops see 1-1 (Mammalia)
Megaladapis see 1-1 (Mammalia)
Megalania see 1-3-7 (Squamata)
Megaloceros [=*Sinomegacerus*] see 1-1 (Mammalia)
Megalocnus see 1-1 (Mammalia)
Megalosaurus see 1-3-1 (Saurischia)
Meganeura see 2-6 (Uniramia)
Megantereon see 1-1 (Mammalia)
Megapnosaurus [=*Syntarsus*] see 1-3-1 (Saurischia)
Megaraptor see 1-3-1 (Saurischia)
Megatherium see 1-1 (Mammalia)
Megazostrodon see 1-1 (Mammalia)
Meiolania see 1-3-15 (Chelonia)
Mekosuchus see 1-3-5 (Crocodylia)
Mene see 1-5 (Osteichthyes)
Merychippus see 1-1 (Mammalia)
Mesadactylus see 1-3-4 (Pterosauria)
Mesodon see 1-5 (Osteichthyes)
Mesonyx see 1-1 (Mammalia)
Mesopithecus see 1-1 (Mammalia)
Mesosaurus see 1-3-16 (Early Reptiles)
Metamynodon see 1-1 (Mammalia)
Metoposaurus see 1-4 (Amphibia)
Metriorhynchus see 1-3-5 (Crocodylia)
Micreschara see 2-7-4 (Gastropoda)
Microceratodus see 1-5 (Osteichthyes)
Microceratops see *Graciliceratops* see 1-3-2 (Ornithischia)
Microraptor see 1-3-1 (Saurischia)
Microvenator see 1-3-1 (Saurischia)
Minmi see 1-3-2 (Ornithischia)

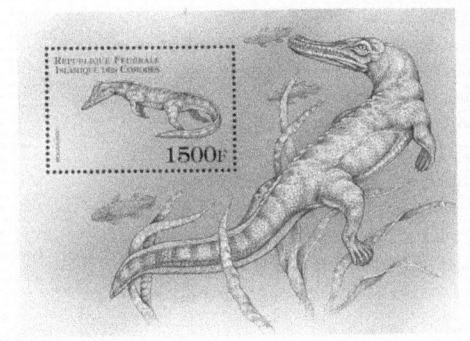

Miohippus see 1-1 (Mammalia)
Mixosaurus see 1-3-13 (Ichthyosauria)
Moeritherium see 1-1 (Mammalia)
Mollusc, unspecified fossil see 2-7-5 (Other Mollusca)
Mongolemys see 1-3-15 (Chelonia)
Mongolotherium see 1-1 (Mammalia)
Monoclonius see 1-3-2 (Ornithischia)
Monocyathus see 2-10 (Archaeocyatha)
Mononykus see 1-2 (Aves)
Montanoceratops see 1-3-2 (Ornithischia)
Mosasaur, unspecified see 1-3-7 (Squamata)
Mosasaurus see 1-3-7 (Squamata)
Moschops see 1-3-10 (Therapsida)
Muraenosaurus see 1-3-12 (Sauropterygia)
Mussaurus see 1-3-1 (Saurischia)
Muttaburrasaurus see 1-3-2 (Ornithischia)
Muzquizopteryx see 1-3-4 (Pterosauria)
Myliobatis see 1-6 (Chondrichthyes)
Mylodon see 1-1 (Mammalia)

N

Nanotyrannus see 1-3-1 (Saurischia)
Nassa [=*Nassarius*] see 2-7-4 (Gastropoda)
Nassarius see *Nassa* see 2-7-4 (Gastropoda)
Natalus see 1-1 (Mammalia)
Natunaornis see 1-2 (Aves)
Nautiloid, unspecified see 2-7-2 (Other Cephalopoda)
Neithea see 2-7-3 (Bivalvia)
Nematonotus see 1-5 (Osteichthyes)
Nesophontes see 1-1 (Mammalia)
Nessiteras see 1-3-12 (Sauropterygia)
Neusticosaurus see 1-3-12 (Sauropterygia)
Ninjemys see 1-3-15 (Chelonia)
Nodosaurus see 1-3-2 (Ornithischia)
Nostoceras see 2-7-1 (Ammonoidea)
Nothosaurus see 1-3-12 (Sauropterygia)
Nothotheriops see 1-1 (Mammalia)
Numidopleura see 1-5 (Osteichthyes)
Nyctosaurus see 1-3-4 (Pterosauria)

O

Odobenocetops see 1-1 (Mammalia)
Odontopleura see 2-3 (Trilobita)
Olenoides see 2-3 (Trilobita)
Omeisaurus see 1-3-1 (Saurischia)
Omphalosaurus see 1-3-13 (Ichthyosauria)
Onsong fish, fossil see 1-5 (Osteichthyes)

Oolitica see 2-7-4 (Gastropoda)
Opabinia see 2-12 (Early Invertebrata)
Ophioceras see 2-7-2 (Other Cephalopoda)
Ophthalmosaurus see 1-3-13 (Ichthyosauria)
Opisthias see 1-3-8 (Sphenodontia)
Opisthocoelicaudia see 1-3-1 (Saurischia)
Ornimegalonyx see 1-2 (Aves)
Ornithischian, unspecified see 1-3-2 (Ornithischia)
Ornithocheirus see 1-3-4 (Pterosauria)
Ornithodesmus see 1-3-4 (Pterosauria)
Ornitholestes see 1-3-1 (Saurischia)
Ornithomimus see 1-3-1 (Saurischia)
Ornithopod, unspecified see 1-3-2 (Ornithischia)
Ornithosuchus see 1-3-6 (Thecodontia)
Orycterocetus see 1-1 (Mammalia)
Osteoborus see 1-1 (Mammalia)
Ostrea see 2-7-3 (Bivalvia)
Oudenodon see 1-3-10 (Therapsida)
Ouranosaurus see 1-3-2 (Ornithischia)
Oviraptor see 1-3-1 (Saurischia)

P

Pachycephalosaurus see 1-3-2 (Ornithischia)
Pachyophis see 1-3-7 (Squamata)
Pachyplichas see 1-2 (Aves)
Pachyrhinosaurus see 1-3-2 (Ornithischia)
Pakicetus see 1-1 (Mammalia)
Paladin see *Kaskia* see 2-3 (Trilobita)
Palaelodus see 1-2 (Aves)
Palaeobatrachus see 1-4 (Amphibia)
Palaeochiropteryx see 1-1 (Mammalia)
Palaeomastodon see 1-1 (Mammalia)
Palaeosaniwa see 1-3-7 (Squamata)
Palaeospondylus see 1-7 (Placodermi)
Panderichthys see 1-5 (Osteichthyes)
Panoplosaurus see 1-3-2 (Ornithischia)
Paracybeloides see 2-3 (Trilobita)
Paracyclotosaurus see 1-4 (Amphibia)
Paradoxides see 2-3 (Trilobita)
Paranthropus [=*Zinjanthropus*] see 1-1 (Mammalia)
Parapuzosia see 2-7-1 (Ammonoidea)
Parasaurolophus see 1-3-2 (Ornithischia)
Paraulacosphinctes see 2-7-1 (Ammonoidea)
Parksosaurus see 1-3-2 (Ornithischia)
Patagosaurus see 1-3-1 (Saurischia)
Pecten see 2-7-3 (Bivalvia)
Peloneustes see 1-3-12 (Sauropterygia)
Pelycosaur, unspecified see 1-3-11 (Pelycosauria)

Pentaceratops see 1-3-2 (Ornithischia)
Perisphinctes see 2-7-1 (Ammonoidea)
Perissoptera see 2-7-4 (Gastropoda)
Peteinosaurus see 1-3-4 (Pterosauria)
Petrolacosaurus see 1-3-16 (Early Reptiles)
Phobetor see 1-3-4 (Pterosauria)
Phobosuchus see *Deinosuchus* see 1-3-5 (Crocodylia)
Pholidogaster see 1-4 (Amphibia)
Phororhacos see *Phorusrhacus* see 1-2 (Aves)
Phorusrhacus [=*Phororhacos*] see 1-2 (Aves)
Phuwiangosaurus see 1-3-1 (Saurischia)
Piatnitzkysaurus see 1-3-1 (Saurischia)
Pinacosaurus see 1-3-2 (Ornithischia)
Pinna see 2-7-3 (Bivalvia)
Pistosaurus see 1-3-12 (Sauropterygia)
Pithecanthropus see 1-1 (Mammalia)
Placerias see 1-3-10 (Therapsida)
Placochelys see 1-3-14 (Placodontia)
Placodus see 1-3-14 (Placodontia)
Platecarpus see 1-3-7 (Squamata)
Plateosauravus see *Euskelosaurus* see 1-3-1 (Saurischia)
Plateosaurus see 1-3-1 (Saurischia)
Platybelodon see 1-1 (Mammalia)
Platygonus see 1-1 (Mammalia)
Platyhystrix see 1-4 (Amphibia)
Platymantis see 1-4 (Amphibia)
Platypittamys see 1-1 (Mammalia)
Platypleuroceras see 2-7-1 (Ammonoidea)
Plesictis see 1-1 (Mammalia)
Plesiosaur, unspecified see 1-3-12 (Sauropterygia)
Plesiosaurus see 1-3-12 (Sauropterygia)
Pleurocoelus [=*Astrodon*] see 1-3-1 (Saurischia)
Pleurotomaria see 2-7-4 (Gastropoda)
Pliohippus see 1-1 (Mammalia)
Pliosaur, unspecified see 1-3-12 (Sauropterygia)
Pliosaurus see 1-3-12 (Sauropterygia)
Plotosaurus see 1-3-7 (Squamata)
Polacanthus see 1-3-2 (Ornithischia)
Poloneustes see 1-3-12 (Sauropterygia)
Postosuchus see 1-3-5 (Crocodylia)
Prenocephale see 1-3-2 (Ornithischia)
Pristichampsus see 1-3-5 (Crocodylia)
Proavis see 1-2 (Aves)
Probactrosaurus see 1-3-2 (Ornithischia)
Proborhyaena see 1-1 (Mammalia)
Procarcharodon see *Carcharocles* see 1-6 (Chondrichthyes)
Procompsognathus see 1-3-1 (Saurischia)
Proconsul see 1-1 (Mammalia)
Procoptodon see 1-1 (Mammalia)
Proeucalycoceras see 2-7-1 (Ammonoidea)

Those flying reptiles known as pterosaurs and the ferocious sabre-tooth tigers are among the most iconic and readily recognisable of all prehistoric animals. There were many species of pterosaur, split into two quite separate lineages, both represented in this impressive sheet of Lesotho stamps – the earlier rhamphorhynchoids, sporting a long tail and whose beaks brimmed with teeth, and the later pterodactyloids, which lacked a tail and whose beaks were toothless. The sabre-tooths or machairodontids (they were not related to tigers) were once very diverse and plentiful too, and culminated in the massive American *Smilodon*, as portrayed in this stunning Afghanistan miniature sheet, which was the size of a lion, with enormous canine teeth.

Prohyrax see 1-1 (Mammalia)
Prolecanites see 2-7-1 (Ammonoidea)
Propachyrucos see 1-1 (Mammalia)
Propalaeotherium see 1-1 (Mammalia)
Prosaurolophus see 1-3-2 (Ornithischia)
Protarchaeopteryx see 1-2 (Aves)
Protembolotherium see 1-1 (Mammalia)
Prothylacynus see 1-1 (Mammalia)
Protoavis see 1-2 (Aves)
Protoceratops see 1-3-2 (Ornithischia)
Protohydrochoerus see 1-1 (Mammalia)
Protorosaurus see 1-3-16 (Early Reptiles)
Protostega see 1-3-15 (Chelonia)
Protosuchus see 1-3-5 (Crocodylia)
Pseudomelania see 2-7-4 (Gastropoda)
Pseudophillipsia see 2-3 (Trilobita)
Psittacosaurus see 1-3-2 (Ornithischia)
Pteranodon see 1-3-4 (Pterosauria)
Pteraspis see 1-8 (Agnatha)
Pterodactyl, unspecified see 1-3-4 (Pterosauria)
Pterodactylus see 1-3-4 (Pterosauria)
Pterodaustro see 1-3-4 (Pterosauria)
Pterosaur, unspecified see 1-3-4 (Pterosauria)
Pterosaurus see 1-3-4 (Pterosauria)
Pterotrigonia see 2-7-3 (Bivalvia)
Ptychoparia see 2-3 (Trilobita)
Pugilina see 2-7-4 (Gastropoda)
Purussaurus see 1-3-5 (Crocodylia)
Pycnosteroides see 1-5 (Osteichthyes)
Pyrotherium see 1-1 (Mammalia)

Q

Quetzalcoatlus see 1-3-4 (Pterosauria)

R

Redlichia see 2-3 (Trilobita)
Reineckia see 2-7-1 (Ammonoidea)
Rhamphorhynchus see 1-3-4 (Pterosauria)
Rhinoceros, fossil see 1-1 (Mammalia)
Rhoetosaurus see 1-3-1 (Saurischia)
Rhomaleosaurus see 1-3-12 (Sauropterygia)
Roemoceras see 2-7-1 (Ammonoidea)
Rotula see 2-1 (Echinodermata)
Rubidgea see 1-3-10 (Therapsida)
Rutiodon see 1-3-6 (Thecodontia)

S

Sabinosaurus see 1-3-2 (Ornithischia)
Sabre-tooth tiger, unspecified see 1-1 (Mammalia)
Sahelanthropus see 1-1 (Mammalia)
Saichania see 1-3-2 (Ornithischia)
Saltasaurus see 1-3-1 (Saurischia)
Saltoposuchus see 1-3-6 (Thecodontia)
Saltopus see 1-3-1 (Saurischia)
Sanctacaris see 2-12 (Early Invertebrata)
Sanmartinoceras see 2-7-1 (Ammonoidea)
Sarcopterygian, unspecified see 1-5 (Osteichthyes)
Sarcosuchus see 1-3-5 (Crocodylia)
Sauroctonus see 1-3-10 (Therapsida)
Saurolophus see 1-3-2 (Ornithischia)
Sauropelta see 1-3-2 (Ornithischia)
Sauropodomorph, unspecified see 1-3-1 (Saurischia)
Sauropod, unspecified see 1-3-1 (Saurischia)
Saurornithoides see 1-3-1 (Saurischia)
Saurornitholestes see 1-3-1 (Saurischia)
Scapanorhynchus see 1-6 (Chondrichthyes)
Scaphognathus see 1-3-4 (Pterosauria)
Scaphonyx see 1-3-9 (Rhynchosauria)
Scelidosaurus see 1-3-2 (Ornithischia)
Schwagerina see 2-11 (Protozoa)
Scipionyx see 1-3-1 (Saurischia)
Scleromochlus see 1-3-4 (Pterosauria)
Scolosaurus see *Euoplocephalus* see 1-3-2 (Ornithischia)
Scutellosaurus see 1-3-2 (Ornithischia)
Sea urchin, fossil see 2-1 (Echinodermata)
Segisaurus see 1-3-1 (Saurischia)
Segnosaurus see 1-361 (Saurischia)
Seismosaurus see 1-3-1 (Saurischia)
Selenopeltis see 2-3 (Trilobita)
Seymouria see 1-4 (Amphibia)
Shantungosaurus see 1-3-2 (Ornithischia)
Shark, unspecified prehistoric see 1-6 (Chondrichthyes)
Sharovipteryx see 1-3-4 (Pterosauria)
Shonisaurus see 1-3-13 (Ichthyosauria)
Shunosaurus see 1-3-1 (Saurischia)
Siamosaurus see *Spinosaurus* see 1-3-1 (Saurischia)
Siamotyrannus see 1-3-1 (Saurischia)
Sieberella see 2-2 (Brachiopoda)
Silvisaurus see 1-3-2 (Ornithischia)
Sinanthropus see Homo see 1-1 (Mammalia)
Sinomegacerus see *Megaloceros* see 1-1 (Mammalia)
Sinosauropteryx see 1-3-1 (Saurischia)
Sivatherium see 1-1 (Mammalia)
Smilodectes see 1-1 (Mammalia)
Smilodon see 1-1 (Mammalia)

Solaster see 2-1 (Echinodermata)
Sordes see 1-3-4 (Pterosauria)
Spathobathis see *Aellopos* see 1-6 (Chondrichthyes)
Spinosaurus [=*Spinosaurus*] see 1-3-1 (Saurischia)
Spirifer see 2-7-3 (Bivalvia)
Spirocerus see 1-1 (Mammalia)
Sponge, prehistoric see 2-9 (Porifera)
Spriggina see 2-12 (Early Invertebrata)
Squalicorax see 1-6 (Chondrichthyes)
Starfish, fossil see 2-1 (Echinodermata)
Staurikosaurus see 1-3-1 (Saurischia)
Stegoceras see 1-3-2 (Ornithischia)
Stegodon see 1-1 (Mammalia)
Stegodont, unspecified see 1-1 (Mammalia)
Stegomastodon see 1-1 (Mammalia)
Stegosaurus see 1-3-2 (Ornithischia)
Stegotetrabelodon see 1-1 (Mammalia)
Steneosaurus see 1-3-5 (Crocodylia)
Stenonychosaurus see *Troodon* see 1-3-1 (Saurischia)
Stenopterygius see 1-3-13 (Ichthyosauria)
Stethacanthus see 1-6 (Chondrichthyes)
Struthiomimus see 1-3-1 (Saurischia)
Struthiosaurus see 1-3-2 (Ornithischia)
Stygimoloch see 1-3-2 (Ornithischia)
Stylinodon see 1-1 (Mammalia)
Styracosaurus see 1-3-2 (Ornithischia)
Suchomimus see 1-3-1 (Saurischia)
Supersaurus [=*Ultrasauros*] see 1-3-1 (Saurischia)
Sylviornis see 1-2 (Aves)
Syndyoceras see 1-1 (Mammalia)
Syntarsus see *Megapnosaurus* see 1-3-1 (Saurischia)
Synthetoceras see 1-1 (Mammalia)

T

Talarurus see 1-3-2 (Ornithischia)
Tapirus see 1-1 (Mammalia)
Tarbosaurus see 1-3-1 (Saurischia)
Tazoudasaurus see 1-3-1 (Saurischia)
Tchadanthropus see *Homo* see 1-1 (Mammalia)
Teleoceras see 1-1 (Mammalia)
Telmatosaurus see 1-3-2 (Ornithischia)
Temnodontosaurus see 1-3-13 (Ichthyosauria)
Tenontosaurus see 1-3-2 (Ornithischia)
Teratornis see 1-2 (Aves)
Teratosaurus see 1-3-6 (Thecodontia)
Terebratula see 2-2 (Brachiopoda)
Testudinites see 1-3-15 (Chelonia)
Tetralophodon see 1-1 (Mammalia)
Thaumatosaurus see 1-3-12 (Sauropterygia)

Dinosaurs and other Prehistoric Animals on Stamps

Thecodontian, unspecified see 1-3-6 (Thecodontia)
Thecodontosaurus see 1-3-1 (Saurischia)
Theropod, unspecified see 1-3-1 (Saurischia)
Thoatherium see 1-1 (Mammalia)
Thoracosaurus see 1-3-5 (Crocodylia)
Thrinaxodon see 1-3-10 (Therapsida)
Thyestes see 1-8 (Agnatha)
Thylacoleo see 1-1 (Mammalia)
Timimus see 1-3-1 (Saurischia)
Titanohyrax see 1-1 (Mammalia)
Titanosaurus see 1-3-1 (Saurischia)
Titanotylopus see 1-1 (Mammalia)
Tommotia see 2-7-2 (Other Cephalopoda)
Torosaurus see 1-3-2 (Ornithischia)
Tortoise, fossil see 1-3-15 (Chelonia)
Toxodon see 1-1 (Mammalia)
Trachodon see *Anatotitan* see 1-3-2 (Ornithischia)
Tragocerus see 1-1 (Mammalia)
Tribrachidium see 2-12 (Early Invertebrata)
Triceratops see 1-3-2 (Ornithischia)
Trigonia see 2-7-3 (Bivalvia)
Trilobite, unspecified see 2-3 (Trilobita)
Trinacromerum see 1-3-12 (Sauropterygia)
Triplagnostus see 2-3 (Trilobita)
Tristychius see 1-6 (Chondrichthyes)
Tritylodon see 1-3-10 (Therapsida)
Troodon [=*Stenonychosaurus*] see 1-3-1 (Saurischia)
Tropeognathus see 1-3-4 (Pterosauria)
Tsintaosaurus see 1-3-2 (Ornithischia)
Tuojiangosaurus see 1-3-2 (Ornithischia)
Turritella see 2-7-4 (Gastropoda)
Tylosaurus see 1-3-7 (Squamata)
Tyrannosaur, unspecified see 1-3-1 (Saurischia)
Tyrannosaurus see 1-3-1 (Saurischia)
Tytthostonyx see 1-2 (Aves)

U

Uintatherium see 1-1 (Mammalia)
Ultrasauros see *Supersaurus* see 1-3-1 (Saurischia)
Ultrasaurus see 1-3-1 (Saurischia)
Ursus see 1-1 (Mammalia)
Utahraptor see 1-3-1 (Saurischia)

V

Varanosaurus see 1-3-11 (Pelycosauria)
Varnerxiphactinus see 1-5 (Osteichthyes)
Velociraptor see 1-3-1 (Saurischia)

Vinctifer see *Belonostomus* see 1-5 (Osteichthyes)
Virgotrigonia see 2-7-3 (Bivalvia)
Vitirallus see 1-2 (Aves)
Viviparus see 2-7-4 (Gastropoda)
Volia see 1-3-5 (Crocodylia)
Vulcanodon see 1-3-1 (Saurischia)

Wasp, prehistoric see 2-6 (Uniramia)
Wellesiosaurus see 1-3-12 (Sauropterygia)
Woolungasaurus see 1-3-12 (Sauropterygia)
Wuerhosaurus see 1-3-2 (Ornithischia)

Xenacanthus see 1-6 (Chondrichthyes)
Xenopus see 1-4 (Amphibia)
Xiphactinus see 1-5 (Osteichthyes)
Xystridura see 2-3 (Trilobita)

Yandusaurus see 1-3-2 (Ornithischia)
Yangchuanosaurus see 1-3-1 (Saurischia)
Yingshanosaurus see 1-3-2 (Ornithischia)

Zalambdalestes see 1-1 (Mammalia)
Zambiasaurus see 1-3-10 (Therapsida)
Zinjanthropus see *Paranthropus* see 1-1 (Mammalia)
Zygorhiza see 1-1 (Mammalia)

CLASSIFICATION OF ANIMALS LISTED IN THIS CATALOGUE

SECTION 1: Vertebrates

Phylum: CHORDATA (Backboned animals)

Class No. 1 MAMMALIA (Mammals)

Class No. 2 AVES (Birds)

Class No. 3 REPTILIA (Reptiles)

    Order/Category No. 1 **SAURISCHIA** (Lizard-hipped dinosaurs)
    Order/Category No. 2 **ORNITHISCHIA** (Bird-hipped dinosaurs)
    Order/Category No. 3 **UNSPECIFIED DINOSAURS**
    Order/Category No. 4 **PTEROSAURIA** (Pterosaurs - Flying reptiles)
    Order/Category No. 5 **CROCODYLIA** (Crocodilians)
    Order/Category No. 6 **THECODONTIA** (Thecodontians)
    Order/Category No. 7 **SQUAMATA** (Lizards and Snakes)
    Order/Category No. 8 **SPHENODONTIA** (Sphenodontids)
    Order/Category No. 9 **RHYNCHOSAURIA** (Rhynchosaurs)
    Order/Category No. 10 **THERAPSIDA** (Therapsids - Mammal-like reptiles)
    Order/Category No. 11 **PELYCOSAURIA** (Pelycosaurs - Sail reptiles)
    Order/Category No. 12 **SAUROPTERYGIA** (Plesiosaurs and Nothosaurs)
    Order/Category No. 13 **ICHTHYOSAURIA** (Ichthyosaurs - Fish reptiles)
    Order/Category No. 14 **PLACODONTIA** (Placodontians)
    Order/Category No. 15 **CHELONIA** (Turtles and Tortoises)
    Order/Category No. 16 **EARLY REPTILES**

Class No. 4 AMPHIBIA (Amphibians)

Class No. 5 OSTEICHTHYES (Bony Fishes)

Class No. 6 CHONDRICHTHYES (Cartilaginous Fishes - Sharks and Rays)

Class No. 7 PLACODERMI (Placoderms - Armoured Fishes)

Class No. 8 AGNATHA (Jawless Fishes - Lampreys and Ostracoderms)

SECTION 2: Invertebrates

Phylum No. 1 ECHINODERMATA (Echinoderms - Starfishes, Sea Urchins, etc)

Phylum No. 2 BRACHIOPODA (Brachiopods - Lamp Shells)

Phylum No. 3 TRILOBITA (Trilobites)

Phylum No. 4 CHELICERATA (Chelicerates - Sea Scorpions, Arachnids, etc)

Phylum No. 5 CRUSTACEA (Crustaceans)

Phylum No. 6 UNIRAMIA (Insects, Millipedes, Centipedes, etc)

Phylum No. 7 MOLLUSCA (Molluscs)

Class/Category No. 1 AMMONOIDEA (Ammonite Cephalopods)
Class/Category No. 2 OTHER CEPHALOPODA (Nautiloids, Belemnites, etc)
Class/Category No. 3 BIVALVIA (Bivalves - Clams, etc)
Class/Category No. 4 GASTROPODA (Gastropods - Snails, etc)
Class/Category No. 5 OTHER MOLLUSCS

Phylum No. 8 CNIDARIA (Jellyfishes, Corals, etc)

Phylum No. 9 PORIFERA (Sponges)

Phylum No. 10 ARCHAEOCYATHA (Archaeocyathans)

Phylum No. 11 PROTOZOA (Protozoans/Single-celled animals)

Phylum/Category No. 12 EARLY INVERTEBRATES

LISTING OF STAMPS BY ANIMAL GENUS

LISTING OF STAMPS BY ANIMAL GENUS

SECTION 1: Vertebrates

Phylum: CHORDATA
(Backboned animals)

Class No. 1 MAMMALIA (Mammals)

Aceratherium
    Macedonia 4
Amebelodon
    Congo Republic 15
    Gambia 92
Ancyclotherium
    Liberia 106
Andrewsarchus
    St Kitts **MS**20
Archaeohyrax
    Guyana 16
Archidiskodon
    Antigua 55
    Romania 4
Arctodus
    Canada 14
    Maldive Islands 120
Argyrolagus
    Antigua 52
Arsinotherium
    Congo Republic 4
    Egypt 1
    Malagasy Republic 4
    Nevis 24
    Uzbekistan 7
    Vietnam 22
Artigasia
    Uruguay 11
Astrapotherium
    Turks and Caicos Islands **MS**9
Australopithecine, unspecified
    Palau 36 37 43
Australopithecus
    Cambodia 38 39 40 41
    Cuba 4 29
    Ethiopia 7
    North Korea 24
    Palau 40 44
    South Africa 6 7 8 10
    Uzbekistan **MS**9
Baluchitherium, see *Indricotherium*
Basilosaurus
    Comoro Islands 24
Bison
    Romania 3
Borhyaena
    Turks and Caicos Islands 4
Brontops
    Antigua 56
    Vietnam 26
Brontotherium
    Liberia 104
    Nevis **MS**40
    Poland 17
Canis
    Cuba 41
Capromeryx
    Maldive Islands 115
Cetotherium
    Comoro Islands 26
Chalicotherium
    Micronesia 30

Russia 2
Chriacus
　　Antigua 51
Coelodonta
　　Afghanistan 17
　　Antigua **MS**67
　　China (People's Republic) 4
　　Cuba 40
　　Kazakhstan **MS**7
　　Lesotho **MS**44
　　Liberia **MS**111
　　Maldive Islands 114
　　Poland 28
　　St Vincent 76 **MS**95
　　Sweden 3
Coryphodon
　　Canada 12
Cuvieronius
　　Guyana 5
　　Turks and Caicos Islands 7
Deer, prehistoric
　　Niuafo'ou 14
Deinotherium
　　Bulgaria 5
　　Congo Republic 2
　　Czech Republic 5
　　Micronesia 29
　　Moldova 1
　　Nevis 21
　　Romania 6 7
　　Tanzania **MS**14
　　Vietnam 25
Diacodexis
　　Antigua 48
Diapithecine, unspecified
　　Palau 41
Diprotodon
　　Australia 24
Doedicurus
　　Argentine Republic 8
　　Cambodia 2
　　Uruguay 10
Dryopithecus
　　Uzbekistan **MS**9
Elephant, fossil
　　Turkish Cypriot Posts 1
Elephas
　　Djibouti Republic 1
　　Tunisia 6
Embolotherium
　　Mongolia 10
Entelodon
　　Guyana 179
　　Kazakhstan 1
　　Mongolia 12
Eohippus, see *Hyracotherium*
Equus
　　Afghanistan 12
Eremotherium
　　El Salvador 5
Eurhinodelphis
　　Antigua **MS**53
　　Comoro Islands 18
　　Tristan da Cunha **MS**2a,c
Geocapromys
　　Cuba 12
Glossotherium
　　Maldive Islands 113
　　Uruguay 5
Glyptodon
　　Guyana 4
　　Maldive Islands 117
　　Uruguay 2
Gomphotherium
　　Aden Protectorate States –
　　　　Qu'aiti State in Hadhramaut 5
　　Croatia 3
　　Democratic Congo 3
　　El Salvador 1
　　France 1
Ground sloth, unspecified
　　El Salvador 8 9 10
　　Guinea-Bissau 24
　　St Vincent 75
Hemicyon
　　Antigua 47
Hesperocyon
　　Gambia 91
Hipparion
　　Afghanistan 18
　　Bulgaria 3
　　Mongolia 14
　　Niger 19 23
Hippopotamus
　　Cyprus 1
　　Indonesia 7
Hippopotamus, fossil
　　Sri Lanka 1
　　Turkish Cypriot Posts 1
Hominid, unspecified

    Antigua **MS**54
    Chad **MS**20 34 **MS**35
    Guinea-Bissau 34 35 36 37 38
        MS39

Homo
    Aden Protectorate States –
        Qu'aiti State in Hadhramaut 7
    Andorra (French Post Offices) 1
    Cambodia 43 44 45
    Chad 1
    China (People's Republic) 4
    Croatia 6 7
    Cuba 3 5 6 7 30 31 32
    France 2
    Georgia **MS**38
    Germany 6
    Gibraltar 5 6
    Great Britain 1
    Greece 2
    Hungary 11
    Indonesia 1 2 3 4 5 6
    Italy 1
    Kenya 4 5
    Palau 38 39 42 45 46 47
    South Africa 11 12
    Uzbekistan **MS**9 (x6)
    Yugoslavia 4

Homotherium
    Antigua 33

Human, Gibraltar prehistoric
    Gibraltar 1 2 3

Human, unspecified prehistoric
    Guyana 65
    Kenya 1 **MS**52
    Kenya, Uganda and Tanganyika 2
    North Korea 14 15
    Tonga 1

Hyaenodon
    Gambia 89
    Micronesia 28

Hyrachyus
    Cambodia 5

Hyracotherium
    Afghanistan 8
    Antigua 57
    Comoro Islands **MS**69
    St Vincent 73
    United States of America 10

Icaronycthris
    Gambia 85

Ictitherium
    Antigua 45

Indricotherium [=*Baluchitherium*]
    Chad 19
    Gambia 93
    Kampuchea 7
    Micronesia 27
    Mongolia 4
    Russia 3
    St Vincent 69
    Vietnam 24

Kanuites
    Antigua 50

Leptictidium
    Antigua 44
    Tanzania 80

Loxodonta
    Libya 14
    Nevis 23

Machairodus
    Aden Protectorate States –
        Qu'aiti State in Hadhramaut 1
    Bulgaria 6
    Poland 18

Macrauchenia
    Antigua 34
    Argentine Republic 9
    Guyana 11
    Maldive Islands 116
    Nevis 26
    Uruguay 3

Mammal, unspecified fossil
    Comoro Islands **MS**17
    Niuafo'ou 8 **MS**10
    North Korea 9

Mammoth, unspecified
    Guyana 21

Mammut
    Bulgaria 4
    Congo Republic 16
    Manama 3
    United States of America 1 8

Mammuthus
    Afghanistan 13
    Bequia **MS**13
    Bhutan 27
    Bulgaria 1
    Canada 15
    China (People's Republic) 4
    Cuba **MS**44

Democratic Congo 2 5
Dominica 54 57 **MS**66
El Salvador 4
France 9 **MS**10
Fujeira **MS**15
Grenada **MS**78
Grenadines of Grenada **MS**48
Guinea-Bissau 4
Guyana 59
Hungary 10
Ireland (Republic) 1 **MS**3 4
Jersey 1 2
Libya 15
Madagascar **MS**8
Maldive Islands **MS**122
Manama **MS**9
Mongolia 8 24
Nicaragua 2
Niuafo'ou 9 14
Poland 19
Romania 2
St Kitts **MS**20
St Vincent 96 130 131 132
Sweden 4
Tanzania **MS**14
United States of America 11
Vietnam 23
Yemen Republic 3

Marsupial, unspecified fossil
   Australia 10

Mastodont, unspecified
   El Salvador 7
   Georgia 19 35
   Guyana 19
   Maldive Islands 121
   Mongolia 6
   St Vincent 78

Megacerops
   Canada 13

Megaladapis
   Micronesia 4

Megaloceros [=*Sinomegacerus*]
   Afghanistan 14
   China (People's Republic) 3
   Cuba 39
   France 8 **MS**10
   Guinea-Bissau 7
   Ireland (Republic) 2 **MS**3 5
   Isle of Man 2
   Kazakhstan 6

Romania 5
Tonga 1

Megalocnus
   Cuba 1 13

Megantereon
   Gibraltar 4

Megatherium
   Argentine Republic 7
   Ecuador 2
   Guyana 8

Megazostrodon
   Comoro Islands **MS**69

Merychippus
   Afghanistan 10

Mesonyx
   Cambodia 1

Mesopithecus
   Macedonia 2

Metamynodon
   Niger 22

Miohippus
   Afghanistan 9

Moeritherium
   Bhutan 25
   Guyana 172
   Liberia 105
   Micronesia **MS**31
   Niger 20

Mongolotherium
   Mongolia 7

Mylodon
   Cambodia 3
   Chile 4
   Guyana 12

Natalus
   Guyana 4

Nesodon
   Maldive Islands 118

Nesophontes
   Cuba 14

Nothotheriops
   Maldive Islands 112

Odobenocetops
   Liberia **MS**111

Orycterocetus
   Tristan da Cunha **MS**2

Osteoborus [=*Borophagus*]
   El Salvador 6

Pakicetus
   Comoro Islands 21

Dinosaurs and other Prehistoric Animals on Stamps

Palaeochiropteryx
    West Germany 1
Palaeomastodon
    Congo Republic 15
Paranthropus
    Cambodia 42
    Cuba 28
    Ethiopia 1
    Great Britain 1
    Kenya 3
    South Africa 9
    Tanzania 1
    Uzbekistan **MS**9
Pithecanthropus, see *Homo*
Platybelodon
    Bhutan 26
    Congo Republic 18
    Guinea-Bissau 22
    Hungary 9
    Nevis 22
Platygonus
    Maldive Islands 111
Platypittamys
    Guyana 18
Plesictis
    Antigua 46
Pliohippus
    Afghanistan 11
Proborhyaena
    Uruguay 13
Proconsul
    Cuba 33
    Guyana 61
    Kenya 6
    Kenya, Uganda and Tanganyika 1
    Niger 21
Procoptodon
    Australia 27
    Nevis 25
Prohyrax
    Namibia 3
Propachyrucos
    Uruguay 14
Propalaeotherium
    Antigua 58
    West Germany 2
Protembolotherium
    Yemen Republic 1
Prothylacynus
    Turks and Caicos Islands 3

Protohydrochoerus
    Guyana 15
    Turks and Caicos Islands 1
Pyrotherium
    Guyana 17
Rhinoceros, fossil
    North Korea 27
    Sri Lanka 1
Sabre-tooth tiger, unspecified
    Gambia **MS**94
    Guinea 5 8
    Niuafo'ou 9 14
    St Vincent 72
Sahelanthropus
    Chad 49 50 51 52 **MS**53
Sinanthropus, see *Homo*
Sinomegacerus, see *Megaloceros*
Sivatherium
    Maldive Islands 110
Smilodectes
    Guyana 7
Smilodon
    Afghanistan **MS**19
    Cuba 43
    Ecuador 1
    El Salvador 2
    France 6 **MS**10
    Grenada 69
    Grenadines of Grenada 39
    Guyana 13
    Liberia 103
    Madagascar 6 29
    Maldive Islands **MS**122
    Peru 2 3
    St Kitts 17
    Turks and Caicos Islands 5
    United States of America 9
    Uruguay 8
Spirocerus
    Mongolia 13
Stegodon
    Gambia 84
    India 1
Stegomastodon
    Uruguay 15
Stegotetrabelodon
    Libya 10 11 **MS**21
Stylinodon
    Antigua 49

Syndyoceras
 St Vincent 79
Synthetoceras
 Afghanistan 16
 Comoro Islands 15
Tapirus
 Maldive Islands 119
Tchadanthropus, see *Homo*
Teleoceras
 Guyana 10
Tetralophodon
 Libya 1
 Uganda 7
Thoatherium
 Turks and Caicos Islands 6
Thylacoleo
 Australia 25
Titanohyrax
 Libya 4
Titanotylopus
 Guyana 9
Toxodon
 Argentine Republic 10
 El Salvador 3
 Peru 2 3
 Turks and Caicos Islands 8
 Uruguay 1 4
Tragocerus
 Macedonia 3
Uintatherium
 Afghanistan 3
 Cambodia 4
 Comoro Islands 12
 Gambia 90
 Grenada **MS**78
 Grenadines of Grenada **MS**48
 Madagascar 7 31
 Manama 1
 Nicaragua 5
 Tanzania 33
 Vietnam 27
Ursus
 Afghanistan 15
 Bulgaria 2
 Cuba 42
 Guinea 4
 Macedonia 1
 Monaco 3
 Romania 1 33 **MS**34
 Tonga 1

Zambdalestes
 Dominica 52
Zinjanthropus, see *Paranthropus*
Zygorhiza
 Comoro Islands 23

Class No. 2 AVES (Birds)

Aptornis
 New Zealand 10
Aquila
 Cuba 11
Archaeopteryx
 Bhutan 30
 Bulgaria 14
 Central African Republic
  12 29 60 79
 Chad 38
 Comoro Islands 58
 Congo Republic 10
 Dominica 37 **MS**66
 East Germany 2
 Gabon 29 **MS**66 67
 Gambia 15 26 86
 Georgia 21
 Ghana 47
 Great Britain 7
 Grenada 41 **MS**65 75
 Grenadines of Grenada 14 45
 Guinea-Bissau 11 23
 Guyana 36 46 58 67 134 146 169
 Laos 9
 Lesotho 16 **MS**17 31
 Liberia 36 63 74
 Madagascar 9
 Maldive Islands 58
  MS86 100 **MS**139
 Mali 3 6 9
 Micronesia 15 16 **MS**18
 Mozambique **MS**11
 Niger 17
 Niuafo'ou 8 **MS**10
 North Korea 10
 Palau 27 52 **MS**73
 Poland 16
 Romania 13
 St Vincent 14 65 83 114
 São Tomé e Principe 17
 Sierra Leone 5 31 56 **MS**73

Tanzania 36 74 **MS**76 85
Uganda 12
United States of America 2
Vietnam 29
Archaeotrogon
    Guyana 2
Devincenzia
    Uruguay 7
Diamantornis
    Namibia 2
Diatryma, see *Gastornis*
Dinornis
    Afghanistan 7
    Cuba 8
    Laos 11
    Madagascar 1
    New Zealand 12
        MS13 **MS**15 **MS**16
    St Vincent 70
Euryapteryx
    Comoro Islands 16
Gastornis [=*Diatryma*]
    Comoro Islands 11 **MS**69
    Gambia 82
    Mali 46
    Manama 7
    Palau 26
    Tajikistan 6
    Tanzania 31
    Yemen Republic 2
Genyornis
    Australia 23
Harpagornis
    New Zealand 11
Hesperornis
    Gambia 74
    Laos 8
    St Vincent 30 92
    Sierra Leone 13 **MS**21
Iberomesornis
    Equatorial Guinea 14
Ichthyornis
    Dominica 45
    Micronesia 2
    Palau 33
Mononykus
    St Vincent **MS**128
Natunaornis
    Fiji 2
Ornimegalonyx
    Cuba 9
Pachyplichas
    New Zealand 14
Palaelodus
    Guyana 1
Phorusrhacus [=*Phororhacos*]
    France 7 **MS**10
    Guinea-Bissau 20
    Guyana 6
    Laos 5 10
    Mali 37
    Turks and Caicos Islands 2
    Uzbekistan 8
    Yemen Republic 6
Protarchaeopteryx
    Grenada **MS**63
Proavis
    Madagascar 11
Protoavis
    Guyana 49
    St Vincent 9 61
    São Tomé e Principe **MS**14
Sylviornis
    New Caledonia 1
Teratornis
    Guyana 3
    Laos **MS**12
Tytthostonyx
    Gambia 88
Vitirallus
    Fiji 3

Class No. 3 REPTILIA (Reptiles)

Order/Category No. 1
SAURISCHIA
(Lizard-hipped dinosaurs)

Acrocanthosaurus
    Chad 46
    Grenada 46
    Sierra Leone 54
Afrovenator
    Antigua 13
    Barbuda 11
    Mozambique **MS**11
    Papua New Guinea **MS**8
Alamosaurus

Central African Republic **MS**25
Gabon 93
Grenada 6
Guyana 145
Albertosaurus
    Azerbaijan 4
    Canada 1 10 16
    Central African Republic 57 77
    Comoro Islands 44
    Gabon 44
    Gambia 53
    Ghana **MS**28
    Grenada 55
    Grenadines of Grenada 16
    Guinea 68
    Liberia 24
    Maldive Islands 135
    St Vincent 18
    Sierra Leone 62
    Singapore 3
    Tanzania 56
Alioramus
    Grenada 53
    Guinea 70
Allosaurus [=*Antrodemus*]
    Antigua **MS**11
    Australia 4 **MS**7
    Azerbaijan 6
    Barbuda **MS**9
    Bhutan 20
    Brazil 6
    Central African Republic 7 74
    Comoro Islands 42
    Congo Republic 29 **MS**31
    Cuba 27
    France 3 **MS**54
    Fujeira 6 10
    Gabon 38 87
    Gambia 3 **MS**13
    Ghana 22
    Grenada 21 32 **MS**64
    Grenadines of Grenada **MS**20
    Guinea 33
    Guyana 4639 **MS**64 75 **MS**115
        141 155 161
    Hong Kong 1
    Liberia 43 83 92
    Libya 27
    Madagascar 21 36
    Maldive Islands **MS**23 92

    Mali 29
    Manama 6
    Micronesia 17 **MS**18
    Mongolia **MS**22
    Niger 8
    North Korea 5
    Palau 53
    Romania 22
    St Vincent 4 119
    Sierra Leone 52 **MS**70
    Solomon Islands 6
    Tanzania 21 53 66
    Uganda 17
    United States of America 2 17
    Vietnam 14
    Zambia 24
    Zimbabwe 2
Amargasaurus
    Angola 33
    Argentine Republic 2
    Palau 68
    São Tomé e Principe 35
Anchisaurus
    Gabon 88
    Ghana 2
    Guinea 11
    Guinea-Bissau **MS**17
    Guyana 39
    Maldive Islands 96
    Nevis 16
    St Vincent 16
    Tanzania 24
Angaturama
    Brazil 4
Antrodemus, see *Allosaurus*
Apatosaurus [=*Brontosaurus*]
    Aden Protectorate States –
        Qu'aiti State in Hadhramaut 4
    Angola 19
    Antigua **MS**11
    Barbuda **MS**9
    Benin 2 17
    Bhutan 7
    Bulgaria 7
    Central African Republic
        1 17 55 73
    Chad 29
    Congo Republic **MS**14
    Cuba 16
    Czech Republic 2

Dominica 36
Fujeira 14
Gabon 26 **MS**113
Georgia 1 20
Ghana **MS**51
Grenada 17
Grenadines of Grenada 2
Guyana 66 **MS**115
Hungary 6
Laos 18
Lesotho 38
Liberia 38 77
Maldive Islands 22
Manama 8
Micronesia 23
Montserrat 3
Nevis 27
North Korea 4
Palau 50
Poland 3
Romania 8 20
St Kitts 13 **MS**20
St Vincent 57 100
San Marino 1
São Tomé e Principe 5
Senegal 2
Sierra Leone **MS**72
Singapore 2
Somalia 1
Tanzania 4 55
Uganda 9 34 42
United States of America 2 7
Vietnam 20
Zambia 10

Argentinosaurus
    Bequia 9
    Chad 22
    Gabon **MS**113
    Solomon Islands 4

Astrodon, see *Pleurocoelus*

Avimimus
    Cambodia 22
    Guinea-Bissau 9 **MS**17
    Maldive Islands 27 105
    Mali 20
    Nevis 6
    Sierra Leone 58

Barapasaurus
    Maldive Islands 33

Barosaurus
    Dominica 34
    Liberia 88
    Maldive Islands 33

Baryonyx
    Antigua 62
    Benin 19
    Central African Republic 56
    Chad 18
    Dominica 22 51
    Gambia 30 59
    Guinea 50
    Liberia 9
    Libya 5
    Maldive Islands 43 84 138
    Mozambique **MS**3 **MS**12
    St Vincent 25
    São Tomé e Principe **MS**36
    Solomon Islands 1
    Tanzania 26
    Zambia 19

Beipiaosaurus
    Mozambique **MS**14

Bothriospondylus
    Mozambique **MS**4

Brachiosaurus
    Angola 6 **MS**11 21 31
    Antigua 4
    Barbuda 2
    Bequia 5
    Bhutan 13 16
    Cambodia **MS**37
    Central African Republic
        8 66 104 **MS**107
    Comoro Islands 61
    Congo Republic 3 11
    Dominica **MS**53
    Gabon 47 102
    Gambia 57
    Germany 4 5
    Grenada 20 31 42
    Grenadines of Grenada
        8 **MS**9 13 32
    Guinea **MS**43
    Guinea-Bissau 32
    Guyana 82 151 157 **MS**171
    Kampuchea 5
    Kiribati 4
    Lesotho 28
    Liberia 30 76 94
    Madagascar **MS**28 37

Malawi **MS**54
Maldive Islands
19 **MS**23 69 **MS**109
Micronesia 11 **MS**18
Mongolia **MS**22
Mozambique **MS**11
Poland 6
St Vincent 20 101
San Marino 2
São Tomé e Principe **MS**14
Sierra Leone 9 23 47 **MS**70
Tanzania **MS**71 82
Togo 4 **MS**8 9
Uganda 4 15 35 43
United States of America 15
Vietnam 16
Brontosaurus, see *Apatosaurus*
Byronosaurus
Mozambique **MS**13
Camarasaurus
Cambodia 18
Comoro Islands 50
Dominica 21
Gabon 82
Grenada 51
Grenadines of Grenada 26
Guyana 85
Liberia 1
Micronesia 3
Nevis 28
Nicaragua 12
Romania 18
St Vincent 2 29
Sierra Leone **MS**71
Tanzania 18 63 89
United States of America 14
Carcharodontosaurus
Guinea 80 **MS**81
Papua New Guinea 6
Carnosaur, unspecified
New Zealand
2 6 **MS**57 **MS**58 **MS**59
Poland 20
Carnotaurus
Angola 24
Antigua **MS**30
Argentine Republic 1 12
Barbuda **MS**28
Cuba 45
Equatorial Guinea 13

Gabon 75
Gambia 61 70
Madagascar 27
Mali 32
Micronesia 22
Caudipteryx
Grenada **MS**64
Ceratosaurus
Afghanistan 6
Benin 21
Cambodia 19
Comoro Islands 38 **MS**69
Dominica 18 39
Gambia 42
Georgia 2
Grenada 23
Guinea 16 42 **MS**43
Guinea-Bissau 29
Guyana 84
Laos 2
Lesotho 10 30
Madagascar 2
Maldive Islands 101
Mali 14 44
Palau 49
St Vincent 107
São Tomé e Principe **MS**14
Sierra Leone 22
Tanzania 22 **MS**83
United States of America 12
Vietnam 18
Zambia 17
Cetiosaurus
Central African Republic 16
Gabon **MS**113
Gambia 6 **MS**13
Guyana 144
Maldive Islands 104
Morocco 1
Tanzania 17 49
Uganda 33 41
Coelophysis
Antigua 65
Azerbaijan 1
Cambodia 12
Chad 27
Comoro Islands 39
Dominica 12
Gabon 15
Gambia 22 28 39 60 75

Ghana 7 **MS**9 27
Guyana 70 110 153 182
Lesotho **MS**44
Liberia 91
Mali 38
Micronesia **MS**31
St Vincent 21 63 122
Sierra Leone 66
Tanzania 30 96
Togo 3 **MS**8
Turks and Caicos Islands 11
Zambia 22
Coelosaur, unspecified
   Micronesia 2
Coelurosaur, unspecified
   Antigua 60
Coelurus
   Benin 19
   Tanzania 78
Compsognathus
   Antigua 38
   Bhutan 24
   Central African Republic 13 38 43
   Comoro Islands 4
   Dominica 11 **MS**66
   Gambia 62 63
   Grenada 24 49
   Guyana 88 **MS**114 159
   Liberia 5 78
   Madagascar 26
   Maldive Islands 81
   Nevis 12
   Nicaragua 19
   Palau 72
   St Vincent 52
   Sierra Leone 28
   Uganda 23
   United States of America 2
   Zaire 2
   Zambia 25
Cryolophosaurus
   Grenada **MS**64
Daspletosaurus
   Cambodia **MS**30
   Gabon 100
   Ghana 23
   Maldive Islands 41
   Mali **MS**26
   Nevis **MS**40
   St Vincent **MS**127

United States of America 33
Zambia 18
Deinonychus
   Antigua 7 42
   Barbuda 5
   Benin 12
   Bhutan 8 28
   Bolivia 1
   Cambodia 23
   Central African Republic
      MS71 91
   Chad 44
   Comoro Islands 41
   Dominica 25
   Equatorial Guinea **MS**12
   Gabon 6 79 95
   Gambia 5 **MS**69 **MS**94
   Georgia 3 **MS**10
   Grenada 67
   Grenadines of Grenada 19 37
   Guinea 22
   Guinea-Bissau 30
   Guyana 45 69 133
   Lesotho 34 35
   Liberia **MS**34 90
   Madagascar **MS**15
   Maldive Islands 7 66 127 137
   Mali 33
   Micronesia **MS**18 **MS**31
   Mozambique **MS**11
   Nevis 10
   Nicaragua 14
   Niger 6
   Palau **MS**73
   St Kitts 12
   St Vincent 22 71 103
   Sierra Leone 29 **MS**35 41
   Tanzania 39
   Togo 10
   Uganda 36 44
   Zambia 5
Dicraeosaurus
   Germany 1
   Guinea 18 34
   Guyana 50 **MS**114
   São Tomé e Principe 9
Dilophosaurus
   Cambodia 16
   Chad 21
   Comoro islands 36

Dominica 23
Gabon 89 108
Grenada 43
Guinea 26 37 45
Kiribati 3
Malawi **MS**54
Maldive Islands 26
Mali 15 34
St Vincent 94 120
São Tomé e Principe 13
Togo 5 **MS**8 11 15
Turks and Caicos Islands
    15 **MS**18
Uganda 24
Diplodocus
    Benin 18
    Bhutan 3
    Cambodia 34
    Central African Republic 58
    Congo Republic 11
    Dominica 38
    Equatorial Guinea **MS**8 **MS**16
    Gabon 2
    Ghana 42
    Grenadines of Grenada 11
    Guyana **MS**64
    Liberia 46
    Maldive Islands 3 59
    Montserrat 2
    Mozambique **MS**11(x 2)
    Romania 23
    St Vincent **MS**17 55 **MS**66 **MS**95
    Senegal 1
    Sierra Leone **MS**70
    Solomon Islands 2
    Tanzania 10 35 73 **MS**76
    Uganda 30
    United States of America 2
    Vietnam 10
Dromaeosaurid, unspecified
    Dominica 24
    Guinea 33
Dromaeosaurus
    Chad 4 12
    Japan (Fukui Prefecture) 3
    Liberia 57 79
    Maldive Islands 63
    Mali 22
Dromiceiomimus
    Comoro Islands 13

Gabon 45 96
Guinea 28
Liberia 40
Maldive Islands 49
Mali 42
Tanzania 87
Dryptosaurus
    Central African Republic 78
    Maldive Islands 50
Elaphrosaurus
    Angola 16
    Dominica 41
    Ghana 6 **MS**59
    Grenada 25
    Maldive Islands 35
    Mozambique **MS**4
Elopteryx
    Romania 28 **MS**32
Eoraptor
    Argentine Republic 3
    Grenada **MS**64
    Kiribati 5
Erlikosaurus
    Libya 16
Euskelosaurus [=*Plateosauravus*]
    Lesotho 3
Eustreptospondylus
    Guyana 176
    Madagascar 12
    Nevis 3
    St Vincent 124
Gallimimus
    Comoro Islands 62
    Grenadines of Grenada 25
    Kyrgyzstan 3
    Malawi **MS**54
    Maldive Islands **MS**57
    Micronesia 8
    Poland 23
    Romania 19
    St Vincent 46
    Tanzania 93
    Zambia 11
Garudimimus
    Gambia 78
Gasosaurus
    Lesotho 14
Giganotosaurus
    Argentine Republic 5
    Central African Republic

106 **MS**107
Chad **MS**33
Guinea 79 **MS**81
Kiribati 8
Papua New Guinea 4
St Vincent **MS**129
São Tomé e Principe 35
Gorgosaurus
    Bequia 2
    Bulgaria 20
    Central African Republic 20
    Guinea 20
    Vietnam 129
Gryponyx, see *Massospondylus*
Halticosaurus
    Grenadines of Grenada **MS**35
Herrerasaurus
    Cambodia 15
    Central African Republic
        62 **MS**100 103
    Comoro Islands 66
    Georgia 25
    Ghana 26
    Grenada **MS**63
    Grenadines of Grenada 17
    Guyana 138
    Madagascar 9
    Maldive Islands 82
    St Vincent 109
    Sierra Leone **MS**71
Hylaeosaurus
    Mozambique **MS**3
Hypselosaurus
    Palau 63
Irritator
    Mozambique **MS**13
Lufengosaurus
    China (People's Republic) 2
Mamenchisaurus
    Lesotho 29
    Maldive Islands 9
    Mongolia 21
Massospondylus
    Canada 8
    Gabon 90
    Lesotho 2 5 15
    Maldive Islands 107
    St Vincent **MS**128
    Zimbabwe 3
Megalosaurus

    Comoro Islands 37
    Gabon 86
    Guinea 13
    Maldive Islands 29 **MS**109
    North Korea 18
    Romania 15
    Tanzania 48
    Uganda 48 **MS**59 38 46
Megapnosaurus [=*Syntarsus*]
    Maldive Islands 95
    St Vincent **MS**128
Megaraptor
    South Korea 1
Microraptor
    Grenada 77
    Grenadines of Grenada 47
Microvenator
    Maldive Islands 46
Mussaurus
    Cuba 38
Nanotyrannus
    St Vincent 27
Opisthocoelicaudia
    Gabon 46
    Guinea 30
    Liberia 49
    Mongolia 18
Ornitholestes
    Antigua 61
    Chad 3 11
    Comoro Islands 6
    Gambia 31 39 46
    Guinea 31
    Guinea-Bissau **MS**17
    Guyana 81 186
    Maldive Islands 89
    Mozambique **MS**3
    St Vincent 58 64 123
    Sierra Leone 30
    Tanzania 62
    Zambia 20
Ornithomimosaurus
    Chad 25
    Guyana **MS**114
Ornithomimus
    Chad 8 16
    Congo Republic 6
    Dominica 48
    Gambia 10 17 66
    Georgia 18 36

Guyana 78
Palau **MS**73
St Vincent 8
Sierra Leone 27
Tanzania 25 46
United States of America 25
Oviraptor
Antigua 23 32
Azerbaijan 3
Barbuda 21
Bequia 8
Bhutan 10
Cuba 46
Gabon 11
Guyana 29 76
Liberia 20
Libya 6
Maldive Islands 64 71
Nevis 2
Niger **MS**11
Papua New Guinea 2
St Vincent 62 98
Tanzania 44
Zambia 26
Patagosaurus
Argentine Republic 6
Central African Republic 94
São Tomé e Principe 10
Phuwiangosaurus
Thailand 2 **MS**6
Piatnitzkysaurus
Maldive Islands 39
Plateosauravus, see *Euskelosaurus*
Plateosaurus
Angola 20
Antigua 63
Cambodia 14
Fujeira 3 8
Gambia 29
Ghana 34
Guinea 10
Guyana **MS**64 112
Kuwait 1 2
Lesotho 13
Libya 18
Madagascar 16 39
Maldive Islands **MS**57
Manama 4
Micronesia **MS**18
Nicaragua 10

Romania 26
St Vincent 67
Sierra Leone 45 **MS**72
Sweden 1
Tanzania 2 9 42
Pleurocoelus [=*Astrodon*]
Chad 43
Maldive Islands 42 108
Procompsognathus
Lesotho 11
Mozambique **MS**4
Rhoetosaurus
Australia 11
Saltasaurus
Gabon **MS**66 84 111
Gambia 50
Guinea 47
Guyana 74
Laos 15
Liberia 75
Maldive Islands 70
Mali 21
Micronesia 26
Nevis 11
North Korea **MS**20 **MS**21
St Vincent 99
Tanzania 16
Zambia MS28
Saltopus
Cuba 36
Sauropod, unspecified
Brazil 3
Central African Republic 26 28
Guyana 63
Hungary 4
Malawi 3
Mongolia **MS**23
New Zealand 1 2
Niuafo'ou 4 11
Poland 29
São Tomé e Principe 26
Thailand 1 7
Sauropodomorph, unspecified
Lesotho 6
Saurornithoides
Guinea 36
Mali 19 39
Saurornitholestes
Cambodia 24
Scipionyx

Mozambique **MS**14
Segisaurus
    Azerbaijan 1
Segnosaurus
    Azerbaijan 3
    Laos 13
    Madagascar 10 14
    Nevis 8
    St Vincent 104
Seismosaurus
    Bequia 6
    Chad 45
    Gambia **MS**69 101
    Ghana **MS**10
Shunosaurus
    Angola 32
    Guinea-Bissau 12
    Liberia **MS**23
    Papua New Guinea **MS**57
    Uganda **MS**28
Siamosaurus, see *Spinosaurus*
Siamotyrannus
    Thailand 3 **MS**56
Sinosauropteryx
    Grenada **MS**63
    Guyana 183
Spinosaurus [=*Siamosaurus*]
    Angola 7 **MS**12
    Cambodia 20
    Central African Republic 35
    Cuba 52
    Dominica 46 55
    Gambia 9 **MS**38 40
    Georgia 14 34
    Grenada 11 57 **MS**63
    Grenadines of Grenada 1 **MS**59
    Guinea 24 53 75 **MS**78
    Guyana 38 142 180
    Liberia **MS**62
    Maldive Islands 56
    Micronesia **MS**18
    Nauru 3
    Niger 4
    St Vincent 3 56
    Tajikistan 8
    Tanzania 19
    Thailand 4 **MS**6
Staurikosaurus
    Gambia 23
    Guyana 26 54 113

    Libya 19
    Madagascar 19
Stenonychosaurus, see *Troodon*
Struthiomimus
    Antigua 35
    Bequia 7
    Central African Republic 23 63
    Comoro Islands 10
    Gabon 39 81
    Ghana 30
    Grenada 39
    Guinea 73
    Guyana **MS**115
    Israel 1 2 3
    Liberia 27
    Papua New Guinea **MS**57
    St Vincent 68
    São Tomé e Principe 41
    Sierra Leone 44
    Tanzania 68
    Togo 17
Suchomimus
    Grenada 68
    Grenadines of Grenada 38
    Micronesia **MS**13
    São Tomé e Principe 34
Supersaurus [=*Ultrasauros*]
    Ghana 11 12
    Liberia 96
Syntarsus, see *Megapnosaurus*
Tarbosaurus
    Antigua 28
    Barbuda 26
    Central African Republic 24
    Comoro Islands 63
    Czech Republic 3
    Gambia 56
    Ghana 24
    Guinea 19
    Guyana 102 181
    Hungary 5
    Kampuchea 6
    Liberia **MS**23
    Mongolia 1 20
    Poland 20 31
    Uzbekistan 6
Tazoudasaurus
    Morocco 2
Thecodontosaurus
    Gabon 110

Theropod, unspecified
    Antigua 59
    Benin 26 31 32
    Brazil 2
    Central African Republic 27 28
    Cuba 16
    Ghana 40
    Guinea-Bissau 8 10 13 14 16
     MS17 25 27 31
    Lesotho 8
    Mongolia 30 34 35
    Poland 29
    São Tomé e Principe 24 27 28 33
    Thailand 1

Timimus
    Australia 3 **MS**7

Titanosaurus
    Brazil 5
    Chile 3
    Guinea 38
    Uruguay 6

Troodon [=*Stenonychosaurus*]
    Central African Republic **MS**25
    Cuba **MS**57
    Equatorial Guinea 15
    Gambia 44 64
    Grenada 47
    Grenadines of Grenada 21
    Guinea 29
    Libya 7
    Madagascar 18
    Maldive Islands 10 68 94
    Mali 30
    Micronesia 21
    Romania 17
    St Vincent 102
    São Tomé e Principe 40
    Sierra Leone **MS**70
    Zambia 21

Tyrannosaurid, unspecified
    Azerbaijan 2

Tyrannosaurus
    Aden Protectorate States –
        Qu'aiti State in Hadhramaut 3
    Angola 23 **MS**37
    Antigua 5 19 20
    Azerbaijan 7
    Barbuda 3 17 18
    Benin 3 5
    Bhutan 1 5
    Bulgaria 18
    Canada **MS**17
    Central African Republic
        33 68 90
    Chad **MS**48
    Comoro Islands **MS**17 40
    Congo Republic 6 12
    Cuba 21
    Dahomey 3
    Dominica 7 31
    Equatorial Guinea 10
    Gabon 25 41 105 **MS**113
    Gambia **MS**38
    Georgia 9 15 33
    Ghana **MS**28 44
    Great Britain 4
    Grenada 8 9 28 **MS**62
    Grenadines of Grenada
        3 **MS**9 **MS**35
    Guinea **MS**25 **MS**74
    Guinea-Bissau 5
    Guyana 4635 **MS**64 71 **MS**115
    Kyrgyzstan 1
    Laos 1 20
    Lesotho **MS**44
    Liberia 50 **MS**62 84 87 97 108
    Madagascar **MS**28 38
    Malagasy Republic 2
    Malawi **MS**4
    Maldive Islands
        6 13 **MS**23 60 77 **MS**86
    Micronesia 9 **MS**18a,b,c 20
    Mongolia 28
    Montserrat 1
    Mozambique **MS**53 **MS**36
    Nauru 5
    Nevis 20
    Nicaragua 9
    Niuafo'ou 5 12
    North Korea 2 **MS**20 **MS**21
    Palau 26 56
    Papua New Guinea 3
    Poland 10
    Romania 12 24
    St Kitts 19
    St Vincent
        MS17 **MS**66 89 **MS**126
    San Marino 5
    São Tomé e Principe 4 8
    Senegal 5

Dinosaurs and other Prehistoric Animals on Stamps

    Sierra Leone 39 46 **MS**53
    Tajikistan 1
    Tanzania 32 60 72 **MS**76 77 98
    Togo 13 **MS**18
    Uganda 18 **MS**40
    United States of America 4 27
    Vietnam 4
    Yemen Republic **MS**58
    Zaire **MS**5 **MS**6
    Zambia 23
Ultrasauros, see *Supersaurus*
Ultrasaurus
    Kiribati 1
Utahraptor
    Central African Republic 67
    Guinea **MS**55
    Guyana 178
    St Vincent **MS**127
Velociraptor
    Bhutan 21
    Central African Republic 75
    Congo Republic **MS**26
    Cuba **MS**50
    Dominica 63
    Gabon 68
    Gambia 45
    Georgia 16 32
    Ghana 25
    Grenada **MS**62
    Guinea-Bissau 28
    Guyana 154 **MS**184
    Kyrgyzstan 6
    Liberia 58 **MS**85
    Malawi **MS**54
    Maldive Islands 55
    Mali 24
    Mozambique **MS**3
    Nauru 7
    Palau 59
    Poland 27
    St Vincent 110 **MS**128
    Togo **MS**7
    Uganda 10
    Zaire 4
Vulcanodon
    Dominica 42
Yangchuanosaurus
    Antigua 64
    Azerbaijan **MS**8
    Benin 22

    Cuba 51
    Dominica **MS**53
    Gabon 97
    Gambia 27
    Guyana 107 **MS**140
    Libya 9

Order/Category No. 2
ORNITHISCHIA
(Bird-hipped dinosaurs)

Acanthopholis
    Comoro Islands 8
    Mali 40
    St Vincent 4
Agathaumas
    Gambia 51
    Grenada 50
Agilisaurus
    Palau 67
Anatosaurus, see *Anatotitan*
Anatotitan [=*Anatosaurus*] [=*Trachodon*]
    Aden Protectorate States –
        Qu'aiti State in Hadhramaut 3
    Angola 22
    Benin 1
    Central African Republic 22 51 72
    Dominica 49
    Ghana 5 41
    Grenada 56
    Guinea-Bissau 1
    Guyana 73 **MS**184
    Laos 6 16
    Maldive Islands 16 54
    Mali 18
    St Vincent 23 49 60
    Sierra Leone 12
    Tajikistan 3
    Tanzania 41 65
    Uzbekistan 5
Anchiceratops
    Democratic Congo 9
    Guinea **MS**32
    Liberia 54
    Tajikistan 5
Ankylosaur, unspecified
    New Zealand 4
    São Tomé e Principe 33
Ankylosaurus
    Benin 30

Bequia 11
Central African Republic 3
Dominica 56
Equatorial Guinea 5
Grenadines of Grenada 19
Liberia 28
North Korea 1
Palau 58
Papua New Guinea 1
St Vincent 51
Sierra Leone **MS**71
Solomon Islands 7
Tanzania 64
Vietnam 19
Arrhinoceratops
Gabon **MS**113
Atlascopcosaurus
Australia 3 6 **MS**7(x 2)
Bactrosaurus
Chad 26
Cuba 35
Gambia **MS**38
Sierra Leone 68
Bagaceratops
Guinea 38
Brachylophosaurus
Central African Republic 96
Camptosaurus
Central African Republic 82
Dominica 1 19
Gabon 85
Gambia 7 76
Ghana 45
Grenada 54
Grenadines of Grenada 22
Guinea 15
Madagascar 25
Niger 7
St Vincent 28
Tanzania 69
United States of America 2 13
Centrosaurus
Antigua 14
Barbuda 12
Cambodia 9
Grenada 58
Guinea 46
Guinea-Bissau 15
Liberia 18 89
Nevis 31

Papua New Guinea 5
St Vincent 111
Solomon Islands 5
Uganda 32
Zambia 14
Chasmosaurus
Central African Republic 102
Equatorial Guinea 9
Lesotho 33
Liberia 19 29
Maldive Islands 52
Mongolia 15
New Zealand 15
St Vincent 19
São Tomé e Principe 15
Corythosaurus
Angola 25
Antigua **MS**30 36
Azerbaijan 4
Barbuda **MS**28
Benin 27
Bhutan 17
Central African Republic 6 18
Chad 6 14
Comoro Islands 68
Cuba 20
Dominica 3 **MS**9
Equatorial Guinea 4
Gabon 8 52 69
Ghana 29
Grenadines of Grenada 28
Guinea 23 48
Guyana 33 160
Liberia 21
Madagascar 33
Maldive Islands 78 103
Mongolia 27
North Korea 16
Palau 69
Poland 8
São Tomé e Principe 16 **MS**22
Sierra Leone 38 **MS**70
Tanzania 67 80
United States of America 24
Vietnam 12
Dryosaurus [=*Dysalotosaurus*]
Central African Republic 50
Gambia 1 32
Germany 3
Grenada 48

Grenadines of Grenada 24
Guinea 41
Liberia 52 66
Maldive Islands 31
Mali 16
Palau 70
Tanzania 29
Zaire 3
Dysalotosaurus, see *Dryosaurus*
Edmontonia
    Bulgaria 16
    Comoro Islands 9
    Maldive Islands 53
    Mali 27
    Papua New Guinea **MS**57
    United States of America 21
    Zambia 15
Edmontosaurus
    Bhutan 6
    Dominica 2
    Gabon 50
    Gambia 103
    Grenadines of Grenada **MS**35
    Guyana 149
    Liberia 55
    Nevis 5 30
    St Kitts 18
    Sierra Leone 55
    Tanzania 8
Einiosaurus
    United States of America 22
Euoplocephalus [=*Scolosaurus*]
    Cambodia 32
    Central African Republic 21
        MS25 40 97
    Chad 7 15
    Cuba 24
    Dominica 6 11
    Gambia 21
    Georgia 6
    Grenadines of Grenada 30
    Guyana 27 86
    Kyrgyzstan 4
    Laos 4
    Maldive Islands 20 80 130
    Mauritania **MS**18
    Mozambique **MS**11
    Nauru 6
    Nevis 15 32
    Nicaragua 13

    Palau 71
    St Vincent 80
    Turks and Caicos Islands 17
    Vietnam 20
Fabrosaurus
    Gambia 4
    Transkei 5
Fulgurotherium
    Georgia 28
Gasparinisaura
    Argentine Republic 4
Gastonia
    Papua New Guinea **MS**7
Graciliceratops [=*Microceratops*]
    Cambodia 29
    Gambia **MS**94
Gryposaurus [=*Kritosaurus*]
    Central African Republic 44
    Chad 23
    Maldive Islands 45
    Nevis 1
    Niger 10
    Palau 61
Hadrosaur, unspecified
    Cuba 25 27
    Grenadines of Grenada 27
    Maldive Islands **MS**23
Hadrosaurus
    Angola 28
    Georgia 26
    Grenada 13
    Guyana 103
    Madagascar 40
    Nevis 13 39
    Palau 65
    Sierra Leone 50 57
Heterodontosaurus
    Central African Republic **MS**25
    Chad 2 10
    Congo Republic 25
    Gambia 19
    Ghana 3
    Guyana 43 **MS**114
    Libya 13
    Mali 17 45
    St Vincent 13
    Sierra Leone 32
    Tanzania 28 70
    Zambia 7
Homalocephale

Central African Republic 47
Liberia 11
Mozambique **MS**11
St Kitts 15
Huayangosaurus
   Maldive Islands 37
Hypacrosaurus
   Dominica 32
   Grenadines of Grenada **MS**20
   St Vincent 106
Hypsilophodon
   Angola 30
   Bhutan 9
   British Antarctic Territory 15
   Madagascar 23 35
   Mozambique **MS**11
   Nevis 38
   St Vincent 108
   Sierra Leone 7 36
   Tanzania 50
   Uganda 3 **MS**59
   Vietnam 31
Iguanodon
   Angola 17 27
   Azerbaijan 5
   Belgium 1
   Bhutan 18
   Brazil 6
   Bulgaria 15
   Cambodia 31
   Chile 1
   Comoro Islands 14
   Congo Republic 30 **MS**31
   Croatia 1 2
   Cuba 17 49
   Gabon 76
   Ghana 1
   Great Britain 2
   Grenadines of Grenada 29
   Guinea 2 39
   Guyana 139
   Japan (Fukui Prefecture) 3
   Laos 3
   Liberia 95
   Madagascar 17 42
   Maldive Islands
      15 **MS**23 76 99 136
   Mali 2 5 **MS**26 28
   Micronesia 1 2
   Mongolia 19 32

   Mozambique **MS**54
   Nevis 29
   Niger 3
   Papua New Guinea **MS**57
   Romania 21
   St Vincent 24 87 105
   San Marino 8
   São Tomé e Principe 32
   Sierra Leone 6 48 60 61 64
   Solomon Islands 8
   South Korea 2
   Tanzania 11 15 43
   Uganda 2 **MS**40
   Vietnam 3
   West Berlin 1 2 3 4
Kentrosaurus [=*Kentrurosaurus*]
   Central African Republic 54
   Chad 32
   Comoro Islands 3
   Congo Republic 1 22
   Gambia 11 41
   Germany 2
   Ghana 36
   Guinea 77 **MS**78
   Guyana 109 116
   Lesotho 9
   Malawi 1
   Maldive Islands 32
   Micronesia 25
   Nevis 9
   Sierra Leone 10
   Uganda 1 25
Kentrurosaurus, see *Kentrosaurus*
Kritosaurus, see *Gryposaurus*
Lambeosaurus
   Ghana 14 49
   Grenada 10
   Grenadines of Grenada 28
   Guinea 54
   Madagascar 32
   Mozambique **MS**11
   St Vincent 121
   Sierra Leone 37
   Tanzania 47 95
   Uganda 31
   Zambia 13
Leaellynasaura
   Australia 2 **MS**7 9
   Guyana 41
   Lesotho 32

Maldive Islands 93
Leptoceratops
    Central African Republic 99
    Georgia 22
    Maldive Islands **MS**139
Lesothosaurus
    Angola 19 **MS**14
    Bhutan 19
    Congo Republic 20
    Gambia 54 55
    Guyana 44 111 117
    Lesotho 7 12 **MS**17
    Maldive Islands 85
    Mali 12 31
    St Vincent 12 59
    Sierra Leone 33
    Tanzania 23
Maiasaura
    Angola 18
    Grenada **MS**37
    Guinea 52
    Maldive Islands 36
    Sierra Leone 43
Microceratops, see *Graciliceratops*
Minmi
    Australia 6 **MS**7
    Guyana 42
    Kiribati 6
    Nevis 7
Monoclonius
    Angola 35
    Bulgaria 22
    Central African Republic 49
    Cuba 19
    Dominica 10
    Gabon 12
    Georgia 17 37
    Ghana 43
    Maldive Islands 17
    Mozambique **MS**11
    São Tomé e Principe 19
    Sierra Leone **MS**34
Montanoceratops
    Antigua 40
    Cambodia 8
    Georgia 27
    Maldive Islands 48 62
Muttaburrasaurus
    Australia 5 **MS**7
    Cambodia 27

    Cuba 54
    Democratic Congo 4
    Guyana **MS**114
    Laos 14
    Nevis 18
    North Korea 19
Nodosaurus
    Central African Republic 45
    Liberia 7
    Maldive Islands 47
    Mozambique **MS**4
    Niger 9
Ornithischian, unspecified
    São Tomé e Principe 29
Ornithopod, unspecified
    Guinea-Bissau 18 **MS**19
    Niuafo'ou 4 11
Ouranosaurus
    Angola 8 **MS**13 29
    Antigua 43
    Cambodia 21
    Central African Republic 80
    Chad 18
    Ghana 4
    Grenada 38
    Guinea 17 44 76 **MS**78
    Liberia 51
    Mali 25 47
    Nevis 17 33
    Niger 1 12
Pachycephalosaurus
    Antigua 12
    Barbuda 10
    Benin 29
    Cuba 53
    Gabon 6 48 71
    Ghana 48
    Grenadines of Grenada 5
    Guinea 51
    Guyana 147
    Liberia 10 53
    Maldive Islands 75
    St Vincent 93
    São Tomé e Principe 38
    Tanzania 27
    Togo 2 **MS**8 16
Pachyrhinosaurus
    Central African Republic **MS**25
    Gabon 112
    Ghana 18

Lesotho 34
Liberia 17
Micronesia 24
São Tomé e Principe 31
Sierra Leone 59 **MS**72
Panoplosaurus
Grenadines of Grenada 33
Guyana 31
Parasaurolophus
Angola 15
Antigua 6 21 22
Azerbaijan 7
Barbuda 4 19 20
Bequia 4
Central African Republic 59 92
Comoro Islands 64
Cuba 26 47
Dominica 8 47
Gabon 33 49 64 72
Gambia 96
Georgia 4 23
Ghana 15
Grenada 12 40
Grenadines of Grenada 7 23
Guinea 35 **MS**55
Guyana 83 148 170
Liberia 25 45 80 **MS**98
Maldive Islands 11 72
Micronesia **MS**18b,d
Mongolia 5
Mozambique **MS**11
Nauru 1
Nevis 34
Palau 54
Romania 16
St Kitts **MS**20
St Vincent 86 **MS**126
São Tomé e Principe 1
Tajikistan 4
Tanzania 57 97
Uganda **MS**28 39
United States of America 20
Vietnam 32
Zambia 16
Parksosaurus
Maldive Islands 51
Pentaceratops
Antigua 27
Azerbaijan 2
Barbuda 25

Dominica 17
Gabon 51 77 101
Georgia 24
Grenada 33
Maldive Islands 44
Singapore 1
Pinacosaurus
Central African Republic 53
Chad 5 13
Liberia 59
St Vincent 97
Polacanthus
Guinea 21
Guyana 104
Liberia 109
Niger 5
Tajikistan 7
Togo 1 **MS**8
Prenocephale
Cambodia 25
Gambia 73
Poland 26
Probactrosaurus
Liberia 8
Mongolia 17
Prosaurolophus
Antigua 39
Protoceratops
Afghanistan 4
Antigua 9 24 25 26
Barbuda 7 22 23 24
Bulgaria 11
Cambodia 7
Central African Republic **MS**71
Comoro Islands 52
Gabon 30
Gambia 65
Great Britain 5
Grenada 34
Guinea 49
Guyana 30
Kyrgyzstan 5
Laos 17
Liberia 42
Madagascar 4 30
Mongolia 3 7
Nauru 8
Niger **MS**11
Poland 25
St Vincent 53 112

    Sierra Leone **MS**34
    Tanzania 90
    Zambia 6
Psittacosaurus
    Antigua 31
    Benin 25
    Bequia 3
    Cambodia 6
    Dominica 43 65
    Gabon 40 94
    Grenada 45 66
    Grenadines of Grenada 36
    Guinea 27
    Guyana 32 105
    Liberia 41
    Libya 12
    Madagascar 20
    Maldive Islands 73
    Mali 35 36
    Micronesia 15
    Mongolia 11
    Mozambique 8
    Nevis 35
    North Korea 17
    Papua New Guinea **MS**7
    St Vincent 74
    São Tomé e Principe 39
    Tanzania 91
    Thailand 5 **MS**6
    Uganda 11
    Vietnam 30
    Zambia 27
Sabinosaurus
    Mexico 2
Saichania
    Cuba 56
    Gambia 68
    Poland 24
    Sierra Leone 67
Saurolophus
    Gambia 2
    Georgia 5
    Ghana 13
    Guyana **MS**114
    Kazakhstan 2
    Kyrgyzstan 2
    Malagasy Republic **MS**6
    Poland 22
    Russia 4
    Sierra Leone 26

    Tanzania 88
    Zambia 12
Sauropelta
    Central African Republic 101
    Comoro Islands 65
    Cuba 48
    Dominica **MS**30 33
    Madagascar 11
Scelidosaurus
    Ghana 32
    Guinea 14
    Guyana 108
    Liberia 39
    Maldive Islands 12 87
    Nevis 37
    St Vincent **MS**127
    Tanzania 52
Scolosaurus, see *Euoplocephalus*
Scutellosaurus
    Chad 24
    Congo Republic 21
    Democratic Congo 1
    Gambia 81
    Guyana 87
    Mali 13
    St Vincent **MS**127
    São Tomé e Principe 13
    Togo 6 **MS**8
    Zaire 1
Shantungosaurus
    Cambodia 28
    Liberia 61
Silvisaurus
    Tanzania 12
Stegoceras
    Cambodia 35
    Gabon 80
    Ghana 39
    Grenada 60
    Guyana 89 118
    Sierra Leone 25
    Tanzania 92
Stegosaurus
    Afghanistan 5
    Angola 26
    Antigua 10 41 **MS**67
    Azerbaijan 6
    Barbuda 8
    Benin 4 6
    Bequia 12

Bhutan 11 23
Bosnia and Herzegovina 3
Brazil 6
Bulgaria 8
Cambodia 36
Central African Republic
    4 15 30 69 **MS**100
Comoro Islands 43 67
Congo Republic 8 23 28 **MS**31
Cuba 18 55
Czech Republic 1
Dahomey 2
Dominica 4 20 40 64
Equatorial Guinea 2
Fujeira 4 9 13
Gabon 28 73 109
Gambia 18 52 67 102
Georgia 7
Great Britain 3
Grenada 19 61
Grenadines of Grenada 10 34
Guinea 6
Guinea-Bissau 6
Guyana 40 **MS**64 77
Hungary 8
Kiribati 7
Laos 19
Liberia 22 **MS**34 56 60
    MS98 110 **MS**111
Libya 25
Madagascar 22 34
Malagasy Republic 3
Malawi 2
Maldive Islands 1 14 79 102
Manama 2
Micronesia 7
Mongolia 16 25
Mozambique **MS**53 **MS**54
Nevis **MS**19 36
Niuafo'ou 7 **MS**10
North Korea 1 5
Palau 51
Poland 5
Romania 11 25
St Kitts 16
St Vincent **MS**17 47 85 **MS**126
San Marino 6
São Tomé e Principe 2 21 **MS**42
Senegal 4
Sierra Leone 51

Somalia 3
Tajikistan 2
Tanzania 5 6 20 59 79 84 86
Togo 12
Turks and Caicos Islands 16
Uganda 26
United States of America 2 6 16
Vietnam 5
Zambia 8

Struthiosaurus
    Angola 36
    Romania 14 27 30 **MS**32

Stygimoloch
    Gambia 43
    Zambia **MS**28

Styracosaurus
    Afghanistan 2
    Antigua 29
    Barbuda 27
    Bulgaria 17
    Cambodia 10
    Canada 9
    Central African Republic 19 52
    Chad 9 17
    Comoro Islands 7
    Cuba 25
    Democratic Congo 7 **MS**8
    Equatorial Guinea 6 **MS**12
    Gabon 78
    Gambia 58
    Ghana 17
    Guyana **MS**64 **MS**140
    Liberia 26
    Madagascar 5 **MS**43
    Maldive Islands
        8 83 106 128 **MS**139
    Manama 5
    Mozambique **MS**512
    North Korea **MS**20 **MS**21
    Poland 7
    St Vincent **MS**66
    Sierra Leone **MS**34 49 **MS**72
    Tanzania 34 40
    Uzbekistan 4
    Vietnam 9

Talarurus
    Mongolia 2 26

Telmatosaurus
    Romania 29 **MS**32

Tenontosaurus

Dinosaurs and other Prehistoric Animals on Stamps

    Bequia 1
    Comoro Islands 51
    Grenada **MS**78
    Grenadines of Grenada **MS**48
    Guinea 40
    Libya 8
    Madagascar **MS**15
    Maldive Islands 18 34
    Nevis 4
    Sierra Leone 40
Torosaurus
    Dominica 5 **MS**9
    Gabon 70
    Guyana 162 **MS**171
    Liberia 6 44 81 107
    Micronesia **MS**18
    Mozambique 9
Trachodon, see *Anatotitan*
Triceratops
    Angola **MS**37
    Antigua 8 **MS**67
    Barbuda 6
    Benin 28
    Bequia 10
    Bhutan 12 22 **MS**31
    Bulgaria 12
    Cambodia 11
    Central African Republic
        2 39 64 95
    Congo Republic 27 **MS**31
    Cuba 22 27
    Dominica **MS**30 50
    Equatorial Guinea 7 11
    Fujeira 2 7 11
    Gabon 7 99
    Gambia **MS**38 46 100
    Georgia 8
    Ghana 16
    Great Britain 6
    Grenada 7 36 59 **MS**65
    Grenadines of Grenada 4 31
    Guinea **MS**7 69
    Guyana 72 150
    Liberia 33 82
    Madagascar 13 24 41
    Malagasy Republic 5
    Malawi **MS**4
    Maldive Islands 4 21 **MS**23 67 74
    Mali 7 8
    Micronesia 12 14

    Mongolia **MS**29 33
    Mozambique 10
    Namibia **MS**5
    Nauru 4
    Nevis **MS**19
    Nicaragua 3
    Niuafo'ou 5 12
    Palau 57 62
    Romania 10
    St Kitts 11
    St Vincent **MS**17
        MS66 88 **MS**126
    San Marino 9
    São Tomé e Principe 3
    Senegal 3
    Sierra Leone **MS**34 42 **MS**53 69
    Somalia 4 **MS**5
    Tanzania 7 61
    Togo 14
    Turks and Caicos Islands
        12 **MS**18
    Uganda 22
    Vietnam 7
    Zambia 9
Tsintaosaurus
    Central African Republic 48
    Mali 23
    Uganda 16
    Vietnam 28
Tuojiangosaurus
    Angola 34
    Cambodia 17
    Central African Republic 48
    Guyana 28
    Nevis 14
Wuerhosaurus
    Cambodia 26
    Lesotho 43
Yandusaurus
    Maldive Islands 88
Yingshanosaurus
    Palau 64

```
Order/Category No. 3
```
UNSPECIFIED DINOSAURS

Dinosaur, unspecified
    Georgia 27
    Guinea-Bissau 21
    Kuwait 3

Lesotho 1
Palau **MS**60a,b

Order/Category No. 4
PTEROSAURIA
(Pterosaurs - Flying reptiles)

Anurognathus
    Bhutan 15
    Gabon 5
    Gambia 47
    Grenadines of Grenada 15
    Nicaragua 26
Batrachognathus
    Palau 30
Campylognathus
    Palau 28
Cearadactylus
    Guyana 23
    Maldive Islands 132
    St Vincent 215
Criorhynchus
    Democratic Congo 6
    Gabon 42
    Gambia 99
    Guyana 90 91 131
Ctenochasma
    Palau 34
Dimorphodon
    Benin 8
    Bhutan 2 29
    Central African Republic 11
    Comoro Islands 30 49
    Dominica 14
    Gabon 27 92
    Ghana **MS**51
    Grenada 15 30
    Guinea 67
    Guyana 68 135 152
    Hungary 7
    Liberia 4
    Madagascar 10
    Maldive Islands 28 90
    Nicaragua 16 25
    Niger 15
    Palau 22
    St Vincent 1 42
    São Tomé e Principe 20
    Sierra Leone 3
    Tanzania 45
    Uganda 21
    Yemen Republic 5
Dorygnathus
    Palau 21
Dsungaripterus
    Antigua 37
    Benin 16
    Cuba 51
Eudimorphodon
    Comoro Islands 34 60
    Gabon 3
    Ghana 21
    Guinea 65
    Guyana 24 91 133
    Lesotho 37
    Liberia 3 65
    Madagascar 12
    St Vincent 7 115
Gallodactylus
    Palau 29
Germanodactylus
    Grenada 14
Hatzegopteryx
    Romania 31 **MS**32
Mesadactylus
    Chad 40
    Comoro Islands 29
Muzquizopteryx
    Mexico 1
Nyctosaurus
    Lesotho 36
    Palau 23
Ornithocheirus
    Australia 1 **MS**7 8
    Central African Republic 65
    Liberia 86
Ornithodesmus
    Comoro Islands 35
    Lesotho 42
    Palau 25
Peteinosaurus
    Comoro Islands 59
    Gabon 53
    Gambia 72 95
    Ghana 19
    Guyana 130
    Lesotho 39
    Palau 32
    Tanzania 94

Phobetor
    Azerbaijan **MS**8
    Grenada 5
Pteranodon
    Aden Protectorate States –
        Qu'aiti State in Hadhramaut 2
    Antigua 3 25 **MS**53
    Barbuda 1 23
    Bequia **MS**13
    Bhutan 14 **MS**31
    Central African Republic
        MS25 89
    Chad 41
    Comoro Islands 27 32 48
    Congo Republic 13
    Cuba 15 53
    Dominica 44 **MS**53
    Equatorial Guinea 3
    Gabon 13 14 74 104
    Gambia 14 48 83
    Georgia 11 31
    Ghana 33
    Grenada 1 3 **MS**26
    Grenadines of Grenada 6 12
    Guyana 22 47 79 129 143 158
        MS171
    Laos **MS**7
    Lesotho 4
    Liberia 48 **MS**85 93 94
    Libya 26
    Madagascar 14
    Maldive Islands 5 61 97
    Micronesia 5 **MS**18
    Mongolia 28
    Mozambique **MS**54
    Nicaragua 7 8 11 29
    Niger 18
    Niuafo'ou 7 **MS**10
    North Korea 1
    Palau 18 19 55
    Poland 29
    St Vincent 6 10 **MS**66 82 113
    San Marino 3
    São Tomé e Principe **MS**7 8
    Sierra Leone 2 24 63
    Solomon Islands 3
    Somalia 2
    Sweden 2
    Tanzania 3 58
    Uganda 6 14 29

    United States of America 5
    Vietnam 8
Pterodactyl, unspecified
    Mozambique **MS**11
    Palau 20
Pterodactylus
    Bhutan 13
    Bulgaria 19
    Comoro Islands 33 47
    Cuba 52
    East Germany 1
    Gabon 37 43 91
    Georgia 13 29
    Ghana 31
    Grenada 18
    Guyana 25
    Liberia 35
    Maldive Islands 131
    Nicaragua **MS**36
    Palau 24
    St Vincent 43 45 **MS**129
    Sierra Leone 4
    Turks and Caicos Islands 14
Pterodaustro
    Bhutan 4
    Guyana 132
    Liberia 12
    Nicaragua 28
    Palau 66
    Uganda 27
Pterosaur, unspecified
    Ascension 1 2 3 4
    Central African Republic 76
    Falkland Islands 1 2 3 4
    Grenada 74 76
    Grenadines of Grenada 44 46
    Guinea-Bissau **MS**33
    Maldive Islands 133
    Mauritius 1 2 3 4 **MS**5
    Micronesia **MS**18
    Mozambique **MS**11
    New Zealand 3
    Niuafo'ou 4 11
    North Korea 6
    St Helena 1 2 3 4
    São Tomé e Principe 23 25 34
Quetzalcoatlus
    Bequia **MS**13
    Central African Republic **MS**25
    Chad 43

Comoro Islands 28 46
Cuba 55
Gambia 71
Ghana 20
Grenada 2 52
Guinea-Bissau **MS**26
Guyana 35 48 **MS**115 128
Liberia 64
Maldive Islands 40
Nauru 2
Niger 14
St Vincent 11 54
Tanzania **MS**100
Uganda 13
Rhamphorhynchus
   Aden Protectorate States –
     Qu'aiti State in Hadhramaut 6
   Benin 13
   Bulgaria 10
   Central African Republic 10 61
     MS71 88
   Chad 37
   Comoro Islands 31 45
   Dahomey 1
   Dominica 15 35
   Equatorial Guinea 3
   Gabon 83
   Gambia 16 49
   Georgia 12 30
   Ghana 8
   Grenada 16
   Grenadines of Grenada 13
   Guyana 37 80 177
   Kampuchea 4
   Kiribati 2
   Lesotho 27
   Liberia 47
   Madagascar 13
   Maldive Islands 91
   Mozambique **MS**11
   Nicaragua 27
   Palau 2 4 5 35 48
   Poland 9
   St Vincent 5 44 81
   São Tomé e Principe **MS**14
   Sierra Leone 1 **MS**35 **MS**70
   Tanzania **MS**13 51
   United States of America 2
   Uzbekistan 3
   Vietnam 11

Scaphognathus
   Benin 15
   Cuba 54
   Gabon 103
   Palau 31
Scleromochlus
   Gambia 12
Sharovipteryx
   Comoro Islands 56
   Guyana 136
   Niger 16
Sordes
   Benin 14
   Cuba 56
   Gabon 1
   Grenada 29
   Guinea 66
   Guyana 34
   Kazakhstan 4
   Maldive Islands 134
   Nicaragua 24
   Niger 13
   Russia 1
   Sierra Leone 65
   Tanzania 37 75 **MS**76
Tropeognathus
   Chad 42
   Grenada 4
   Lesotho 40

Order/Category No. 5
CROCODYLIA (Crocodilians)

Alligator, unspecified giant prehistoric
   Dominica 16
Crocodylus
   Cuba 10
   Namibia 4
Deinosuchus [=*Phobosuchus*]
   Gabon 32
   São Tomé e Principe 34
Diplocynodon
   West Germany 3
Diplosaurus
   Cambodia 33
Geosaurus
   Central African Republic 84
Goniopholis
   United States of America 18

Mekosuchus
    New Caledonia 2
Metriorhynchus
    Ascension 6 11
    Nicaragua 17
Phobosuchus, see *Deinosuchus*
Pristichampsus
    West Germany 3
Protosuchus
    Cuba 37
Purussaurus
    Peru **MS**5
Sarcosuchus
    Central African Republic
        105 **MS**107
    Chad 18
    Niger 2 29
Steneosaurus
    Chad 36
    St Vincent 26 37
    Sierra Leone 15
Thoracosaurus
    Sweden 2
Volia
    Fiji 1

Order/Category No. 6
THECODONTIA
(Thecodontians)

Chasmatosaurus
    Gambia 87
    Transkei 7
Desmatosuchus
    Central African Republic
        MS42
Erythrosuchus
    Ghana 38
Euparkeria
    Cambodia 13
    Guinea 9
    Guyana 156
    South Africa 3 **MS**5
Hesperosuchus
    Ghana 50
Lagosuchus
    Guyana **MS**115 137
    Tanzania 99
Longisquama
    Benin 7 23

    Gabon 10
Ornithosuchus
    Cuba 34
    Gambia 8 **MS**13
    Ghana 35
    Guinea 12
Postosuchus
    São Tomé e Principe **MS**14
Rutiodon
    Central African Republic 32
    Maldive Islands 38
Saltoposuchus
    Central African Republic 9
Teratosaurus
    Micronesia **MS**18
Thecodontian, unspecified
    St Vincent 50

Order/Category No. 7
SQUAMATA (Lizards/snakes)

Angolosaurus
    Angola 1
Clidastes
    Tristan da Cunha **MS**1
Kuehneosaurus
    Central African Republic 37
    Maldive Islands 30
Megalania
    Australia 26
Mosasaur, unspecified
    British Antarctic Territory 16
    Mozambique **MS**5
    St Vincent 77
Mosasaurus
    Ascension 7 12
    Barbados 4
    Guyana 101
    Kazakhstan 5
    Liberia 32
    Madagascar 3
    Maldive Islands 65
    Montserrat 9
    Sierra Leone 19
    Somalia **MS**12
    Vietnam 6
Pachyophis (snake)
    Yugoslavia 2
Palaeosaniwa
    United States of America 26

Platecarpus
    Canada 11
    Mozambique **MS5**
    Nicaragua **MS36**
    Tristan da Cunha **MS1**
Plotosaurus
    Mozambique **MS5**
Tylosaurus
    Aden Protectorate States –
        Qu'aiti State in Hadhramaut 2
    Central African Republic**MS25**
    Guinea 3
    Nicaragua 8
    Niger 26
    St Vincent 34

```
Order/Category No. 8
SPHENODONTIA
(Sphenodontids)
```

Opisthias
    United States of America 19

```
Order/Category No. 9
 RHYNCHOCEPHALIA
(Rhynchocephalians)
```

Scaphonyx
    Chad 30
    Mali 10

```
Order/Category No. 10
THERAPSIDA
(Therapsids -
Mammal-like reptiles)
```

Cynodont, unspecified
    Guyana 60
    Mozambique **MS11**
Cynognathus
    Central African Republic 36
    Libya 17
    Mali 11
    North Korea 3
    Poland 15
Diarthrognathus
    Gambia 25

    Guyana 56
Diictodon
    Transkei 6
Endothiodon
    Mozambique 2
Estemmenosuchus
    Gambia 33
    Guyana 57
Kannemeyeria
    Chad 28
Luangwa
    Zambia 3
Lystrosaurus
    Antigua 66
    British Antarctic Territory 1
    Central African Republic 34
    Chad 31
    Gambia 20
    Guyana 52
    Libya 20
    Mozambique **MS11**
    São Tomé e Principe 11
    Sierra Leone **MS71**
    South Africa 2 **MS5**
Moschops
    Comoro Islands 2
    Congo Republic 5
    Guyana 51
Oudenodon
    Zambia 1
Placerias
    Central African Republic 31
Rubidgea
    Transkei 8
    Zambia 1
Sauroctonus
    Comoro Islands 5
    Kampuchea 2
Thrinaxodon
    South Africa 4 **MS5**
Tritylodon
    Lesotho 4
Zambiasaurus
    Zambia 2

```
Order/Category No. 11
PELYCOSAURIA
(Pelycosaurs - Sail reptiles)
```

Dimetrodon
    Central African Republic 70 98
    Equatorial Guinea 1
    Gabon 4
    Grenada 44 **MS**78
    Grenadines of Grenada **MS**48
    Guinea 1
    Guyana 53
    Maldive Islands 2
    Mali 1 4
    Montserrat 4
    Mozambique **MS**4
    Nicaragua 4
    North Korea 3
    St Kitts 14
    St Vincent 84
    São Tomé e Principe 6
    Tanzania **MS**38 54 **MS**76
    Uganda 37 45
    Vietnam 15
    Zambia 4
Edaphosaurus
    Antigua 1 2
    Bulgaria 9
    Comoro Islands 1
    Fujeira 1 5 12
    Guinea-Bissau 2
    Kampuchea 1
    Poland 1
    São Tomé e Principe 18
    Vietnam 21
    Yemen Republic 4
Pelycosaur, unspecified
    Cuba 23
Varanosaurus
    Mali 41

Order/Category No. 12
SAUROPTERYGIA
(Plesiosaurs and Nothosaurs)

'Aramberri monster'
    Mexico 3
Ceresiosaurus
    Comoro Islands 55
    Gabon 55
    Guyana 94 119
    Lesotho 18
    Mozambique **MS**5
    Turks and Caicos Islands 25
Cryptoclidus
    Central African Republic 14
    Congo Republic 7
    Mozambique **MS**5
    Poland 2
    St Vincent 39
Dolichorhynchops
    St Vincent 32
Elasmosaurus
    Ascension 8 13
    Barbados 3
    Grenada **MS**37
    Guinea **MS**74
    Guyana 92
    Liberia 67
    Maldive Islands 25
    Montserrat 6
    St Vincent 117
    San Marino 4
    Turks and Caicos Islands 15 19
Hydrotherosaurus
    St Kitts 4 9
Keichousaurus
    Chad 39
Kronosaur, unspecified
    Palau 13 16 17
Kronosaurus
    Antigua 15
    Argentine Republic **MS**11
    Barbuda 13
    Benin 20
    Guinea 57
    Liberia 15
    St Vincent 118
    Turks and Caicos Islands 30
Liopleurodon
    Guinea 83 **MS**85
    Nicaragua 32
    St Kitts 3 8
    Turks and Caicos Islands 26
Macroplata
    Gabon 107
    Gambia 34
    Maldive Islands **MS**139
    Turks and Caicos Islands 24
Mauisaurus
    New Zealand 5
Muraenosaurus
    Gambia 36

Maldive Islands **MS**139
Turks and Caicos Islands 28
Nessiteras
   Maldive Islands **MS**24
Neusticosaurus
   Switzerland 5
Nothosaurus
   Guyana 97 120
   Liberia 72
   Montserrat 8
   Sierra Leone 8
   Somalia 11
Peloneustes
   Benin 11
   Uganda 5
Pistosaurus
   Gabon 13
Plesiosaur, unspecified
   Ascension 1 2 3 4
   British Antarctic Territory 16
   Falkland Islands 1 2 3 4
   France 5
   Guyana 62
   Lesotho 45
   Mauritius 1 2 3 4
   Monaco 1
   Nicaragua 1 23
   Palau 3 4 6 7 8 9 10 11
      12 14 15 74
   St Helena 1 2 3 4
Plesiosaurus
   Antigua 17
   Ascension 9 14
   Barbados 1
   Barbuda 15
   Bulgaria 13
   Central African Republic 86
   Chile 2
   Gabon 35
   Grenada 22 72
   Grenadines of Grenada 42
   Kazakhstan 3
   Montserrat 7
   Mozambique **MS**5
   Niuafo'ou **MS**13
   Romania 9
   St Vincent 35 91
   São Tomé e Principe 37
   Sierra Leone 11
   Turks and Caicos Islands 20

   Vietnam 1
Pliosaur, unspecified
   Equatorial Guinea **MS**8
   Gabon 56
   Guyana 166
   Liberia 70
Pliosaurus
   Nevis **MS**40
Rhomaleosaurus
   Guyana 93 121
   Lesotho 19
   Tanzania **MS**100
Thaumatosaurus
   San Marino 7
Trinacromerum
   Tristan da Cunha **MS**1
Wellesiosaurus
   Japan 1
Woolungasaurus
   Australia 15

Order/Category No. 13
ICHTHYOSAURIA
(Ichthyosaurs - Fish reptiles)

Cymbospondylus
   Gabon 20
   Guinea 56
   Liberia 99
Eurhinosaurus
   Guinea 59
   St Vincent 38
   Sierra Leone 17
Grendelius
   Gambia 97
   Guyana 96 122 175
Ichthyosaur, unspecified
   France 5
   Gabon 31 58
   Guyana 165 **MS**171
   Liberia 73
   Monaco 1
   Nicaragua 1
   Palau 74
   Somalia 6
Ichthyosaurus
   Antigua 16
   Ascension 5 10
   Barbados 2
   Barbuda 14

Benin 20
Bhutan **MS**31
Central African Republic 83
Comoro Islands 20
Gabon 106
Grenada 71
Grenadines of Grenada 41
Guinea 58
Maldive Islands 124
Mozambique **MS**5
Nicaragua 18
North Korea 7
St Vincent 90
São Tomé e Principe 37
Turks and Caicos Islands 21
Yemen Republic 7

Mixosaurus
Comoro Islands 54
Gabon 62
Guinea 64
Guyana 98 123
Lesotho 21
Sierra Leone 20

Omphalosaurus
Turks and Caicos Islands 10

Ophthalmosaurus
Benin 11
Guinea 61
Guyana 174 **MS**184

Shonisaurus
Gambia 35
Guinea 62
Maldive Islands 125
Micronesia 6
Nicaragua 33
St Vincent 116
São Tomé e Principe 12

Stenopterygius
Comoro Islands 19
Guinea 60
St Vincent 36
São Tomé e Principe **MS**7
Sierra Leone 16

Temnodontosaurus
Guinea 63

Order/Category No. 14
PLACODONTIA
(Placodontians)

Henodus [sic *Honodus*]
Mozambique **MS**6
Sierra Leone 14
Turks and Caicos Islands 27

Placochelys
Gabon 18
Hungary 3
Mozambique **MS**5
Nicaragua 35

Placodus
Guyana 99 125
Mali 43
St Kitts 2 7
Sierra Leone 18
Somalia 9
Turks and Caicos Islands 29

Order/Category No. 15
CHELONIA
(Turtles and Tortoises)

Archelon
Antigua 18
Barbados 5
Barbuda 16
Gambia 37
Guinea 84 **MS**85
Liberia 100
Maldive Islands 126
Micronesia 10
Mozambique **MS**5
New Zealand 21
Tristan da Cunha **MS**1
Turks and Caicos Islands 22

Caretta
St Kitts 5 10

Geochelone
Namibia 1

Labidosaurus
Guinea 72

Meiolania
New Caledonia 3

Mongolemys
Mongolia 9

Ninjemys
Australia 13

Protostega
St Vincent 41

Testudinites
Uruguay 12

Tortoise, unspecified fossil
    Wallis and Fortuna Islands 1

```
Order/Category No. 16
```
EARLY REPTILES

Askeptosaurus
    Grenada 35
    Turks and Caicos Islands 23
Batrachosaurus
    St Vincent 125
Bradysaurus
    South Africa 1 **MS**5
Coelurosauravus
    Comoro Islands 53
Hylonomus
    Canada 6
Hypsognathus
    Ghana 37
Mesosaurus
    Afghanistan 1
    Bulgaria 21
    Comoro Islands 25 **MS**69
    Guinea 71
    Guinea-Bissau 3
    Guyana 4659 95 124
    Nicaragua 31
    Niger 28
    Poland 4
    St Kitts 1 6
    St Vincent 31
    Somalia 10
    Turks and Caicos Islands **MS**9
    Uruguay 9
    Uzbekistan 2
Petrolacosaurus
    Mozambique **MS**4
Protorosaurus
    Gabon 98

```
Class No. 4 AMPHIBIA
(Amphibians)
```

Acanthostega
    Gabon 54 65
Andrias
    Switzerland 2
Cacops [=*Giantoneris*]
    Gambia 24 79
    Guyana 55
    Liberia 69
Crassigyrinus
    Nicaragua 34
Diplocaulus
    Gabon 61
Eogyrinus
    Guyana 168
Eryops
    Benin 10
    Guyana 164
Gerrothorax
    Gabon 60
Giantoneris, see *Cacops*
Ichthyostega
    Congo Republic 9
    Gambia 80
    Guyana 163
    Liberia 68
    Niuafo'ou 6 **MS**10
    Poland 13
Mastodonsaurus
    Central African Republic **MS**25
    Kampuchea 3
    Poland 14
Metoposaurus
    Niger 25
Palaeobatrachus
    Czechoslovakia 2
    East Germany 4
    Niger 25
Paracyclotosaurus
    Australia 14
Pholidogaster
    Gabon 59
Platyhystrix
    Grenadines of Grenada 18
Platymantis
    Fiji 4
Seymouria
    Vietnam 13
Xenopus
    Libya 3

```
Class No. 5 OSTEICHTHYES (Bony
Fishes)
```

Aipichthyoides
    Israel **MS**4

Archaeoteuthis
    Switzerland 4
Belonostomus
    Brazil 1
Caturus
    St Vincent 40
Chaetodon
    Yugoslavia 3
Clupea
    Hungary 1
Coelacanth, prehistoric
    Guyana 100 127
Dapedius
    Luxembourg 4
Enchodus
    Gabon 21
Eurypholis
    Grenada 70
    Grenadines of Grenada 40
Eusthenopteron
    Canada 5
    Niuafo'ou 6 **MS**10
    Poland 12
Fish, unspecified fossil
    Ascension 1 2 3 4
    Falkland Islands 1 2 3 4
    Libya 2
    Mauritius 639 640 641 642
    Niuafo'ou 1 **MS**10
    St Helena 1 2 3 4
    Slovenia 6
    Somalia 6
    Zimbabwe 1
Griphognathus
    Nicaragua 22
Gyroptychius
    Nicaragua 22
Lepisosteus
    Gambia **MS**94
Mene
    Greece 1
    Libya 22
    Monaco 2
Mesodon
    Libya 23
Microceratodus
    Angola 3
Nematonotus
    Lebanon 2
Numidopleura
    Tunisia 3
Onsong fish, fossil
    North Korea 8
Panderichthys
    Gambia 77
Pycnosteroides
    Liberia 13
Sarcopterygian, unspecified fossil
    Comoro Islands **MS**69
Varnerxiphactinus
    Grenada 73
    Grenadines of Grenada 43
Vinctifer, see *Belonostomus*
Xiphactinus
    Liberia 101

Class No. 6 CHONDRICHTHYES (Cartilaginous Fishes - Sharks and Rays)

Aellopos [=*Spathobathis*]
    Gabon 35
Carcharocles [=*Carcharodon*]
    [=*Procarcharodon*]
    Angola 2
    Dominica 27
    New Caledonia 4 **MS**5a,b,c
    Tristan da Cunha **MS**2
Carcharodon, see *Carcharocles*
Cladoselache
    Gabon 36
Deltoptychius
    Gabon 32
Hexanchus
    Tristan da Cunha **MS**2
Ischyodus
    Gabon 17
Myliobatis
    Tristan da Cunha **MS**2
Procarcharodon, see *Carcharocles*
Scapanorhynchus
    Gabon 34
Shark, unspecified prehistoric
    Denmark 2 **MS**5
    Liechtenstein 4
Spathobathis, see *Aellopus*
Squalicorax
    St Vincent 33
Stethacanthus

        Gabon 57
        Guyana 126
        Lesotho 22
Tristychius
        Grenada **MS**37
Xenacanthus
        Comoro Islands 22
        Gabon 16
        Nicaragua **MS**36

Class No. 7 PLACODERMI
(Placoderms - Armoured Fishes)

Bothriolepis
        Madagascar 44
        Nicaragua **MS**36
Dinichthys
        Dominica 26
        Nicaragua 6
        Poland 11
Dunkleosteus
        Benin 9 24
        Gabon 19
        Grenada 27
        Guyana 167
        Lesotho 23
        Liberia 71 102
        Sierra Leone **MS**73
Mcnamaraspis
        Australia 12
Palaeospondylus
        Gabon 24

Class No. 8 AGNATHA
(Agnathans -
Lampreys and Ostracoderms)

    Conodont, unspecified
        Canada 7
Pteraspis
        Nicaragua 19
Thyestes
        Russia 5

SECTION 2: Invertebrates

Phylum No. 1 ECHINODERMATA
(Starfishes, Sea Urchins, etc)

Ascocystites
        Czech Republic **MS**54
Carolicrinus
        Czech Republic **MS**54
Crinoid, unspecified fossil
        Somalia 8
Echinocorys
        Denmark 3 **MS**5
Echinoderm, unspecified fossil
        Bosnia and Herzegovina 1
        Croatia 3
Rotula
        Angola 5
Sea urchin, fossil
        Liechtenstein 3
Solaster
        Isle of Man 3
Starfish, fossil
        Slovenia 4

Phylum No. 2 BRACHIOPODA
(Brachiopods - Lamp Shells)

Brachiopod, unspecified fossil
        Mauritania 1 3
        Somalia 8
Karavankina
        Slovenia 2
Lingulella
        British Antarctic Territory 3
Sieberella
        Czech Republic **MS**4
Terebratula
        Ethiopia 2 3

Phylum No. 3 TRILOBITA
(Trilobites)

Asaphus
        Aland Islands 1
Cheirurus
        Czech Republic **MS**4
Deiphon

Czech Republic **MS**4
Kaolishania
    China (People's Republic) 1
Lyriaspis
    British Antarctic Territory 5
Odontopleura
    East Germany 3
Olenoides
    Gambia **MS**103
Paladin
    Slovenia 3
Paracybeloides
    Gabon 22
Paradoxides
    Canada 3
Pseudophillipsia
    Tunisia 1
Ptychoparia
    North Korea 13
Redlichia
    North Korea 12
Selenopeltis
    Czechoslovakia 4
Trilobite, unspecified
    Ascension 1 2 3 4
    Central African Republic 85
    Falkland Islands 1 2 3 4
    French Territory of
        the Afars and the Issas 1
    Guinea 82 **MS**85
    Mauritania 2 4
    Mauritius 1 2 3 4
    Niuafo'ou 3 **MS**10
    St Helena 1 2 3 4
    Somalia 7
    United States of America 3
Triplagnostus
    British Antarctic Territory 4
Xystridura
    Dominica 29

Phylum No. 4 CHELICERATA
(Chelicerates -
Sea Scorpions, Arachnids, etc)

Eurypterus
    Canada 4

Phylum No. 5 CRUSTACEA
(Crustaceans)

Calcinoplanx
    North Korea 22
Crustacean, Cambrian
    Niuafo'ou 3 **MS**10
Eryon
    Libya 24
Hoploparia
    British Antarctic Territory 14

Phylum No. 6 UNIRAMIA
(Insects, Millipedes,
Centipedes, etc)

Bibio
    Slovenia 5
Dragonfly, unspecified giant prehistoric
    Uganda 20
Insect, unspecified prehistoric
    Central African Republic 41
Libanobythus
    Lebanon 1
Meganeura
    Central African Republic 81
    Comoro Islands 57
    Gabon 9
    Niuafo'ou 6 **MS**10
    Uzbekistan 1
Wasp, prehistoric
    Poland 21

Phylum No. 7 MOLLUSCA
(Molluscs)

Class/Category No. 1
AMMONOIDEA
(Ammonite Cephalopods)

Ainoceras
    British Antarctic Territory 12
Ammonite, unspecified
    Argentine Republic 12
    Ascension 1 2 3 4
    Bosnia and Herzegovina 2
    Czechoslovakia 5

Falkland Islands 1 2 3 4
French Territory of the
   Afars and the Issas 1
Japan 2
Liberia 32
Liechtenstein 2
Malagasy Republic 1
Mauritius 1 2 3 4
Nicaragua 20
Palau **MS**1
St Helena 1 2 3 4
Somalia 7

Anolcites
   Austria 2

Berbericeras
   Algeria 1

Calliphylloceras
   Italy 2

Coeloceras
   Luxembourg 3

Echioceras
   Gabon 63

Gaudryceras
   Transkei 1

Gunnarites
   British Antarctic Territory 13

Hemihaploceras
   Italy 2

Heraclites
   Austria 2

Hildoceras
   Italy 2

Hypacanthoplites
   Liechtenstein 1

Hypophylloceras
   Czechoslovakia 1

Lewesiceras
   Central African Republic 87

Lytoceras
   Switzerland 1

Lytodiscoides
   Mozambique 1

Mantelliceras
   Tunisia 5

Nostoceras
   Angola 4

Parapuzosia
   Denmark 1 **MS**5

Paraulacosphinctes
   Austria 1

Perisphinctes
   Cuba 2

Platypleuroceras
   Netherlands 1

Proeucalycoceras
   Israel **MS**4

Prolecanites
   Isle of Man 4

Reineckia
   Hungary 2

Roemoceras
   Peru 4

Sanmartinoceras
   British Antarctic Territory 7

Class/Category No. 2 OTHER CEPHALOPODA

Aturia
   Yugoslavia 1
Belemnite, unspecified
   Lesotho 26
   Somalia **MS**12

Belemnopsis
   British Antarctic Territory 6
Nautiloid, unspecified
   Dominica 28
   Gabon 23
   Liberia 14 16
   Nicaragua 23

Ophioceras
   Czech Republic **MS**4

Tommotia
   Lesotho 24

Class/Category No. 3 BIVALVIA (Bivalves - Clams, etc)

Aucellina
   British Antarctic Territory 9

Chlamys, fossil
   Czechoslovakia 3

Clinocardium
   North Korea 23

Cucullaea
   Ethiopia 4

Gryphaea

    Luxembourg 2
    Switzerland 3
Mediterraneotrigonia
    Tunisia 2
Neithea
    Transkei 3
Ostrea, fossil
    Ethiopia 5
    North Korea 11
Pecten, fossil
    Luxembourg 1
Pinna, fossil
    British Antarctic Territory 8
Pterotrigonia
    British Antarctic Territory 10
Trigonia, fossil
    Ethiopia 6
Virgotrigonia
    Peru 1

Class/Category No. 4
GASTROPODA
(Gastropods - Snails, etc)

Euamophalus
    Aland Islands 2
Gastropod, unspecified
    Slovenia 7
Micreschara
    Tunisia 4
Nassa [=*Nassarius*]
    Isle of Man 1
Oolitica
    Austria 2
Perissoptera
    British Antarctic Territory 11
Pleurotomaria
    Denmark 4 **MS5**
Pseudomelania
    Transkei 1
Pugilina
    Transkei 4
Turritella, fossil
    Algeria 2
Viviparus, fossil
    Croatia 4

Class/Category No. 5
OTHER MOLLUSCS

Molluscs, unspecified fossil
    Croatia 3
    North Korea 26

Phylum No. 8 CNIDARIA
(Jellyfishes, etc)

Coral, unspecified fossil
    North Korea 25
    Somalia 8
Jellyfish, prehistoric
    Niuafo'ou 2

Phylum No. 9 PORIFERA
(Sponges)

Sponge, prehistoric
    Niuafo'ou 2

Phylum No. 10 ARCHAEOCYATHA
(Archaeocyathans)

Monocyathus
    British Antarctic Territory 2

Phylum No. 11 PROTOZOA
(Single-celled animals)

Schwagerina
    Slovenia 1

Phylum/Category No. 12
EARLY INVERTEBRATES

Anomalocaris
    China (People's Republic) 5
    Lesotho 20
Charniodiscus
    Australia 21 **MS22**
Dickinsonia

Australia 17 **MS**22
Inaria
Australia 20 **MS**22
Kimberella
Australia 19 **MS**22
Opabinia
Canada 2
Sanctacaris
Lesotho 25
Spriggina
Australia 18 **MS**22
Tribrachidium
Australia 16 **MS**22

APPENDIX I
A SELECTION OF CRYPTOZOOLOGICAL STAMPS

As noted in the Introduction to this catalogue, a number of mystery beasts (cryptids) have been put forward at one time or another as prehistoric survivors, e.g. a popular identity for the Loch Ness monster is an evolved modern-day plesiosaur, and the bigfoot has often been suggested to be a surviving *Gigantopithecus*. Consequently, it seemed nothing if not apt to include in this catalogue a selection of various former and present-day cryptids that have appeared on stamps. Former cryptids include such famous examples as the okapi, coelacanth, and Vu Quang ox, which although well known to local people were once dismissed as mythical beasts by zoologists until formally discovered and found to be species hitherto unknown and undescribed by science. Also included are some major new and rediscovered animals, such as the giant rift tubeworms, takahe, and Chacoan peccary.

I have not included stamps depicting traditional mythical beasts such as dragons, unicorns, centaurs, flying horses, etc. However, I have included the Black Dog, though I freely confess that it is much more likely to be a zooform entity (i.e. paranormal) than a strictly corporeal cryptid.

Incidentally, an excellent online source of information and illustrations appertaining to cryptozoology and philately can be accessed at: http://www.pibburns.com/cryptost.htm

In the following listing, each stamp is identified by its country of issue, its year of issue, its number (i.e. whether it is the first, second, third, etc stamp depicting a given cryptid to be issued by that country), and its denomination. Please note: the stamps contained in this Appendix are not included in any of this catalogue's listings sections.

Ambun Beast (=Palorchestid Diprotodont?)
Papua New Guinea 1970, 1 5c

Bigfoot/Sasquatch
Canada 1980, 1 39c

Black Dog
Isle of Man 1997, 1 21p
Jersey 1997, 1 31p

Bunyip
Australia 1994, 1 45c, 2 45c, 3 90c, 4 $1.35

Chacoan Peccary *Catagonus wagneri*
Argentine Republic 2002, 1 $1

Dinosaurs and other Prehistoric Animals on Stamps

Coelacanth, Comoros *Latimeria chalumnae*
Comoro Islands 1950, 1 40f; 1954 (Postage Due), 2 5f, 3 10f, 4 20f; 1975,
    5 50f; 1975, 6 50f (*surcharged* **ETAT COMORIEN**); 1977, **MS**7 500f; 1998,
    8 200f, 9 200f, 10 200f, 11 200f; 2006, 12 125f
Gambia 1997, 1 1d50
Guyana 1996, 1 $35; 1996, 2 $30; 1998, 3 $55
Ivory Coast 1979, 1 65f
Kuwait 1997, **MS**1 150f
Liberia 1998, 1 32c
Madagascar 1994, 1 15f
Malagasy Republic 1982, **MS**1 450f; 1990, **MS**2 550f
Mauritania 2000, 1 50um
Mozambique 1998, 1 2000m
North Korea 1993, 1 40ch
Palau 2000, 1 33c
São Tomé e Principe 2007, 1 14000d, **MS**2 14000d
South Africa 1989, 1 16c, 2 30c, 3 50c
Turks and Caicos Islands, 1997 1 $2

Coelacanth, Indonesian *Latimeria menadoensis*
Indonesia 2000, **MS**1 5000r

Congo Peacock *Afropavo congensis*
Belgium 1962, 1 6f+2f
Burundi 1965, 1 3r, 2 10r, 3 10r (airmail); 1979, 4 8f, 5 31f (airmail)
Congo (Kinshasa) 1963, 1 4f
Gambia 1993, 1 2d; 1997, 2 1d50
Hungary 1977, 1 1fo
North Korea 1990, 1 10ch

Giant Forest Hog *Hylochoerus meinertzhageni*
Ivory Coast 1963, 1 15f
Mauritania 1973, 1 250f; 1974, 2 50u
Zambia 2001, 1 2000k

Giant Octopus
France 1982, 1 1f80+40c
Guernsey 1997, 1 26p
St Kitts 2005, 1 $2
St Vincent 2005, 1 $2
Togo 1980, 1 200f

Giant Rift Tubeworm *Riftia pachyptila*
Guyana 1996, 1 $30

FACING PAGE: This varied assortment of cryptozoological stamps include: a thylacine-depicting First Day Cover from Australia; a set of four coelacanth stamps from the Comoro Islands; a set of four Canadian stamps (depicting the bigfoot or sasquatch, the kraken or giant squid, the loup-garou or were-wolf, and Ogopogo the monster of Lake Okanagan) and a miniature sheet from the Maldives depicting one of the famous giant footprints reputedly left behind by the yeti or abominable snowman.

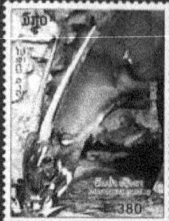

This plate contains a selection of particularly attractive stamps depicting cryptozoological creatures from the present and the past, which are as follows:

Row 1: Congo peacock, coelacanth, sea serpent, okapi; **Row 2:** Yeti, Vu Quang ox, mushrushu/sirrush; **Row 3:** thylacine, mermaid (a local issue stamp from Herm in the Channel Islands), Komodo dragon, takahe; **Row 4:** okapi; **Row 5:** coelacanth (first-ever coelacanth stamp), Ambun beast, Vo Quy's pheasant (male and female).

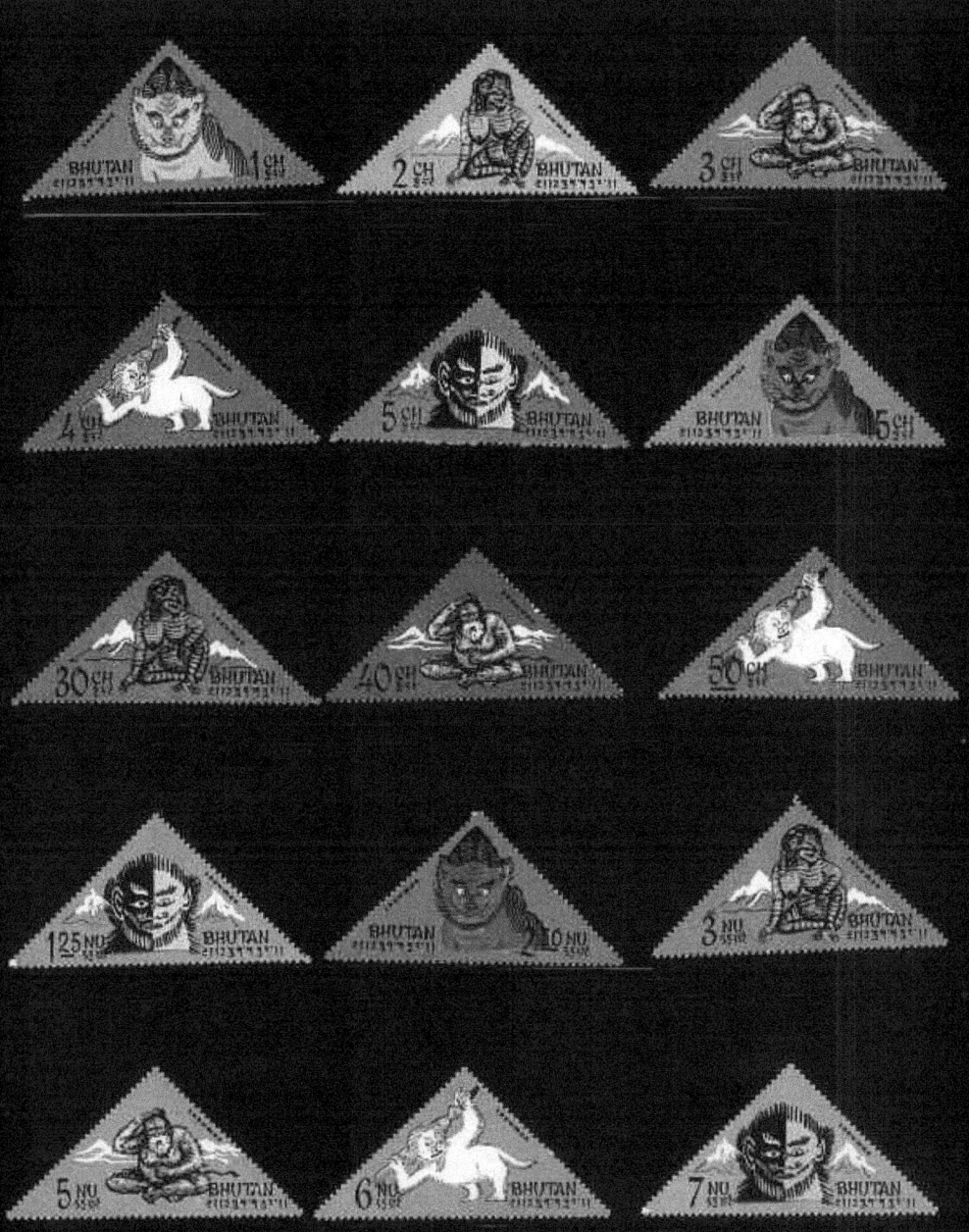

Long associated with reports of the yeti or abominable snowman, Bhutan featured this famous mountain-dwelling cryptozoological creature in a very attractive set of triangular stamps from 1966, and in an even more distinctive 3-D stamp from 1970, (see p. 215) made from plastic!

Many cryptozoologists believe that there are at least two different types of yeti – a human-sized version that may be a ground-dwelling orang utan, and a much bigger, exclusively bipedal form that could be a surviving species of *Gigantopithecus*, a giant prehistoric ape.

Komodo Dragon *Varanus komodoensis*
Belgium 1965, 1 6f+3f
France 2001, 1 3f80 (UNESCO Stamp)
Indonesia 1959, 1 75s; 1985, 2 300r; 1995, 3 150r; 2000, 4 500r, 5 500s, 6
    500r, 7 500r

Kraken/Giant Squid *Architeuthis dux*
Australian Antarctic Territory, 1973, 1 $1
Canada 1990, 1 39c
Central African Republic 2005, 1 300f
Dominica 1983, 1 45c
Guyana 1996, 1 $30
New Zealand 1998, 1 40c; 1999, **MS**2 40c
Palau 1993, 1 29c; 2000, **MS**2 $2
St Pierre and Miquelon 1975, 1 20c
Seychelles 1984, 1 2r
South West Africa 1980, 1 15c

Lake Monster, unspecified
Palau 1993, **MS**1 29c

Lake Okanagan Monster/Ogopogo
Canada 1990, 1 39c

Loch Ness Monster *Nessiteras rhombopteryx*
Maldive Islands 1992, **MS**1 25r
[There is also a First Day Cover issued by Great Britain in 1991 that bears not only the five dinosaur stamps from that year but also a depiction of the Loch Ness monster, portrayed as a plesiosaur]

Mushrushu/Sirrush/Ishtar Gate Dragon
East Germany 1966, 1 20pf

Okapi *Okapia johnstoni*
Belgian Congo 1931, 1 2f50, 2 3f35; 1942, 3 20f, 4 20f; 1959, 5 5f
Belgium 1961, 1 2f+50c
Benin 1996, 1 135f
Burundi 1970, 1 7f, 2 7f, 3 14f (airmail), 4 14f (airmail); 1971, 5 3f, 6
    17f (airmail), 7 17f+1f (*surcharged* **AIDE INTERNATIONALE AUX REFUGIES**)
Central African Republic 1982, 1 110f
Congo (Kinshasa) 1960, 1 5f
Congo Republic (Brazzaville) 1978, 1 35f
Democratic Congo (Kinshasa) 2000, 1 1f
Cuba 1978, 1 4c
East Germany 1980, 1 5pf
Fujeira 1972, 1 20d
Guinea 1997, **MS**1 1000f
Katanga 1960, 1 5f
Zaire 1975, 1 1k, 2 2k, 3 3k, 4 4k, 5 5k; 1984 6 2z, 7 3z, 8 8z, 9 10z, **MS**10
    50z

Dinosaurs and other Prehistoric Animals on Stamps

Sea Serpents/Sea Monsters
Antigua 1992, **MS**1 $6
Guinea 2000, 1 300f, 2 300f
Guyana 1992, 1 $125
Iceland 1989, 1 30k, 2 30k, 3 30k
Nicaragua 1978, 1 3c
Sierra Leone 1996, **MS**1 1500l
South Africa 2001, 1 2r30
South West Africa 1982, 1 15c
Sweden 1991, 1 5k

Takahe *Porphyrio* (=*Notornis*) *mantelli*
New Zealand 1956, 1 8d; 1982, 2 $5
Nicaragua 1991, 1 5c

Thylacine/Tasmanian Wolf *Thylacinus cynocephalus*
Australia 1959, 1 1s2d; 1981, 2 24c; 2008, 3 55C
Equatorial Guinea 1974, 1 40e (airmail)
Laos 1984, 1 3k
Micronesia 1999, 1 33c

Vo Quy's Pheasant *Lophura hatinhensis*
Vietnam 1995, **MS**1, no denomination

Vu Quang Ox/Saola *Pseudoryx nghetinhensis*
Laos 1997, 1 350k, 2 380k, 3 420k
Vietnam 2000, 1 400d, 2 400d, 3 5000d, 4 10000d

Yeti/Abominable Snowman
Bhutan 1966, 1 1ch, 2 2ch, 3 3ch, 4 4ch, 5 5ch, 6 15ch, 7 30ch, 8 40ch, 9 50ch, 10 1n25, 11 2n50, 12 3n, 13 5n, 14 6n, 15 7n; 1970, 16 30ch; 1996, 17 20n
Maldive Islands 1992, **MS**1 25r

A LIVING DRAGON

The **Komodo dragon** (*Varanus komodoensis*) is a species of lizard that inhabits the islands of Komodo, Rinca, Flores, Gili Motang, and Gili Dasami, in central Indonesia. A member of the monitor lizard family (Varanidae), it is the largest living species of lizard, growing to an average length of 2–3 meters (approximately 6.5–10 ft) and weighing around 70 kilograms (154 lb). Their unusual size is attributed to island gigantism, since there are no other carnivorous animals to fill the niche on the islands where they live, and also to the Komodo dragon's low metabolic rate. As a result of their size, these lizards are apex predators, dominating the ecosystems in which they live. Although Komodo dragons eat mostly carrion, they will also hunt and ambush prey including invertebrates, birds, and mammals.

Although the existence on Komodo (and the other above-named islands) of giant lizards dubbed land crocodiles had long been claimed by visiting pearl-fishers and also by criminals exiled here, science refused to believe such stories until 1912. This was when the Governor of Flores shot a Komodo specimen measuring 7 ft 4 in long, and sent it to Major P.A. Ouwens (director of Java's Buitenzorg Botanical Gardens), who formally documented it and named its species *Varanus komodoensis*.

Left: Baby Komodo dragon at London Zoo, October 2007 (CFZ)

PROUD AS A PEACOCK

The only species of peafowl known from Africa, the Congo peacock is a very unusual species, which lacks the spectacular fan-like tail train of other peafowl, and was only recognised by science in 1936, when its discoverer, American ornithologist Dr James Chapin, documented it and named it *Afropavo congensis*. Its remarkable story, however, had begun back in 1913, when Chapin had spied an unfamiliar feather within a native head-dress in the Belgian Congo's (now the Democratic Congo's) Ituri Forest. Unable to identify it, he bought the head-dress and spent a long time attempting to uncover the mysterious species from which this puzzling feather had originated, but did not meet with any success. Finally, he placed the feather in his desk, but never forgot it.

Then in 1936, while visiting Belgium's Tervueren Museum, Chapin spotted a pair of strange but forgotten stuffed birds not on public view, and saw that the female's wings sported the very same feathers as his mystery plume! He realised that their species was unknown to science, and learnt that it did indeed come from the Ituri Forest, where it was referred to by the natives as the mbulu. Its discovery by Chapin was one of the most important ornithological finds of the entire 20th Century, because it is such a dramatically distinctive, unexpected species – far removed both morphologically and geographically from its much more familiar Asian relatives.

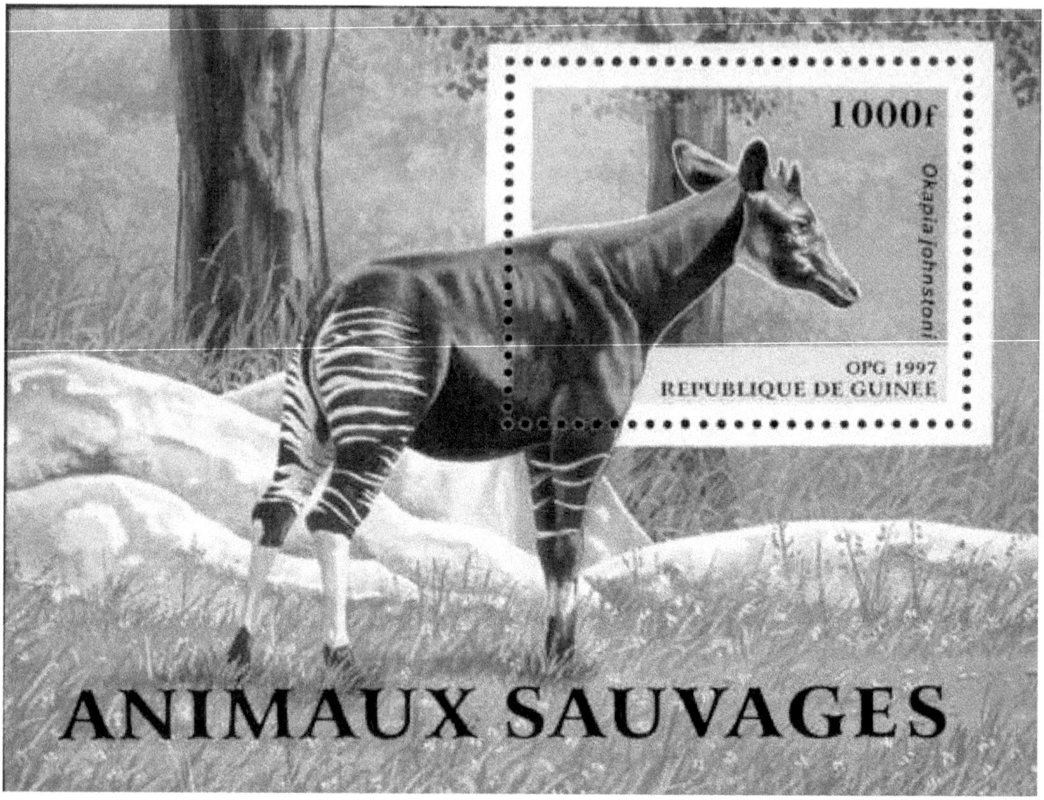
1000f
Okapia johnstoni
OPG 1997
REPUBLIQUE DE GUINEE
ANIMAUX SAUVAGES

Fantasies
of the Sea
Sierra Leone
Le1500
Sea Serpent
Serpents of the Sea
Throughout the ages there have been alleged sightings of sea serpents. A typical eye-witness, Hans Egede, a Norwegian missionary, wrote in 1734 of "a sea monster which raised its head so high ... that its head reached our maintop ... long sharp snout ... blew like a whale, had broad large flippers ... covered with a hard skin ... it was formed like a snake."

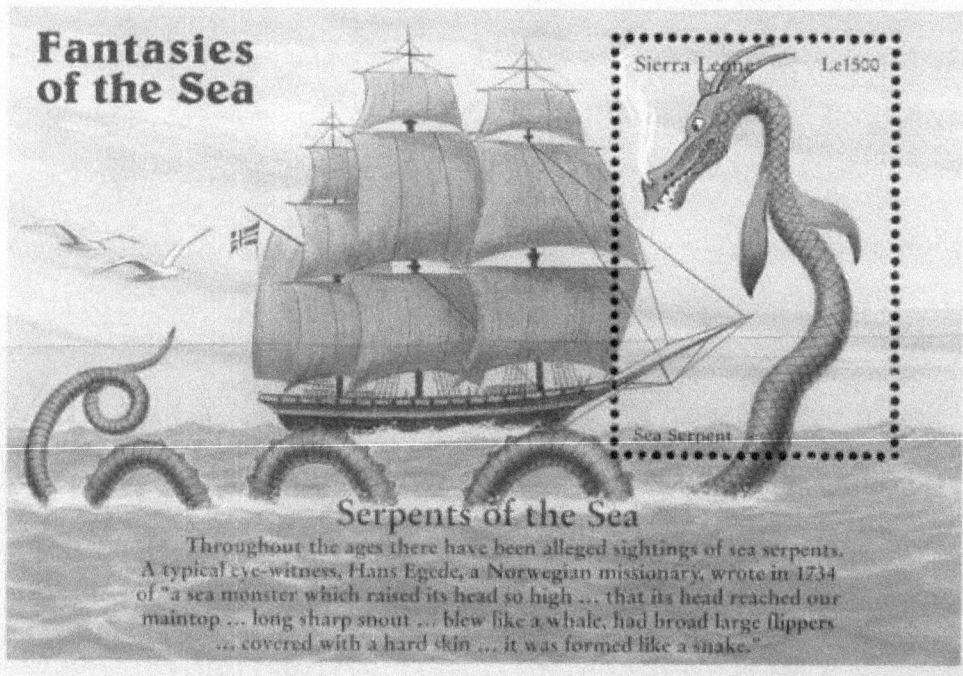

APPENDIX II
TRIVIA

Ever wondered which was the world's very first dinosaur stamp, or which dinosaur appears on more stamps than any other, or which was the first diamond-shaped prehistoric animal stamp? Wonder no more - the answers to these and other tantalisingly trivial queries of the palaeophilatelic kind are here!

FAMOUS FIRSTS

This section is dominated by stamps from Poland's first prehistoric animals set, which was issued in 1965 just a few months before San Marino's. Together with Poland's second such set, issued in 1966, they remain among the most famous stamps to depict prehistoric creatures.

FIRST PREHISTORIC ANIMAL (AND ALSO FIRST PREHISTORIC MAMMAL) STAMP
Stegodon ganesa (mammal)
India 1951, 1 2a (pictured on page 18, and front cover)

FIRST SET OF PREHISTORIC ANIMAL STAMPS
In 1958, China (People's Republic) issued a 3-stamp set featuring *Kaolishania pustulosa* (trilobite) 4f, *Lufengosaurus huenei* (s-dinosaur) 8f, and *Sinomegacerus* [=*Megaloceros*] *pachyospeus* (mammal) 16f.

FIRST PREHISTORIC ANIMAL MINIATURE SHEET
Mammuthus primigenius woolly mammoth (mammal)
Manama 1971, **MS9** 10r

FIRST SABRE-TOOTH TIGER STAMP
Machairodus (mammal)
Poland 1966, 18 6z50

FIRST PREHISTORIC HUMAN STAMP
Zinjanthropus [=*Paranthropus*] *boisei* (mammal)
Tanzania 1965, 1 1s30

FIRST WOOLLY MAMMOTH STAMP
Mammuthus primigenius (mammal)
Poland 1966, 19 7z10

FIRST PREHISTORIC BIRD STAMP
Archaeopteryx (bird)
Poland 1966, 16 2z50

FIRST DINOSAUR (ALSO FIRST S-DINOSAUR) STAMP
Lufengosaurus huenei (s-dinosaur)
China (People's Republic) 1958, 2 8f (pictured on page 18)

FIRST *TYRANNOSAURUS REX* STAMP
Tyrannosaurus rex (s-dinosaur)
Poland 1965, 10 6z50

FIRST *APATOSAURUS* (ALSO FIRST SAUROPOD) STAMP
Apatosaurus [=*Brontosaurus*] (s-dinosaur)
Poland 1965, 3 40g

FIRST *STEGOSAURUS* (ALSO FIRST O-DINOSAUR) STAMP
Stegosaurus (o-dinosaur)
Poland 1965, 5 90g

FIRST CERATOPSIAN (HORNED) DINOSAUR STAMP
Styracosaurus (o-dinosaur)
Poland 1965, 7 1z35

FIRST *TRICERATOPS* STAMP
Triceratops (o-dinosaur)
San Marino 1965, 9 200l

FIRST HADROSAUR (DUCK-BILLED DINOSAUR) STAMP
Corythosaurus (o-dinosaur)
Poland 1965, 8 3z40

FIRST DINOSAUR FOOTPRINTS STAMP
Dinosaur footprints (unspecified)
Lesotho 1970, 1 3c

FIRST PTEROSAUR STAMP
Rhamphorhynchus (pterosaur)
Poland 1965, 9 5z60

FIRST MOSASAUR STAMP
Tylosaurus (lizard)
Aden Protectorate States – Qu'aiti State in Hadhramaut 1968, 2 10f

FIRST THERAPSID STAMP
Cynognathus (therapsid)
Poland 1966, 15 60g

FIRST PELYCOSAUR STAMP
Edaphosaurus (pelycosaur)
Poland 1965, 1 20g

FIRST PLESIOSAUR STAMP

Plesiosaur, unspecified
Monaco 1955, 1 10f

FIRST ICHTHYOSAUR STAMP
Ichthyosaur, unspecified
Monaco 1955, 1 10f

FIRST PLACODONT STAMP
Placochelys (placodont)
Hungary 1969, 3 4fo

FIRST EARLY REPTILE STAMP
Mesosaurus (early reptile)
Poland 1965, 4 609

FIRST PREHISTORIC AMPHIBIAN STAMP
Andrias scheuchzeri (amphibian)
Switzerland 1959, 2 40c+10c

FIRST PREHISTORIC FISH (ALSO FIRST PREHISTORIC BONY FISH) STAMP
Archaeoteuthis (fish)
Switzerland 1961, 4 20c+10c

FIRST PREHISTORIC SHARK STAMP
Procarcharodon [=*Carcharocles*] *megalodon* (shark)
Angola 1970, 2 3e

FIRST PLACODERM STAMP
Dinichthys (placoderm)
Poland 1966, 11 20g

FIRST PREHISTORIC INVERTEBRATE (ALSO FIRST AMMONITE) STAMP
Berbericeras sekikensis (ammonite)
Algeria 1952, 1 15f

FIRST TRILOBITE STAMP
Kaolishania pustulosa (trilobite)
China (People's Republic) 1958, 1 4f

FIRST PALAEONTOLOGIST STAMP
Dr Grigore Antipa with *Deinotherium* (mammal)
Romania 1967, 7 40b

FIRST TRIANGULAR PREHISTORIC ANIMAL STAMP
Machairodus sabre-tooth tiger (mammal)
Aden Protectorate States – Qu'aiti State in Hadhramaut 1968, 1 5f

FIRST DIAMOND-SHAPED PREHISTORIC ANIMAL STAMP
Angolosaurus bocagei (lizard)
Angola 1970, 1 50c

QUETZALCOATLUS - CRÉTACÉ   ALAMOSAURUS - CRÉTACÉ   PACHYRHINOSAURUS - CRÉTACÉ

EUPLOCEPHALUS - CRÉTACÉ

PTERANODON - CRÉTACÉ

RÉPUBLIQUE CENTRAFRICAINE

1000 F
POSTE AÉRIENNE

TYLOSAURE - CRÉTACÉ

TROODON - CRÉTACÉ

HETERODONTOSAURUS - TRIAS

MASTODONSAURUS - TRIAS

ÈRE MÉSOZOÏQUE
TRIAS - JURASSIQUE - CRÉTACÉ

TOP TENS

[These totals are based solely upon the stamps and miniature sheets included in this catalogue; they do not incorporate the many local, unofficial, and other Cinderella dinosaur-depicting stamps and miniature sheets that have been issued by various organisations, persons, etc]

TOP 10 DINOSAURS RELATIVE TO THE TOTAL NUMBER OF STAMPS AND MINIATURE SHEETS DEPICTING THEM

#1	Tyrannosaurus (s-dinosaur)	128 stamps
#2	Stegosaurus (o-dinosaur)	120
#3	Triceratops (o-dinosaur)	94
#4	Brachiosaurus (s-dinosaur)	73
#5	Iguanodon (o-dinosaur)	68
#6	Allosaurus (s-dinosaur)	66
#7	Apatosaurus [=Brontosaurus] (s-dinosaur)	61
#8=	Deinonychus (s-dinosaur)	59
#8=	Parasaurolophus (o-dinosaur)	59
#10	Styracosaurus (o-dinosaur)	42

TOP 10 DINOSAURS RELATIVE TO THE NUMBER OF COUNTRIES THAT HAVE ISSUED STAMPS AND MINIATURE SHEETS DEPICTING THEM

#1	Stegosaurus (o-dinosaur)	64 countries
#2	Tyrannosaurus (s-dinosaur)	63
#3	Triceratops (o-dinosaur)	52
#4	Apatosaurus [=Brontosaurus] (s-dinosaur)	46
#5=	Allosaurus (s-dinosaur)	41
#5=	Iguanodon (o-dinosaur)	41
#7	Brachiosaurus (s-dinosaur)	38
#8	Deinonychus (s-dinosaur)	37
#9	Parasaurolophus (o-dinosaur)	35
#10	Corythosaurus (o-dinosaur)	29

TOP 10 PREHISTORIC ANIMALS RELATIVE TO THE TOTAL NUMBER OF STAMPS AND MINIATURE SHEETS DEPICTING THEM

#1	Tyrannosaurus (s-dinosaur)	128 stamps
#2	Stegosaurus (o-dinosaur)	120
#3	Triceratops (o-dinosaur)	94
#4	Pteranodon (pterosaur)	91
#5	Archaeopteryx (bird)	79
#6	Brachiosaurus (s-dinosaur)	73
#7	Iguanodon (o-dinosaur)	68
#8	Allosaurus (s-dinosaur)	66
#9	Apatosaurus [=Brontosaurus] (s-dinosaur)	61
#10=	Deinonychus (s-dinosaur)	59

#10=   *Parasaurolophus* (o-dinosaur)   59

TOP 10 PREHISTORIC ANIMALS RELATIVE TO THE NUMBER OF COUNTRIES THAT HAVE ISSUED STAMPS AND MINIATURE SHEETS DEPICTING THEM

#1	*Stegosaurus* (o-dinosaur)	64 countries
#2	*Tyrannosaurus* (s-dinosaur)	63
#3	*Triceratops* (o-dinosaur)	52
#4	*Apatosaurus* [=*Brontosaurus*] (s-dinosaur)	46
#5	*Pteranodon* (pterosaur)	45
#6=	*Allosaurus* (s-dinosaur)	41
#6=	*Iguanodon* (o-dinosaur)	41
#8=	*Brachiosaurus* (s-dinosaur)	38
#8=	*Archaeopteryx* (bird)	38
#10	*Deinonychus* (s-dinosaur)	37

TOP 10 COUNTRIES RELATIVE TO THE NUMBER OF PREHISTORIC ANIMAL STAMPS AND MINIATURE SHEETS THAT HAVE BEEN ISSUED BY THEM

#1	Guyana	184 stamps and miniature sheets
#2	Maldive Islands	139
#3	St Vincent	132
#4	Gabon	113
#5	Liberia	111
#6	Central African Republic	107
#7	Gambia	103
#8	Tanzania	100
#9	Guinea	85
#10	Grenada	78

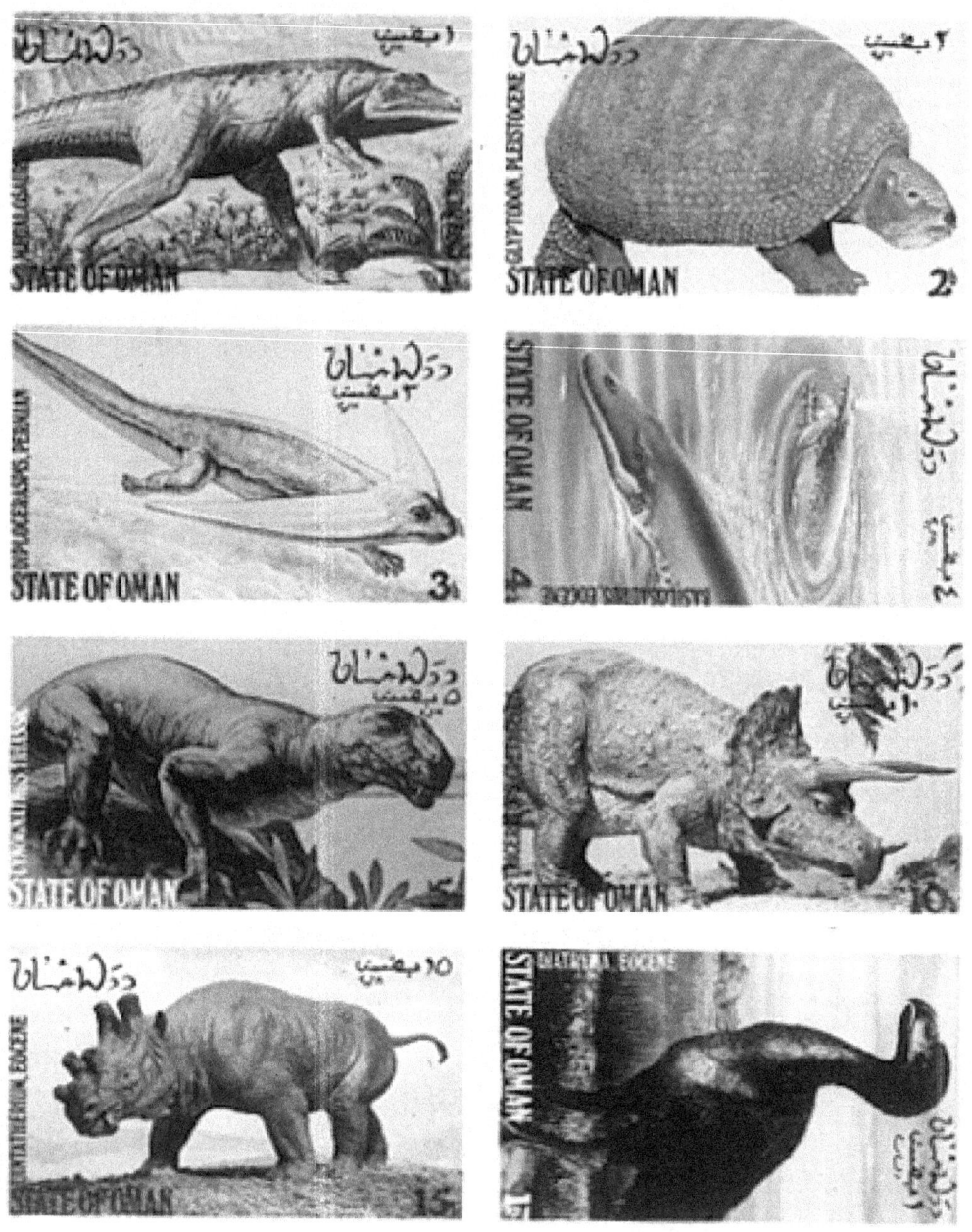

As already noted here, these unofficial stamps are readily distinguished from official Omani stamps by bearing the name 'State of Oman' rather than 'Sultanate of Oman', but from a palaeophilatelic point of view they are noteworthy inasmuch as they depict certain prehistoric animals that so far have been rarely if ever portrayed on real stamps. Most surprising of these overlooked creatures must surely be *Basilosaurus*, a primitive but quite enormous form of exceptionally elongate whale from the Eocene epoch (40-34 million years ago), whose spectacular appearance invariably guarantees it featuring in books and televised documentaries dealing with prehistoric animals. Remarkably, however, this veritable sea monster, which averaged 18 m (60 ft) or so in total length, has currently been depicted on only a single genuine stamp – issued by the Comoro Islands in 1998.

APPENDIX III
A BRIEF WORD CONCERNING UNOFFICIAL PREHISTORIC ANIMAL STAMPS

In addition to the numerous genuine sets of prehistoric animal stamps and miniature sheets now in existence, there are also many unofficial examples on record – enough, in fact, to warrant mention here, even though they are not included in this catalogue's listings. These unofficial – or (to give them their accepted philatelic term) Cinderella - prehistoric animal stamps (most of which are pseudo-stamps) can be split into three major categories.

BOGUS STAMPS (PSEUDO-STAMPS)

Anyone who collects prehistoric animal stamps and miniature sheets will undoubtedly have encountered at one time or another some quite spectacular-looking modern-day sets purportedly issued by various exotic-sounding Russian republics, and also some strangely-named Russian overprinted sets. In reality, however, these handsome stamps and overprints are bogus, issued not by the republics themselves but by private companies aimed directly at stamp collectors, thus serving no valid postal function whatsoever. In short, they are not stamps at all, merely labels specifically designed to look like stamps. Consequently, these pseudo-stamps are not listed in this or any other catalogue of genuine stamps.

Having said that, I do confess to a weakness for these interesting if superficially deceptive items, and over the years, albeit in full knowledge of their bogus status, I have amassed a modest but representative selection, depicting a wide range of prehistoric species. The number of Russian republics and other territories named on them, and including a few entirely fictitious ones, is very considerable, and includes the following examples, but there may well be others that I have so far not encountered. So look out for these prehistoric animal pseudo-stamps, and even though (as I do) you may well appreciate their artistic value, make sure that you also recognise them for what they are – or, rather, what they are not:

Abkhazia, Adigey, Adjaria, Altai (=Altay), Altaj, Amurskava, Baikal, Bashkiria, Bashkortostan, Batum, Bessarabia, Buriatia, Caratchaevo, Chakasia, Chechenia, Cherkesia, Chuashia, Chuvashia, Dagestan, Eastern Siberia, Evenkia, Franz Joseph Land, Gagauzia, Hakasia, Ingushetia, Jewish Republic, Kabarbino-Balkaria, Kalmykia (=Kalmikia), Kamchatka, Kamtshatka, Karachaevo-Cherkesia, Karakalpakia, Karakalpakiston, Karbardino-Balkaria, Karelia, Karjala, Khakasia, Kolguev Islands, Komi, Komsomolsk, Korekia, Koriakia, Kuril Islands, Mari (=Mari-El), Marj-El, Mordavia, Mountain Badakhshan Autonomy, Naxcivan, New Earth, N.M.P. (=Transdinestra), North Ossetia, Novosibirisk Island, Sacha-Yakutia, Saha (=Saha-Yakutia), Sakhalin Island, Sfor-Bosnia, Tartari, Tatarstan, Touva, Transniestra, Udmurtia, Ukrainian Arctic Post, Ural, Westland, Yakutia, and Yakutia-Sacha.

And just to make matters even more confusing, some bogus prehistoric animal stamps have been issued that bear the names of bona fide former Russian republics – most notably Tajikistan and Turkmenistan -

even though these latter now-independent countries have not been involved in any way with regard to the pseudo-stamps' origin of production. If in doubt concerning the authenticity of any stamps bearing these countries' names, check to see whether they are listed in any catalogue of genuine stamps – if they aren't included, they aren't genuine.

REBEL-ISSUE STAMPS

Occasionally, a rebel organisation or movement will issue sets of stamps for the country in which they are operating, sometimes to raise funding for their activities. Obviously, however, these do not experience any official postal use, and so once again, just like bogus stamps, they are best looked upon as pseudo-stamps. Perhaps the best-known example of rebel-issue stamps depicting prehistoric animals is the set of eight stamps and one miniature sheet issued in 1980 within Oman and bearing the name 'State of Oman' (genuine Omani stamps bear the name 'Sultanate of Oman'). The eight stamps are as follows: *Megalosaurus* (s-dinosaur) 1b, *Glyptodon* (mammal) 2b, *Diploceraspis* (amphibian) 3b, *Basilosaurus* (mammal) 4b, *Cynognathus* (therapsid) 5b, *Triceratops* (o-dinosaur) 10b, *Uintatherium* (mammal) 15b, and *Diatryma* [=*Gastornis*] (bird) 1r.

Also in 1980, another Oman-based rebel group issued for propaganda purposes a set of eight prehistoric animal stamps on an imperforate sheet, each stamp bearing the name 'Dhufar' (a southwestern governorate of Oman engaged at that time in left-wing guerrilla activity against the Omani government). The antediluvian stalwarts featured are: *Diatryma* [=*Gastornis*] 1b, *Rhamphorhynchus* (pterosaur) 2b, *Iguanodon* (o-dinosaur) 3b, *Indricotherium* (mammal) 4b, *Saltoposuchus* (thecodontian) 5b, *Dimetrodon* (pelycosaur) 10b, *Mammuthus* woolly mammoth (mammal) 15b, and *Archaeopteryx* (bird) 1r.

Equally contentious are the prehistoric animal stamps of Western Sahara. This controversial region of northwestern Africa is classified by the United Nations as a Non Self-Governing Territory. Most of it is presently occupied and administratively controlled by neighbouring Morocco – a situation opposed by Western Sahara's Polisario Front independence movement, and the government-in-exile of the self-proclaimed Sahrawi Arab Democratic Republic (SADR), another name for this much-disputed territory. Several sets of stamps depicting dinosaurs and other prehistoric fauna have been issued by bodies allied to Western Sahara's independence movement. However, Morocco's postal authorities class all such stamps as illegal, and they are currently not listed in any stamp catalogue, hence their omission from this present one.

LOCAL STAMPS

The most respectable unofficial stamps are those issued for valid local postal use, usually on small offshore islands or when transporting mail from such islands to their country's much bigger mainland. Scotland is famous for many of its Hebdridean islands issuing their own local-use stamps, which pay for the transport of mail from there to the nearest mainland Scottish branch of the UK's national Post Office. These stamp sets include at least four that are of interest to collectors of prehistoric animal stamps.

Set #1 is a three-stamp set of 1981 from the Isle of Pabay, featuring a trio of fossil molluscs – *Pseudopecten* (bivalve) 10p, *Gryphaea* (bivalve) 15p, and *Uptonia* (ammonite) 25p. More ambitious is Set #2, issued by Easdale Island in 1995, comprising two sheets of four stamps, each of which depicts a dinosaur. Set #3, issued by Bernera Islands in 1982, consists of two ammonite stamps. And an unnamed prehistoric reptile somewhat resembling a placodont is one of two stamps on a sheet comprising Set #4, issued in 1982 by Staffa.

Despite their often highly attractive designs and meticulous illustrations of prehistoric animals, the plethora of bogus Russian republic stamps in existence depicting such creatures can usually be readily exposed as such by failing to adhere to one or both of two very prevalent philatelic conventions. Firstly, some are produced in sheets yielding a composite picture (as in the Dagestan and Karakalpakiston examples shown here) like many genuine stamp sheets do, but if bogus sheets are split up into individual stamps, it will soon be found that some of these 'stamps' do not depict any animals on them, instead portraying nothing more than a patch of sky or expanse of ground – a major design oversight that does not happen with genuine composite-picture sheets of stamps. Secondly, even individual bogus stamps that look very like the real thing, such as the Komi, Chechnya (Chechenia), and Buriatia examples seen here, rarely if ever include the names of the animals that they portray – unlike genuine stamps, which almost always do. In addition, as again shown here, some bogus stamps do not even bear any unit of currency, just numbers.

APPENDIX IV
GEOLOGICAL TIME-LINE

Eon	Era	Period		Epoch	m.y.
Phanerozoic	Cenozoic	Quaternary		Holocene	
				Pleistocene	1.5
		Neogene		Pliocene	
				Miocene	23
		Paleogene		Oligocene	
				Eocene	
				Paleocene	65
	Mesozoic	Cretaceous			
		Jurassic			
		Triassic			250
	Paleozoic	Permian			
		Carboniferous	Pennsylvanian		
			Mississippian		
		Devonian			
		Silurian			
		Ordovician			
		Cambrian			540
Precambrian		Proterozoic			2500
		Archean			3800
		Hadean			4600

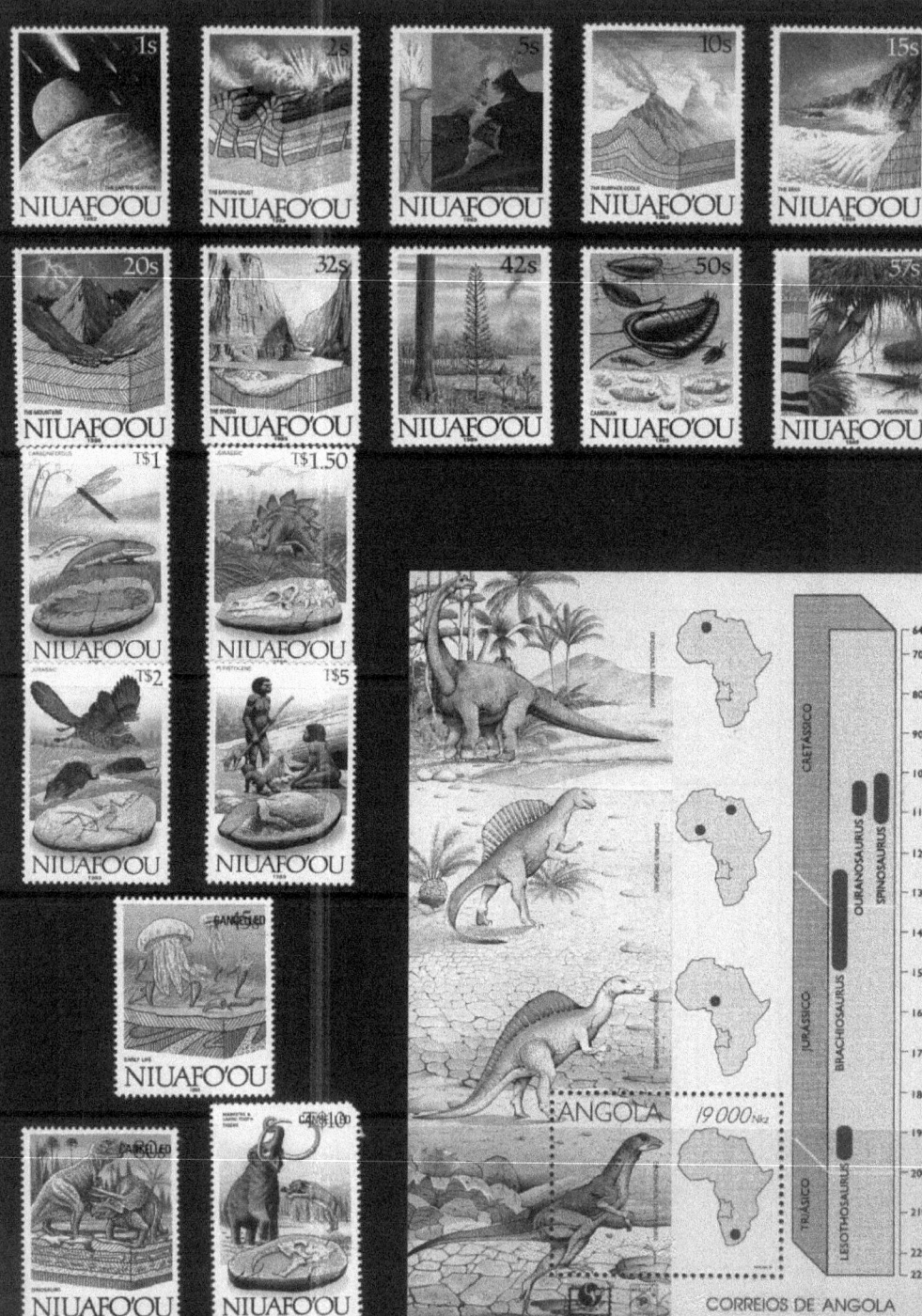

SELECTED BIBLIOGRAPHY

The literature on these fascinating long-vanished creatures is as colossal as their own most stupendous representatives, so I am limiting myself here to providing a brief listing of some of the most useful books (including certain early classics as well as modern-day works) that I have consulted during my preparation of the present catalogue, especially in relation to locating accurate illustrations.

These books all contain detailed bibliographies offering many more references, including scientific papers and articles, that can be accessed for further information, and there are also numerous online palaeontological and philatelic websites. Among the most notable and comprehensive of these latter are 'Prehistoric Life on Stamps' at http://home.hetnet.nl/~tonveijd/ and 'Paleontology Philatelic Catalogue' at http://home.hetnet.nl/~tonveijd/ - both of which I highly recommend to anyone interested in prehistoric animals on stamps.

GENERAL BOOKS

Dorling Kindersley Encyclopedia of Dinosaurs and Prehistoric Life. American Museum of Natural History, 2001
Wild New World. Barton, Bean, Dunleavy, Gray and White, 2002
Dinosaurs and Other Prehistoric Animals. Benton, 1992
Vertebrate Palaeontology. Benton, 2nd ed., 2000
Cassell's Atlas of Evolution. Benton (consultant), 2001
Macmillan Illustrated Encyclopedia of Dinosaurs and Prehistoric Animals. Cox, Savage, Gardiner and Dixon, 2nd ed., 1998
Fauna Prehistoricos y Reptiles. Gimeno, 1996
Prehistoric Life: The Rise of the Vertebrates. Norman, 1994
The Atlas of the Prehistoric World. Palmer, 2000
Vertebrate Life. Pough, Heiser and McFarland, 4th ed., 1996
The Rise of Life: The First 3.5 Billion Years. Reader, 1986
Kadimakara: Extinct Vertebrates of Australia. Rich, van Tets and Knight, 1985
Vertebrate Palaeontology. Romer, 3rd ed., 1966
The Antipodean Ark. Schouteden, Hand and Archer, 1987
In Search of Prehistoric Survivors. Shuker, 1995
The New Zoo: New and Rediscovered Animals of the Twentieth Century. Shuker, 2002
Fossils of the World. Turek, Marek and Benes, 1990
Wildlife of Gondwana. Vickers-Rich and Rich, 1993

DINOSAURS

The Dinosaur Heresies. Bakker, 1986
Dinosaur Stamps of the World. Baldwin and Halstead, 1991
The Penguin Historical Atlas of the Dinosaurs. Benton, 1996
Encyclopedia of Dinosaurs. Currie and Padian (eds), 1997
Encyclopedia of Dinosaurs. Dodson (consultant), 1990
The Evolution and Extinction of the Dinosaurs. Fastovsky and Weishampel, 1996
The Natural History Museum Book of Dinosaurs. Gardom and Milner, 1999
Dinosaurs: The Encyclopedia. Glut, 1997
Walking With Dinosaurs. Haines, 1999
Seismosaurus: The Earth Shaker. Hallett, 1994
Collins Guide to Dinosaurs. Lambert, rev. ed., 1983
The Great Dinosaur Atlas. Lindsay and Fornari, 1991
Dinosaurs of Australia and New Zealand. Long, Schouten and Windberg, 1998
Dinosaurs: The Textbook. Lucas, 1994
The Illustrated Encyclopedia of Dinosaurs. Norman, 1985
Dinosaur! Norman, 1991
Dinosaurs! 8 vols. Norman (consultant), 1992-5
1000 Facts on Dinosaurs. Parker, Flegg and Jessop (eds), 2002
Predatory Dinosaurs of the World. Paul, 1988
Hunting Dinosaurs. Psihoyos, 1994
Feathered Dinosaurs. Sloan, 2000
The Dinosauria. Weishampel, Dodson and Osmólska (eds), 2nd ed., 2004
Feathered Dinosaurs of China. Wenzel, 2004

OTHER PREHISTORIC REPTILES AND AMPHIBIANS

The Reign of the Reptiles. Benton, 1990
Evolution and Palaeobiology of Pterosaurs. Buffetaut and Mazin (eds), 2003
Ancient Marine Reptiles. Callaway and Nicholls (eds), 1996
Gaining Ground: The Origin and Early Evolution of Tetrapods. Clack, 2002
Sea Dragons: Predators of the Prehistoric Oceans. Ellis, 2003
The First Amphibians. Llamas, 1998
Sea Monsters: Prehistoric Predators of the Deep. Marven and James, 2003
The Pterosaurs: From Deep Time. Scrimger and Unwin, 2005
Supercroc. Sloan, 2002
Fossil Amphibians and Reptiles. Swinton, 5th ed., 1973
The Illustrated Encyclopedia of Pterosaurs. Wellnhofer, 1991

PREHISTORIC MAMMALS

Mammoths, Sabretooths, and Hominids: 65 Million Years of Mammalian Evolution in Europe. Agusti and Anton, 2002
A Book of Mammoths. Augusta and Burian, 1963

The Hunt For the Dawn Monkey: Unearthing the Origins of Monkeys, Apes, and Humans. Beard, 2004
The Rise of the Mammals. Benton, 1991
How Humans Evolved. Boyd and Silk, 1997
Reconstructing Human Origins. Convoy, 2005
First in Line: Tracing Our Ape Ancestry. Gundling, 2005
Walking With Beasts. Haines, 2001
Mammoths, Mastodonts, and Elephants. Haynes, 1991
The Cambridge Encyclopedia of Human Evolution. Jones, Martin and Pilbeam (eds), 1992
Pleistocene Mammals of Europe. Kurtén, 1968
Pleistocene Mammals of North America. Kurtén and Anderson, 1980
Mammoths. Lister and Bahn, 1995
The Velvet Claw. Macdonald, 1992
Quaternary Extinctions: A Prehistoric Revolution. Martin and Klein (eds), 1984
Biological Anthropology and Prehistory: Exploring Our Human Ancestry. Moloney and Rice, 2004
Mammal Evolution: An Illustrated Guide. Savage and Long, 1986
A History of Land Mammals in the Western Hemisphere. Scott, rev. ed., 1962
On the Track of Ice Age Mammals. Sutcliffe, 1986
The Fossil Trail. Tattersall, 1995
Extinct Humans. Tattersall and Schwartz, 2000
National Geographic Prehistoric Mammals. Turner, 2004
Evolving Eden: An Illustrated Guide to the Evolution of the African Large Mammal Fauna. Turner and Anton, 2004
Beasts of Eden: Walking Whales, Dawn Horses, and Other Enigmas of Mammal Evolution. Wallace, 2004

PREHISTORIC BIRDS

Prodigious Birds: Moas and Moa-Hunting in Prehistoric New Zealand. Anderson, 1989
The Rise of Birds: 225 Million Years of Evolution. Chatterjee, 1997
Feathered Dragons: Studies on the Transition From Dinosaurs to Birds. Currie, Koppelhus, Shugar and Wright (eds), 2004
The Age of Birds. Feduccia, 1980
The Origin and Evolution of Birds. Feduccia, 1996
New Zealand's Extinct Birds. Gill and Martinson, 1991
Dinosaurs of the Air: The Evolution and Loss of Flight in Dinosaurs and Birds. Paul, 2001
Fossil Birds. Swinton, 3rd ed., 1975

PREHISTORIC FISHES

Fossil Atlas: Fishes. Fricklinger, 1996
Fossil Fishes: The First 500 Million Years. Long, 1994
Discovering Fossil Fishes. Maisey, 1996

Megalodon: Hunting the Hunter. Renz, 2002
Fossil Fish. Young, 2004

PREHISTORIC INVERTEBRATES

The Fossils of the Burgess Shale. Briggs, Erwin and Collier, 1995
Invertebrate Palaeontology and Evolution. Clarkson, 3rd ed., 1993
Arthropod Fossils and Phylogeny. Edgecombe (ed), 1998
Trilobite! Eyewitness To Evolution. Fortey, 2000
Wonderful Life: The Burgess Shale and the Nature of History. Gould, 1989
Invertebrate Fossils. Moore, Lalicker and Fischer, 1952
Trilobites. Levi-Setti, 1993
Ancient Invertebrates and Their Living Relatives. Levin, 1998
The Crucible of Creation: The Burgess Shale and the Rise of Animals. Morris, 1999
Ammonites. Monks, Palmer and Harman (eds), 2002
Principles of Invertebrate Paleontology. Shrock and Twenhofel, 2nd ed., 1953
Trilobites and Their Relatives. Siveter, Fortey and Lane (eds), 2003
Trilobites. Whittington, 2000

ACKNOWLEDGEMENTS

I wish to take this opportunity to thank very sincerely all of those zoological and philatelic colleagues who have freely given greatly-valued help and much-appreciated support during my preparation of this catalogue.

In particular, I would like to thank my friend and publisher Jonathan Downes for enabling this book – a marked departure from my usual output - to see the light of day, by boldly going where no CFZ Press publication has gone before.

I would also like to thank Philip R. 'Pib' Burns for so kindly permitting me to reproduce in this catalogue several of his stamp illustrations as featured on his webpage 'Cryptozoology and Philately', which can be accessed at: http://www.pibburns.com/cryptost.htm.

Equally, I wish to thank the Royal Mail for enabling me to reproduce on my website's information page for this catalogue the Loch Ness Monster First Day Cover signed by LNM researcher Adrian Shine, which is contained within my personal philatelic collection. Re this image: Stamp design © Royal Mail Group Ltd. Reproduced by kind permission of Royal Mail Group Ltd. All rights reserved. NB – No reproduction, copying, or downloading of this image, or any image within this catalogue, is permitted.

Please note: the photograph of the little boy and his stamp collection appearing on this catalogue's title page (and which was an attempt to recreate the charming images that popularly appeared on stamp album covers during the early 1960s when the author, Dr Shuker, was himself a stamp-collecting child) does not depict Dr Shuker, but is a photo of Jonathan Downes's godson, Greg Braund-Phillips, and is included here by kind permission of his parents, Roy and Kaye Braund-Phillips. The publisher would also like to thank Max Blake, Richard Freeman, and Corinna Downes for their help during the preparation of this volume.

Unless otherwise stated (see above), all of the stamps, sheets, and First Day Covers illustrated in this catalogue are from my own philatelic collection.

I would be grateful to receive any additions or corrections from readers and fellow palaeophilatelists, which will be incorporated in future editions of this catalogue.

Every effort has been made to contact copyright holders for images utilised in this catalogue. The author and publisher would welcome details of any omissions, which will be rectified in future editions of this catalogue.

ABOUT THE AUTHOR

Dr Karl P.N. Shuker has collected wildlife stamps since childhood, and has a particular interest in those depicting dinosaurs and other prehistoric fauna, which he now maintains as a separate collection. Born and still living in the West Midlands, England, he graduated from the University of Leeds with a Bachelor of Science (Honours) degree in pure zoology, and from the University of Birmingham with a Doctor of Philosophy degree in zoology and comparative physiology. He now works full-time as a freelance zoological consultant to the media, and as a prolific published writer.

Dr Shuker is currently the author of 14 books and hundreds of articles, principally on animal-related subjects, with an especial interest in cryptozoology and animal mythology, on which he is an internationally-recognised authority. He has also acted as consultant for several major multi-contributor volumes as well as for the world-renowned *Guinness Book of Records/Guinness World Records* (he is currently its Senior Consultant for its Life Sciences section), and he has compiled questions for the BBC's long-running cerebral quiz 'Mastermind'.

Dr Shuker has travelled the world in the course of his researches and writings, and has appeared regularly on television and radio. Aside from work, his diverse range of interests include motorbikes, the life and career of James Dean, quizzes, philately, travel, world mythology, and the history of animation.

He is a Scientific Fellow of the prestigious Zoological Society of London, a Fellow of the Royal Entomological Society, a Member of the International Society of Cryptozoology and other wildlife-related organisations, he is Cryptozoology Consultant to the Centre for Fortean Zoology, and is also a Member of the Society of Authors.

Dr Shuker's personal website can be accessed at www.karlshuker.com and includes a section on wildlife-themed philately. There is also an entry for Dr Shuker in the online encyclopedia Wikipedia.

AUTHOR BIBLIOGRAPHY

Mystery Cats of the World: From Blue Tigers To Exmoor Beasts (Robert Hale: London, 1989)

Extraordinary Animals Worldwide (Robert Hale: London, 1991)

The Lost Ark: New and Rediscovered Animals of the 20th Century (HarperCollins: London, 1993)

Dragons: A Natural History (Aurum: London/Simon & Schuster: New York, 1995; republished Taschen: Cologne, 2006)

In Search of Prehistoric Survivors: Do Giant 'Extinct' Creatures Still Exist? (Blandford: London, 1995)

The Unexplained: An Illustrated Guide to the World's Natural and Paranormal Mysteries (Carlton: London/JG Press: North Dighton, 1996; republished Carlton: London, 2002)

From Flying Toads To Snakes With Wings: From the Pages of FATE Magazine (Llewellyn: St Paul, 1997; republished Bounty: London, 2005)

Mysteries of Planet Earth: An Encyclopedia of the Inexplicable (Carlton: London, 1999)

The Hidden Powers of Animals: Uncovering the Secrets of Nature (Reader's Digest: Pleasantville/Marshall Editions: London, 2001)

The New Zoo: New and Rediscovered Animals of the Twentieth Century [fully-updated, greatly-expanded, new edition of *The Lost Ark*] (House of Stratus Ltd: Thirsk, UK/House of Stratus Inc: Poughkeepsie, USA, 2002)

The Beasts That Hide From Man: Seeking the World's Last Undiscovered Animals (Paraview: New York, 2003)

Extraordinary Animals Revisited: From Singing Dogs To Serpent Kings (CFZ Press: Bideford, 2007)

Dr Shuker's Casebook: In Pursuit of Marvels and Mysteries (CFZ Press: Bideford, 2008)

Dinosaurs and Other Prehistoric Animals on Stamps: A Worldwide Catalogue (CFZ Press: Bideford, 2008).

Consultant and also Contributor

Man and Beast (Reader's Digest: Pleasantville, New York, 1993)

Secrets of the Natural World (Reader's Digest: Pleasantville, New York, 1993)

Almanac of the Uncanny (Reader's Digest: Surry Hills, Australia, 1995)

The Guinness Book of Records/Guinness World Records 1998-present day (Guinness: London, 1997-present day)

Consultant

Monsters (Lorenz: London, 2001)

Contributor

Fortean Times Weird Year 1996 (John Brown Publishing: London, 1996)

Mysteries of the Deep (Llewellyn: St Paul, 1998)

Guinness Amazing Future (Guinness: London, 1999)

The Earth (Channel 4 Books: London, 2000)

Mysteries and Monsters of the Sea (Gramercy: New York, 2001)

Chambers Dictionary of the Unexplained (Chambers: Edinburgh, 2007)

Chambers Myths and Mysteries (Chambers: Edinburgh, 2008)

THE CENTRE FOR FORTEAN ZOOLOGY

So, what is the Centre for Fortean Zoology?

We are a non profit-making organisation founded in 1992 with the aim of being a clearing house for information, and coordinating research into mystery animals around the world. We also study out of place animals, rare and aberrant animal behaviour, and Zooform Phenomena; little-understood "things" that appear to be animals, but which are in fact nothing of the sort, and not even alive (at least in the way we understand the term).

Why should I join the Centre for Fortean Zoology?

Not only are we the biggest organisation of our type in the world, but - or so we like to think - we are the best. We are certainly the only truly global Cryptozoological research organisation, and we carry out our investigations using a strictly scientific set of guidelines. We are expanding all the time and looking to recruit new members to help us in our research into mysterious animals and strange creatures across the globe. Why should you join us? Because, if you are genuinely interested in trying to solve the last great mysteries of Mother Nature, there is nobody better than us with whom to do it.

What do I get if I join the Centre for Fortean Zoology?

For £12 a year, you get a four-issue subscription to our journal *Animals & Men*. Each issue contains 60 pages packed with news, articles, letters, research papers, field reports, and even a gossip column! The magazine is A5 in format with a full colour cover. You also have access to one of the world's largest collections of resource material dealing with cryptozoology and allied disciplines, and people from the CFZ membership regularly take part in fieldwork and expeditions around the world.

How is the Centre for Fortean Zoology organized?

The CFZ is managed by a three-man board of trustees, with a non-profit making trust registered with HM Government Stamp Office. The board of trustees is supported by a Permanent Directorate of full and part-time staff, and advised by a Consultancy Board of specialists - many of whom who are world-renowned experts in their particular field. We have regional representatives across the UK, the USA, and many other parts of the world, and are affiliated with other organisations whose aims and protocols mirror our own.

I am new to the subject, and although I am interested I have little practical knowledge. I don't want to feel out of my depth. What should I do?

Don't worry. We were *all* beginners once. You'll find that the people at the CFZ are friendly and approachable. We have a thriving forum on the website which is the hub of an ever-growing electronic community. You will soon find your feet. Many members of the CFZ Permanent Directorate started off as ordinary members, and now work full-time chasing monsters around the world.

I have an idea for a project which isn't on your website. What do I do?

Write to us, e-mail us, or telephone us. The list of future projects on the website is not exhaustive. If you have a good idea for an investigation, please tell us. We may well be able to help.

How do I go on an expedition?

We are always looking for volunteers to join us. If you see a project that interests you, do not hesitate to get in touch with us. Under certain circumstances we can help provide funding for your trip. If you look on the future projects section of the website, you can see some of the projects that we have pencilled in for the next few years.

In 2003 and 2004 we sent three-man expeditions to Sumatra looking for Orang-Pendek - a semi-legendary bipedal ape. The same three went to Mongolia in 2005. All three members started off merely subscribers to the CFZ magazine.

Next time it could be you!

Project Kerinci, Sumatra - 2003
In search of the bipedal ape Orang Pendek

How is the Centre for Fortean Zoology funded?

We have no magic sources of income. All our funds come from donations, membership fees, works that we do for TV, radio or magazines, and sales of our publications and merchandise. We are always looking for corporate sponsorship, and other sources of revenue. If you have any ideas for fund-raising please let us know. However, unlike other cryptozoological organisations in the past, we do not live in an intellectual ivory tower. We are not afraid to get our hands dirty, and furthermore we are not one of those organisations where the membership have to raise money so that a privileged few can go on expensive foreign trips. Our research teams both in the UK and abroad, consist of a mixture of experienced and inexperienced personnel. We are truly a community, and work on the premise that the benefits of CFZ membership are open to all.

What do you do with the data you gather from your investigations and expeditions?

Reports of our investigations are published on our website as soon as they are available. Preliminary reports are posted within days of the project finishing.

Each year we publish a 200 page yearbook containing research papers and expedition reports too long to be printed in the journal. We freely circulate our information to anybody who asks for it.

Is the CFZ community purely an electronic one?

No. Each year since 2000 we have held our annual convention - the *Weird Weekend* - in Exeter. It is three days of lectures, workshops, and excursions. But most importantly it is a chance for members of the CFZ to meet each other, and to talk with the members of the permanent directorate in a relaxed and informal setting and preferably with a pint of beer in one hand. Since 2006 - the *Weird Weekend* has been bigger and better and held in the idyllic rural location of Woolsery in North Devon.

Since relocating to North Devon in 2005 we have become ever more closely involved with other community organisations, and we hope that this trend will continue. We also work closely with Police Forces across the UK as consultants for animal mutilation cases, and we intend to forge closer links with the coastguard and other community services. We want to work closely with those who regularly travel into the Bristol Channel, so that if the recent trend of exotic animal visitors to our coastal waters continues, we can be out there as soon as possible.

We are building a Visitor's Centre in rural North Devon. This will not be open to the general public, but will provide a museum, a library and an educational resource for our members (currently over 400) across the globe. We are also planning a youth organisation which will involve children and young people in our activities. We work closely with *Tropiquaria* - a small zoo in north Somerset, and have several exciting conservation projects planned.

Apart from having been the only Fortean Zoological organisation in the world to have consistently published material on all aspects of the subject for over a decade, we have achieved the following concrete results:

- Disproved the myth relating to the headless so-called sea-serpent carcass of Durgan beach in Cornwall 1975
- Disproved the story of the 1988 puma skull of Lustleigh Cleave
- Carried out the only in-depth research ever into the mythos of the Cornish Owlman
- Made the first records of a tropical species of lamprey
- Made the first records of a luminous cave gnat larva in Thailand.
- Discovered a possible new species of British mammal - the beech marten.
- In 1994-6 carried out the first archival fortean zoological survey of Hong Kong.
- In the year 2000, CFZ theories where confirmed when an entirely new species of lizard was found resident in Britain.
- Identified the monster of Martin Mere in Lancashire as a giant wels catfish
- Expanded the known range of Armitage's skink in the Gambia by 80%
- Obtained photographic evidence of the remains of Europe's largest known pike
- Carried out the first ever in-depth study of the *ninki-nanka*
- Carried out the first attempt to breed Puerto Rican cave snails in captivity
- Were the first European explorers to visit the `lost valley` in Sumatra
- Published the first ever evidence for a new tribe of pygmies in Guyana
- Published the first evidence for a new species of caiman in Guyana

EXPEDITIONS & INVESTIGATIONS TO DATE INCLUDE:

- 1998 Puerto Rico, Florida, Mexico *(Chupacabras)*
- 1999 Nevada *(Bigfoot)*
- 2000 Thailand *(Giant snakes called nagas)*
- 2002 Martin Mere *(Giant catfish)*
- 2002 Cleveland *(Wallaby mutilation)*
- 2003 Bolam Lake *(BHM Reports)*
- 2003 Sumatra *(Orang Pendek)*
- 2003 Texas *(Bigfoot; giant snapping turtles)*
- 2004 Sumatra *(Orang Pendek; cigau, a sabre-toothed cat)*
- 2004 Illinois *(Black panthers; cicada swarm)*
- 2004 Texas *(Mystery blue dog)*
- 2004 Puerto Rico *(Chupacabras; carnivorous cave snails)*
- 2005 Belize *(Affiliate expedition for hairy dwarfs)*
- 2005 Mongolia *(Allghoi Khorkhoi aka Mongolian death worm)*
- 2006 Gambia *(Gambo - Gambian sea monster, Ninki Nanka and Armitage s skink*
- 2006 Llangorse Lake *(Giant pike, giant eels)*
- 2006 Windermere *(Giant eels)*
- 2007 Coniston Water *(Giant eels)*
- 2007 Guyana *(Giant anaconda, didi, water tiger)*
- 2008 Russia *(almasty, giant snakes)*

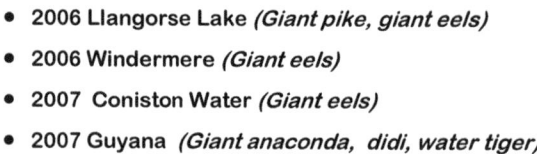

To apply for a <u>FREE</u> information pack about the organisation and details of how to join, plus information on current and future projects, expeditions and events.

Send a stamped and addressed envelope to:

**THE CENTRE FOR FORTEAN ZOOLOGY
MYRTLE COTTAGE, WOOLSERY,
BIDEFORD, NORTH DEVON
EX39 5QR.**

or alternatively visit our website at:
www.cfz.org.uk

Other books available from
CFZ PRESS

THE OWLMAN AND OTHERS - 30th Anniversary Edition
Jonathan Downes - ISBN 978-1-905723-02-7

£14.99

EASTER 1976 - Two young girls playing in the churchyard of Mawnan Old Church in southern Cornwall were frightened by what they described as a "nasty bird-man". A series of sightings that has continued to the present day. These grotesque and frightening episodes have fascinated researchers for three decades now, and one man has spent years collecting all the available evidence into a book. To mark the 30th anniversary of these sightings, Jonathan Downes has published a special edition of his book.

DRAGONS - More than a myth?
Richard Freeman - ISBN 0-9512872-9-X

£14.99

First scientific look at dragons since 1884. It looks at dragon legends worldwide, and examines modern sightings of dragon-like creatures, as well as some of the more esoteric theories surrounding dragonkind.

Dragons are discussed from a folkloric, historical and cryptozoological perspective, and Richard Freeman concludes that: "When your parents told you that dragons don't exist - they lied!"

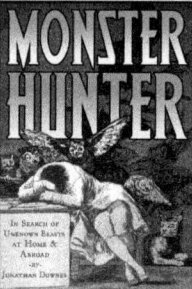

MONSTER HUNTER
Jonathan Downes - ISBN 0-9512872-7-3

£14.99

Jonathan Downes' long-awaited autobiography, *Monster Hunter*...

Written with refreshing candour, it is the extraordinary story of an extraordinary life, in which the author crosses paths with wizards, rock stars, terrorists, and a bewildering array of mythical and not so mythical monsters, and still just about manages to emerge with his sanity intact.......

MONSTER OF THE MERE
Jonathan Downes - ISBN 0-9512872-2-2

£12.50

It all starts on Valentine's Day 2002 when a Lancashire newspaper announces that "Something" has been attacking swans at a nature reserve in Lancashire. Eyewitnesses have reported that a giant unknown creature has been dragging fully grown swans beneath the water at Martin Mere. An intrepid team from the Exeter based Centre for Fortean Zoology, led by the author, make two trips – each of a week – to the lake and its surrounding marshlands. During their investigations they uncover a thrilling and complex web of historical fact and fancy, quasi Fortean occurrences, strange animals and even human sacrifice.

CFZ PRESS, MYRTLE COTTAGE, WOOLFARDISWORTHY BIDEFORD, NORTH DEVON, EX39 5QR
w w w . c f z . o r g . u k

Other books available from
CFZ PRESS

ONLY FOOLS AND GOATSUCKERS
Jonathan Downes - ISBN 0-9512872-3-0

£12.50

In January and February 1998 Jonathan Downes and Graham Inglis of the Centre for Fortean Zoology spent three and a half weeks in Puerto Rico, Mexico and Florida, accompanied by a film crew from UK Channel 4 TV. Their aim was to make a documentary about the terrifying chupacabra - a vampiric creature that exists somewhere in the grey area between folklore and reality. This remarkable book tells the gripping, sometimes scary, and often hilariously funny story of how the boys from the CFZ did their best to subvert the medium of contemporary TV documentary making and actually do their job.

WHILE THE CAT'S AWAY
Chris Moiser - ISBN: 0-9512872-1-4

£7.99

Over the past thirty years or so there have been numerous sightings of large exotic cats, including black leopards, pumas and lynx, in the South West of England. Former Rhodesian soldier Sam McCall moved to North Devon and became a farmer and pub owner when Rhodesia became Zimbabwe in 1980. Over the years despite many of his pub regulars having seen the "Beast of Exmoor" Sam wasn't at all sure that it existed. Then a series of happenings made him change his mind. Chris Moiser—a zoologist—is well known for his research into the mystery cats of the westcountry. This is his first novel.

CFZ EXPEDITION REPORT 2006 - GAMBIA
ISBN 1905723032

£12.50

In July 2006, The J.T.Downes memorial Gambia Expedition - a six-person team - Chris Moiser, Richard Freeman, Chris Clarke, Oll Lewis, Lisa Dowley and Suzi Marsh went to the Gambia, West Africa. They went in search of a dragon-like creature, known to the natives as `Ninki Nanka`, which has terrorized the tiny African state for generations, and has reportedly killed people as recently as the 1990s. They also went to dig up part of a beach where an amateur naturalist claims to have buried the carcass of a mysterious fifteen foot sea monster named 'Gambo', and they sought to find the Armitage's Skink (*Chalcides armitagei*) - a tiny lizard first described in 1922 and only rediscovered in 1989. Here, for the first time, is their story.... With an forward by Dr. Karl Shuker and introduction by Jonathan Downes.

BIG CATS IN BRITAIN YEARBOOK 2006
Edited by Mark Fraser - ISBN 978-1905723-01-0

£10.00

Big cats are said to roam the British Isles and Ireland even now as you are sitting and reading this. People from all walks of life encounter these mysterious felines on a daily basis in every nook and cranny of these two countries. Most are jet-black, some are white, some are brown, in fact big cats of every description and colour are seen by some unsuspecting person while on his or her daily business. 'Big Cats in Britain' are the largest and most active group in the British Isles and Ireland This is their first book. It contains a run-down of every known big cat sighting in the UK during 2005, together with essays by various luminaries of the British big cat research community which place the phenomenon into scientific, cultural, and historical perspective.

CFZ PRESS, MYRTLE COTTAGE, WOOLSERY, BIDEFORD, NORTH DEVON, EX39 5QR
w w w . c f z . o r g . u k

Other books available from
CFZ PRESS

THE SMALLER MYSTERY CARNIVORES OF THE WESTCOUNTRY
Jonathan Downes - ISBN 978-1-905723-05-8

£7.99

Although much has been written in recent years about the mystery big cats which have been reported stalking Westcountry moorlands, little has been written on the subject of the smaller British mystery carnivores. This unique book redresses the balance and examines the current status in the Westcountry of three species thought to be extinct: the Wildcat, the Pine Marten and the Polecat, finding that the truth is far more exciting than the currently held scientific dogma. This book also uncovers evidence suggesting that even more exotic species of small mammal may lurk hitherto unsuspected in the countryside of Devon, Cornwall, Somerset and Dorset.

THE BLACKDOWN MYSTERY
Jonathan Downes - ISBN 978-1-905723-00-3

£7.99

Intrepid members of the CFZ are up to the challenge, and manage to entangle themselves thoroughly in the bizarre trappings of this case. This is the soft underbelly of ufology, rife with unsavoury characters, plenty of drugs and booze." That sums it up quite well, we think. A new edition of the classic 1999 book by legendary fortean author Jonathan Downes. In this remarkable book, Jon weaves a complex tale of conspiracy, anti-conspiracy, quasi-conspiracy and downright lies surrounding an air-crash and alleged UFO incident in Somerset during 1996. However the story is much stranger than that. This excellent and amusing book lifts the lid off much of contemporary forteana and explains far more than it initially promises.

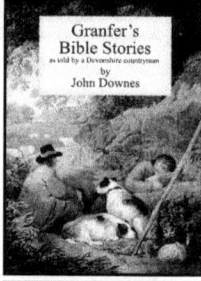

GRANFER'S BIBLE STORIES
John Downes - ISBN 0-9512872-8-1

£7.99

Bible stories in the Devonshire vernacular, each story being told by an old Devon Grandfather - 'Granfer'. These stories are now collected together in a remarkable book presenting selected parts of the Bible as one more-or-less continuous tale in short 'bite sized' stories intended for dipping into or even for bed-time reading. `Granfer` treats the biblical characters as if they were simple country folk living in the next village. Many of the stories are treated with a degree of bucolic humour and kindly irreverence, which not only gives the reader an opportunity to re-evaluate familiar tales in a new light, but do so in both an entertaining and a spiritually uplifting manner.

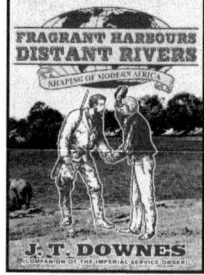

FRAGRANT HARBOURS DISTANT RIVERS
John Downes - ISBN 0-9512872-5-7

£12.50

Many excellent books have been written about Africa during the second half of the 19th Century, but this one is unique in that it presents the stories of a dozen different people, whose interlinked lives and achievements have as many nuances as any contemporary soap opera. It explains how the events in China and Hong Kong which surrounded the Opium Wars, intimately effected the events in Africa which take up the majority of this book. The author served in the Colonial Service in Nigeria and Hong Kong, during which he found himself following in the footsteps of one of the main characters in this book; Frederick Lugard – the architect of modern Nigeria.

CFZ PRESS, MYRTLE COTTAGE, WOOLFARDISWORTHY BIDEFORD, NORTH DEVON, EX39 5QR
w w w . c f z . o r g . u k

Other books available from
CFZ PRESS

ANIMALS & MEN - Issues 1 - 5 - In the Beginning
Edited by Jonathan Downes - ISBN 0-9512872-6-5

£12.50

At the beginning of the 21st Century monsters still roam the remote, and sometimes not so remote, corners of our planet. It is our job to search for them. The Centre for Fortean Zoology [CFZ] is the only professional, scientific and full-time organisation in the world dedicated to cryptozoology - the study of unknown animals. Since 1992 the CFZ has carried out an unparalleled programme of research and investigation all over the world. We have carried out expeditions to Sumatra (2003 and 2004), Mongolia (2005), Puerto Rico (1998 and 2004), Mexico (1998), Thailand (2000), Florida (1998), Nevada (1999 and 2003), Texas (2003 and 2004), and Illinois (2004). An introductory essay by Jonathan Downes, notes putting each issue into a historical perspective, and a history of the CFZ.

ANIMALS & MEN - Issues 6 - 10 - The Number of the Beast
Edited by Jonathan Downes - ISBN 978-1-905723-06-5

£12.50

At the beginning of the 21st Century monsters still roam the remote, and sometimes not so remote, corners of our planet. It is our job to search for them. The Centre for Fortean Zoology [CFZ] is the only professional, scientific and full-time organisation in the world dedicated to cryptozoology - the study of unknown animals. Since 1992 the CFZ has carried out an unparalleled programme of research and investigation all over the world. We have carried out expeditions to Sumatra (2003 and 2004), Mongolia (2005), Puerto Rico (1998 and 2004), Mexico (1998), Thailand (2000), Florida (1998), Nevada (1999 and 2003), Texas (2003 and 2004), and Illinois (2004). Preface by Mark North and an introductory essay by Jonathan Downes, notes putting each issue into a historical perspective, and a history of the CFZ.

BIG BIRD! Modern Sightings of Flying Monsters

£7.99

Ken Gerhard - ISBN 978-1-905723-08-9

From all over the dusty U.S./Mexican border come hair-raising stories of modern day encounters with winged monsters of immense size and terrifying appearance. Further field sightings of similar creatures are recorded from all around the globe. What lies behind these weird tales? Ken Gerhard is a native Texan, he lives in the homeland of the monster some call 'Big Bird'. Ken's scholarly work is the first of its kind. On the track of the monster, Ken uncovers cases of animal mutilations, attacks on humans and mounting evidence of a stunning zoological discovery ignored by mainstream science. Keep watching the skies!

STRENGTH THROUGH KOI
They saved Hitler's Koi and other stories

£7.99

Jonathan Downes - ISBN 978-1-905723-04-1

Strength through Koi is a book of short stories - some of them true, some of them less so - by noted cryptozoologist and raconteur Jonathan Downes. The stories are all about koi carp, and their interaction with bigfoot, UFOs, and Nazis. Even the late George Harrison makes an appearance. Very funny in parts, this book is highly recommended for anyone with even a passing interest in aquaculture, but should be taken definitely *cum grano salis*.

CFZ PRESS, MYRTLE COTTAGE, WOOLSERY, BIDEFORD, NORTH DEVON, EX39 5QR

Other books available from
CFZ PRESS

BIG CATS IN BRITAIN YEARBOOK 2007
Edited by Mark Fraser - ISBN 978-1-905723-09-6

£12.50

People from all walks of life encounter mysterious felids on a daily basis, in every nook and cranny of the UK. Most are jet-black, some are white, some are brown; big cats of every description and colour are seen by some unsuspecting person while on his or her daily business. 'Big Cats in Britain' are the largest and most active research group in the British Isles and Ireland. This book contains a run-down of every known big cat sighting in the UK during 2006, together with essays by various luminaries of the British big cat research community.

CAT FLAPS! Northern Mystery Cats
Andy Roberts - ISBN 978-1-905723-11-9

£6.99

Of all Britain`s mystery beasts, the alien big cats are the most renowned. In recent years the notoriety of these uncatchable, out-of-place predators have eclipsed even the Loch Ness Monster. They slink from the shadows to terrorise a community, and then, as often as not, vanish like ghosts. But now film, photographs, livestock kills, and paw prints show that we can no longer deny the existence of these once-legendary beasts. Here then is a case-study, a true lost classic of Fortean research by one of the country's most respected researchers.

CENTRE FOR FORTEAN ZOOLOGY 2007 YEARBOOK
Edited by Jonathan Downes and Richard Freeman
ISBN 978-1-905723-14-0

£12.50

The Centre For Fortean Zoology Yearbook is a collection of papers and essays too long and detailed for publication in the CFZ Journal *Animals & Men*. With contributions from both well-known researchers, and relative newcomers to the field, the Yearbook provides a forum where new theories can be expounded, and work on little-known cryptids discussed.

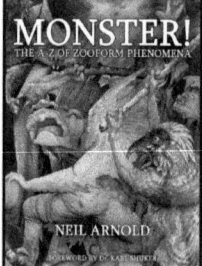

MONSTER! THE A-Z OF ZOOFORM PHENOMENA
Neil Arnold - ISBN 978-1-905723-10-2

£14.99

Zooform Phenomena are the most elusive, and least understood, mystery `animals`. Indeed, they are not animals at all, and are not even animate in the accepted terms of the word. Author and researcher Neil Arnold is to be commended for a groundbreaking piece of work, and has provided the world's first alphabetical listing of zooforms from around the world.

**CFZ PRESS, MYRTLE COTTAGE,
WOOLFARDISWORTHY BIDEFORD,
NORTH DEVON, EX39 5QR
www.cfz.org.uk**

Other books available from
CFZ PRESS

BIG CATS LOOSE IN BRITAIN
Marcus Matthews - ISBN 978-1-905723-12-6

£14.99

Big Cats: Loose in Britain, looks at the body of anecdotal evidence for such creatures: sightings, livestock kills, paw-prints and photographs, and seeks to determine underlying commonalities and threads of evidence. These two strands are repeatedly woven together into a highly readable, yet scientifically compelling, overview of the big cat phenomenon in Britain.

DARK DORSET
TALES OF MYSTERY, WONDER AND TERROR
Robert. J. Newland and Mark. J. North
ISBN 978-1-905723-15-6

£12.50

This extensively illustrated compendium has over 400 tales and references, making this book by far one of the best in its field. Dark Dorset has been thoroughly researched, and includes many new entries and up to date information never before published. The title of the book speaks for itself, and is indeed not for the faint hearted or those easily shocked.

MAN-MONKEY - IN SEARCH OF THE BRITISH BIGFOOT
Nick Redfern - ISBN 978-1-905723-16-4

£9.99

In her 1883 book, *Shropshire Folklore*, Charlotte S. Burne wrote: *'Just before he reached the canal bridge, a strange black creature with great white eyes sprang out of the plantation by the roadside and alighted on his horse's back'*. The creature duly became known as the `Man-Monkey`.

Between 1986 and early 2001, Nick Redfern delved deeply into the mystery of the strange creature of that dark stretch of canal. Now, published for the very first time, are Nick's original interview notes, his files and discoveries; as well as his theories pertaining to what lies at the heart of this diabolical legend.

EXTRAORDINARY ANIMALS REVISITED
Dr Karl Shuker - ISBN 978-1905723171

£14.99

This delightful book is the long-awaited, greatly-expanded new edition of one of Dr Karl Shuker's much-loved early volumes, *Extraordinary Animals Worldwide*. It is a fascinating celebration of what used to be called romantic natural history, examining a dazzling diversity of animal anomalies, creatures of cryptozoology, and all manner of other thought-provoking zoological revelations and continuing controversies down through the ages of wildlife discovery.

**CFZ PRESS, MYRTLE COTTAGE,
WOOLFARDISWORTHY BIDEFORD,
NORTH DEVON, EX39 5QR
w w w . c f z . o r g . u k**

Other books available from
CFZ PRESS

DARK DORSET CALENDAR CUSTOMS
Robert J Newland - ISBN 978-1-905723-18-8

£12.50

Much of the intrinsic charm of Dorset folklore is owed to the importance of folk customs. Today only a small amount of these curious and occasionally eccentric customs have survived, while those that still continue have, for many of us, lost their original significance. Why do we eat pancakes on Shrove Tuesday? Why do children dance around the maypole on May Day? Why do we carve pumpkin lanterns at Hallowe'en? All the answers are here! Robert has made an in-depth study of the Dorset country calendar identifying the major feast-days, holidays and celebrations when traditionally such folk customs are practiced.

CENTRE FOR FORTEAN ZOOLOGY 2004 YEARBOOK
Edited by Jonathan Downes and Richard Freeman
ISBN 978-1-905723-14-0

£12.50

The Centre For Fortean Zoology Yearbook is a collection of papers and essays too long and detailed for publication in the CFZ Journal *Animals & Men*. With contributions from both well-known researchers, and relative newcomers to the field, the Yearbook provides a forum where new theories can be expounded, and work on little-known cryptids discussed.

CENTRE FOR FORTEAN ZOOLOGY 2008 YEARBOOK
Edited by Jonathan Downes and Corinna Downes
ISBN 978 -1-905723-19-5

£12.50

The Centre For Fortean Zoology Yearbook is a collection of papers and essays too long and detailed for publication in the CFZ Journal *Animals & Men*. With contributions from both well-known researchers, and relative newcomers to the field, the Yearbook provides a forum where new theories can be expounded, and work on little-known cryptids discussed.

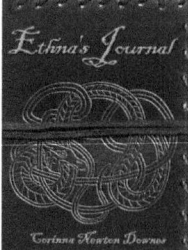

ETHNA'S JOURNAL
Corinna Newton Downes
ISBN 978 -1-905723-21-8

£9.99

Ethna's Journal tells the story of a few months in an alternate Dark Ages, seen through the eyes of Ethna, daughter of Lord Edric. She is an unsophisticated girl from the fortress town of Cragnuth, somewhere in the north of England, who reluctantly gets embroiled in a web of treachery, sorcery and bloody war...

**CFZ PRESS, MYRTLE COTTAGE,
WOOLFARDISWORTHY BIDEFORD,
NORTH DEVON, EX39 5QR
www.cfz.org.uk**

Other books available from
CFZ PRESS

ANIMALS & MEN - Issues 11 - 15 - The Call of the Wild
Jonathan Downes (Ed) - ISBN 978-1-905723-07-2

£12.50

Since 1994 we have been publishing the world's only dedicated cryptozoology magazine, *Animals & Men*. This volume contains fascimile reprints of issues 11 to 15 and includes articles covering out of place walruses, feathered dinosaurs, possible North American ground sloth survival, the theory of initial bipedalism, mystery whales, mitten crabs in Britain, Barbary lions, out of place animals in Germany, mystery pangolins, the barking beast of Bath, Yorkshire ABCs, Molly the singing oyster, singing mice, the dragons of Yorkshire, singing mice, the bigfoot murders, waspman, British beavers, the migo, Nessie, the weird warbling whatsit of the westcountry, the quagga project and much more...

IN THE WAKE OF BERNARD HEUVELMANS
Michael A Woodley - ISBN 978-1-905723-20-1

£9.99

Everyone is familiar with the nautical maps from the middle ages that were liberally festooned with images of exotic and monstrous animals, but the truth of the matter is that the *idea* of the sea monster is probably as old as humankind itself.

For two hundred years, scientists have been producing speculative classifications of sea serpents, attempting to place them within a zoological framework. This book looks at these successive classification models, and using a new formula produces a sea serpent classification for the 21st Century.

CENTRE FOR FORTEAN ZOOLOGY 1999 YEARBOOK
Edited by Jonathan Downes
ISBN 978-1-905723-24-9

£12.50

The Centre For Fortean Zoology Yearbook is a collection of papers and essays too long and detailed for publication in the CFZ Journal *Animals & Men*. With contributions from both well-known researchers, and relative newcomers to the field, the Yearbook provides a forum where new theories can be expounded, and work on little-known cryptids discussed.

CENTRE FOR FORTEAN ZOOLOGY 1996 YEARBOOK
Edited by Jonathan Downes
ISBN 978-1-905723-22-5

£12.50

The Centre For Fortean Zoology Yearbook is a collection of papers and essays too long and detailed for publication in the CFZ Journal *Animals & Men*. With contributions from both well-known researchers, and relative newcomers to the field, the Yearbook provides a forum where new theories can be expounded, and work on little-known cryptids discussed.

**CFZ PRESS, MYRTLE COTTAGE,
WOOLFARDISWORTHY BIDEFORD,
NORTH DEVON, EX39 5QR
w w w . c f z . o r g . u k**

Other books available from
CFZ PRESS

BIG CATS IN BRITAIN YEARBOOK 2008
Edited by Mark Fraser - ISBN 978-1-905723-23-2

£12.50

People from all walks of life encounter mysterious felids on a daily basis, in every nook and cranny of the UK. Most are jet-black, some are white, some are brown; big cats of every description and colour are seen by some unsuspecting person while on his or her daily business. 'Big Cats in Britain' are the largest and most active research group in the British Isles and Ireland. This book contains a run-down of every known big cat sighting in the UK during 2007, together with essays by various luminaries of the British big cat research community.

CFZ EXPEDITION REPORT 2007 - GUYANA
ISBN 978-1-905723-25-6

£12.50

Since 1992, the CFZ has carried out an unparalleled programme of research and investigation all over the world. In November 2007, a five-person team - Richard Freeman, Chris Clarke, Paul Rose, Lisa Dowley and Jon Hare went to Guyana, South America. They went in search of giant anacondas, the bigfoot-like didi, and the terrifying water tiger.

Here, for the first time, is their story...With an introduction by Jonathan Downes and forward by Dr. Karl Shuker.

CENTRE FOR FORTEAN ZOOLOGY 2003 YEARBOOK
Edited by Jonathan Downes and Richard Freeman
ISBN 978 -1-905723-19-5

£12.50

The Centre For Fortean Zoology Yearbook is a collection of papers and essays too long and detailed for publication in the CFZ Journal *Animals & Men*. With contributions from both well-known researchers, and relative newcomers to the field, the Yearbook provides a forum where new theories can be expounded, and work on little-known cryptids discussed.

CENTRE FOR FORTEAN ZOOLOGY 1997 YEARBOOK
Edited by Jonathan Downes and Graham Inglis
ISBN 978 -1-905723-27-0

£12.50

The Centre For Fortean Zoology Yearbook is a collection of papers and essays too long and detailed for publication in the CFZ Journal *Animals & Men*. With contributions from both well-known researchers, and relative newcomers to the field, the Yearbook provides a forum where new theories can be expounded, and work on little-known cryptids discussed.

CFZ PRESS, MYRTLE COTTAGE, WOOLFARDISWORTHY BIDEFORD, NORTH DEVON, EX39 5QR
w w w . c f z . o r g . u k

Other books available from
CFZ PRESS

CENTRE FOR FORTEAN ZOOLOGY 2000-1 YEARBOOK
Edited by Jonathan Downes and Richard Freeman
ISBN 978-1-905723-19-5

£12.50

The Centre For Fortean Zoology Yearbook is a collection of papers and essays too long and detailed for publication in the CFZ Journal *Animals & Men*. With contributions from both well-known researchers, and relative newcomers to the field, the Yearbook provides a forum where new theories can be expounded, and work on little-known cryptids discussed.

THE MYSTERY ANIMALS OF THE BRITISH ISLES: NORTHUMBERLAND AND TYNESIDE
Michael J Hallowell
ISBN 978-1-905723-29-4

£12.50

Mystery animals? Great Britain? Surely not. But is is true.

This is a major new series from CFZ Press. It will cover Great Britain and the Republic of Ireland, on a county by county basis, describing the mystery animals of the entire island group.

The Island of Paradise: Chupacabra, UFO Crash Retrievals, and Accelerated Evolution on the Island of Puerto Rico
Jonathan Downes - ISBN 978-1-905723-32-4

£14.99

In his first book of original research for four years, Jon Downes visits the Antillean island of Puerto Rico, to which he has led two expeditions - in 1998 and 2004. Together with noted researcher Nick Redfern he goes in search of the grotesque vampiric chupacabra, believing that it can - finally - be categorised within a zoological frame of reference rather than a purely paranormal one. Along the way he uncovers mystery after mystery, has a run in with terrorists, art historians, and even has his garden buzzed by a UFO. By turns both terrifying and funny, this remarkable book is a real tour de force by one of the world's foremost cryptozoological researchers.

DR SHUKER'S CASEBOOK
Dr Karl Shuker - ISBN 978-1905723-33-1

£14.99

Although he is best-known for his extensive cryptozoological researches and publications, Dr Karl Shuker has also investigated a very diverse range of other anomalies and unexplained phenomena, both in the literature and in the field. Now, compiled here for the very first time, are some of the extraordinary cases that he has re-examined or personally explored down through the years.

**CFZ PRESS, MYRTLE COTTAGE,
WOOLFARDISWORTHY BIDEFORD,
NORTH DEVON, EX39 5QR
w w w . c f z . o r g . u k**

Other books available from
CFZ PRESS

Dinosaurs and Other Prehistoric Animals on Stamps: A Worldwide Catalogue
Dr Karl P.N.Shuker - ISBN 978-1-905723-34-8

£9.99

Compiled by zoologist Dr Karl P.N. Shuker, a lifelong, enthusiastic collector of wildlife stamps and with an especial interest in those that portray fossil species, it provides an exhaustive, definitive listing of stamps and miniature sheets depicting dinosaurs and other prehistoric animals issued by countries throughout the world. It also includes sections dealing with cryptozoological stamps, dinosaur stamp superlatives, and unofficial prehistoric animal stamps.

CFZ PRESS, MYRTLE COTTAGE,
WOOLFARDISWORTHY BIDEFORD,
NORTH DEVON, EX39 5QR
w w w . c f z . o r g . u k

www.ingramcontent.com/pod-product-compliance
Ingram Content Group UK Ltd.
Pitfield, Milton Keynes, MK11 3LW, UK
UKHW021318180426
11947UKWH00015B/1297